The Little iMac Book

third edition

The Little iMac Book

third edition

John Tollett & Robin Williams

Peachpit Press ▪ Berkeley ▪ California

The Little iMac Book third edition

©2002 Robin Williams

Cover design: John Tollett
Cover illustration: ©2002 John Tollett
Interior design: Robin Williams
All interior illustrations and photographs: ©2002 John Tollett
Production: John Tollett and Robin Williams
Index: Robin Williams and Laura Egley Taylor
Url's Internet Cafe web site **(www.UrlsInternetCafe.com):** ©2002 John Tollett
Editing: Nancy Davis
Prepress: Kate Reber

Peachpit Press

1249 Eighth Street
Berkeley, California 94710
800.283.9444
510.524.2178 voice
510.524.2221 fax
Find us on the World Wide Web at **www.peachpit.com**
To report errors, please send a note to errata@peachpit.com
Peachpit Press is a division of Pearson Education

ISBN 0-321-11630-5

10 9 8 7 6 5 4 3

Printed and bound in the United States of America

Brief contents

detailed contents follow!

To Jimbo Norrena,
my dear friend,
who first suggested I should
do this book.

with love,

R.

Many thanks!

Thanks to Laura Egley Taylor for helping us finish
this book! And to Nancy Davis/Incredible Editor,
and Kate Reber/Prepress Wizardess.

Detailed contents
Start at the Beginning

3 Working at Your Desktop

Things to Do with Your iMac

6   Make a Simple Database   133

7   Make a Simple Spreadsheet   145

The Internet and the World Wide Web

The iMac is Your Digital Hub

21 iMovie: Be a Movie Mogul! 361

More about Your iMac

Introduction by John

The iMac has changed the world—the computer world, the graphic design world, the industrial design world, and the lives of many people around the world. Compelling, innovative design and powerful software inspired countless numbers of new computer users to empower themselves with previously unattainable levels of productivity and creativity. And I'm talking about the *old* iMac—just wait until you get to know the new, flat-panel iMac!

Apple has bundled a ton of fabulous software with Mac OS X (pronounced *Mac oh ess ten*), the operating system that makes other operating systems seem like a nostalgic trip down memory lane.

If you're brand-new to computers, you'll probably take for granted how easy it is to set up your iMac, send email, organize digital photos, burn CDs or DVDs, and even edit home movies.

If you've owned a Mac before and you're familiar with that "old" operating system, Mac OS 9, you'll notice there are more changes in Mac OS X than just the stunningly beautiful new "Aqua" appearance, with its translucent buttons and elegant, uncluttered look. Some of the things you're familiar with have changed. Well, that's not really true. *Everything* you're familiar with has changed. But it's all for the better, and after a few hours you'll start loving the new look and the powerful features of the new iMac.

In this book we've explained a lot about Mac OS X and most of the applications that come with an iMac. You can find even *more* information specifically about OS X in Robin's 824-page book, *The Little Mac OS X Book*. Even though your computer is named "iMac," it's still a Macintosh, and everything in *The Little Mac OS X Book* still applies.

People who are looking for a computer often ask me if an iMac is powerful enough to use on professional projects. **I assure them that a computer does not have to be ugly to be a top-of-the-line professional tool.** This particular iMac is many times faster and more powerful than anything available to professionals in the past. You'll also find that a multitude of great new applications for Mac OS X are constantly being written. After you become comfortable with the iMac, use the Internet to look for OS X applications that you'll find useful, or just fun. There are several web sites I visit everyday to see what new applications are available, or to find new versions of existing software. After you've learned how to get on the Internet and browse web sites, check these out:

www.MacMinute.com

> Up-to-the-minute Mac news and links to new software and software upgrades.

www.MacinTouch.com

> More Mac news, including software releases and discussion forums for Mac software and hardware issues.

www.VersionTracker.com

> Links to new versions of software.

www.MacFixit.com

> Expert Mac information. Subscribe and have access to a massive amount of Macintosh knowledge.

www.MacOSXhints.com

> Lots of Mac OS X tips and tricks.

www.MacAddict.com

> A magazine for those of us addicted to Macintosh. If you're not addicted yet, just wait.

www.Apple.com

> The ultimate Mac site. Visit here for news, shopping, learning, or just drooling.

www.MacWarehouse.com

> A great place to shop online for Mac products. It's quite a thrill to order groovy stuff without leaving your computer, then have it delivered to your door the next day.

Enjoy your iMac. It's more than a tool that increases your productivity—**it will inspire your creativity and your imagination.** If you get tired of creating slide shows and movies; if you get bored building your own music collections and burning customized CDs; if you don't want to watch a musical light show created by iTunes; if roaming around the world on the Internet isn't exciting to you; if you're too tired to play (or create) a DVD—then just sit back and admire the masterpiece of modern art sitting on your desk.

John

Let's Start at the Very Beginning

In the first of these three chapters, John and I will tell you how to get your brand-new iMac **set up and connected to the Internet,** because as soon as you plug it in, the computer wants to go to the Internet.

You *can* set up your iMac with your name and time zone and other stuff right now and **skip the Internet part,** if you like, and when you're ready, read Chapter 15 and follow those directions to get connected.

If you or someone else **already set up** your iMac— if you have already turned it on for the first time and walked through the set-up process—then skip Chapter 1 altogether.

In Chapters 2 and 3, just sit down and work along. I'm going to start from scratch. I'm going to assume you don't know anything about this machine at all. There are some things I'm not going to tell you yet because you can live a long time without knowing them. But I will tell you exactly what you need to know to start being productive and having fun on your great, new iMac, and I'll tell you where to go for more information when you're ready.

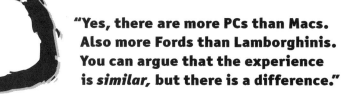

"Yes, there are more PCs than Macs.
Also more Fords than Lamborghinis.
You can argue that the experience
is *similar,* but there is a difference."

Professional designer

Initial Set~up Process

If you haven't already taken your iMac out of the box and plugged it in, do so now. Follow the directions provided in the box. I know the directions tell you to plug the computer directly into the wall, but you really should get a *surge protector* at the hardware store or office supply store (see the illustration to the right). They cost from about $15 up through hundreds of dollars. Plug the power cable from your iMac into the surge protector, then plug the surge protector into the wall. This will help protect your computer from the surges of electricity that happen all the time. If you live in an area that has lightning storms (like John and I do), the only real way to protect your computer is to unplug everything, including any modem and printer cables, right out of the wall.

In this chapter, we're going to turn on the computer, set it up, and get connected to the Internet. If you've already done this, skip this chapter! Head right on over to Chapter 2 and start mousing around.

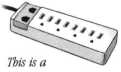

This is a typical inexpensive surge protector. Plug your computer into this and plug this into the wall. If you get a surge protector with phone ports, you should also plug your modem cord into this, then run another cord from this to your phone jack.

Connect your iMac to a phone line

Part of the set-up procedure that follows requires a live Internet connection to complete certain tasks, such as registering with Apple and setting up an iTools account (read about iTools in Chapter 19). To complete the registration process, you don't need to have an Internet Service Provider yet (I'll explain later what that is) or anything special—just **plug in the phone cable** that came in your iMac box (or any phone cable you have lying around the house) into the "modem port" shown below, and plug the other end into a phone jack. That's all you need for now to set up and register your iMac.

Ethernet port: to connect an Ethernet cable.

Modem port: *to connect to a phone line.*

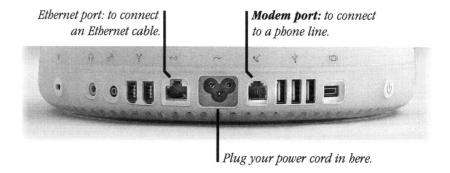

Plug your power cord in here.

Later, after you've read the information in this chapter and have made a decision about what kind of permanent Internet connection you want, you can get that all set up.

If you don't connect your iMac to a phone line at this time, the registration information will be sent when you do connect. But you might as well do it now.

How to turn on your iMac

If you have no idea what the Internet is or the World Wide Web or an ISP, skim through the next few pages before you turn your iMac on for the first time. Then turn on your iMac and start the set-up process.

After you've plugged your iMac in to a power source (preferably through a surge protector, as explained on page 3) and plugged a phone cable in, turn on your iMac: press the **Power button.**

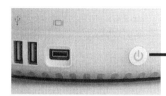

This is the Power button. Slide your hand along the left side of the computer base and you'll feel it.

The Power button is on back-left side of the bubble-bottom* base, next to the other *ports* ("ports" are those places on the back of the base where you plug things in; see Chapter 25 for details about all those ports on the back).

When you're done working on the computer, it's possible to use the Power button to turn it off: press the Power button and hold for five seconds. **BUT** you should only turn it off this way in an emergency! Usually you'll use the Shut Down command, as explained on page 72.

*John's sister, Emma Jean Howell, described the new iMac this way, and it's the best description I've ever heard.

Connecting to the Internet

Now, you can skip the next few pages and get right to the set-up part (page 12), but during the set-up process, you will be asked to make several decisions. If you are brand-new to computers, you might want to have something to base these decisions on. So read or skip the next six pages as necessary for you.

To get to the Internet, your computer must be connected to a "server," a special computer that has information flowing to and from the Internet 24 hours a day. You probably have one of these situations:

> You can connect to the Internet through a **phone line** that is attached to your computer and goes to the phone jack in the wall, or perhaps through another telephone. Typically, your modem will **dial up** your "Internet Service Provider" (as explained on the opposite page). You will most likely connect only for a short time each day, or maybe several times a day—You will *log on* (connect) to the server through your computer, do your Internet and World Wide Web business, then log off.

> If you live in a larger town, you might connect to the Internet through a **broadband** option, something like a television **cable** or **DSL** (Digital Subscriber Line). In that case, you have a special modem supplied by the service you signed up with, and you connect, not with a regular telephone cord, but with a special cord called an *Ethernet cable*. Your connection is "on" all the time (meaning you never have to "dial up" through the phone line).

> Or maybe you work at a business or college that owns their own Internet server, in which case your computer is probably connected to that server 24 hours a day because it is on the company **network.** In that case, you do not "dial up" through a phone line to connect to the Internet—your computer has access all day and night (it's "on" all the time). All you need to do is open your browser or email program.

To get connected to a server, you have to go through a set-up process. The process is different depending on what kind of service you choose to be connected through. The first part of this chapter talks about the options you have for connectivity, then explains what the iMac can set up for you automatically, if you so choose. *Read about your options, because you have to make a choice before you start the set-up process.*

What is an ISP?

The acronym ISP stands for **Internet Service Provider.** There are two basic ways to connect to the Internet—one is through an online service, such as America Online (see the following page). The other is to find an Internet Service Provider (ISP) who gives you special information to enter into your iMac setup at home which will connect *your* computer to *their* servers. The software in your iMac and the numbers the ISP gives you connect your iMac to *their* computers (the ISP's), and *their* computers connect *you* to the Internet, as illustrated below.

*This is you at
your computer.*   *This is an ISP, giving you
access to the Internet.*

There are probably several **local providers** in your area. Ask your friends whom they use for Internet access. You will typically pay a set-up fee to the ISP and a monthly fee for your connection. The fees can vary widely, so you might want to ask around about the cost of a local provider.

A local provider might give you a **dial-up** connection that will go through an existing phone line in your home or office, or a **broadband** option, which is a fast, always-on connection like cable or DSL. If you have a choice, always choose broadband over dial-up—it's phenomenally faster, it doesn't tie up your phone line, and it's always on. Your iMac really likes a connection that's always on. So will you.

To make it easy for you, Apple has arranged with a **national provider,** EarthLink, to offer an Internet connection through your iMac if you don't know a local provider, or if you don't want to use a local provider; see page 10 for details. EarthLink offers dial-up plus a variety of broadband options, depending on where you live.

America Online

What is America Online?

America Online is the most popular "online service" in the world. An online service is a self-contained entity that allows you to connect to the electronic world. Within a service you can exchange email with anyone in the world, join clubs, "chat" with people around the world, get answers to questions, "download" new software (which means to copy it from their computer to yours), set up a web site, and much more.

America Online (also called **AOL**) is a nice, friendly place. It's like a safe, contained village. There are guides to help you, "patrol officers" to make sure people are behaving properly, instructions on how to do things and where to go, help for when you get lost, protection for your children, and more. But America Online is not the Internet, nor is it the World Wide Web. When you are on America Online, you are contained within their system of computers that sits right in Virginia, the home of America Online.

If you think of America Online as a village in Virginia, then the Internet is the big, wide world. In the world, there is no one to help you, to point the way, or to keep you safe. You're on your own. But America Online has a back door. You can slip out that back door and go to the World Wide Web, or access anything else on the Internet, such as mailing lists and newsgroups. From a menu in America Online called "Internet," you can choose to "Go to the Web"; when you do that, you leave America Online and head out into the Internet world. You leave the village. However, AOL has been integrating the web into its village and now it is difficult to tell the boundaries. (I guess this is a good thing. It used to be so uncomplicated. Sigh.)

This is the clean, safe, friendly village of an online service.

Should you use AOL or an ISP?

If you're not yet connected to the Internet, you need to make a choice about how you want to get there: America Online (AOL) **or** an Internet Service Provider (ISP). If you choose America Online, AOL *is* your ISP, and it will be a dial-up connection*.

I used to suggest that if you are new to the online world, start with an online service such as AOL. Become familiar with email, downloading, chatting, sending and receiving files, etc. Poke around the World Wide Web and the rest of the Internet. When you find you are using your online service only to get to the Internet, it's time to get a direct connection through your local ISP. **But now** the iMac has made it so much simpler to get to the web, use email, and to do everything else that it is just about as easy to have a direct Internet connection as it is to use AOL. Many people like the organization of a village, though—the clubs, easy chat rooms, etc. I'm afraid you're going to have to make the decision yourself of which one to sign up with.

You can get a broadband connection through an ISP **in addition to AOL; then you can log on to America Online through your broadband, but you will be paying **for both.** Your AOL bill will be lower, however! See page 11.*

If you decide to use America Online

This is one thing to consider: In Mac OS X there will be lots of times your iMac wants to connect to the Internet and you don't even realize it. If you have a direct connection through a local or national ISP (instead of AOL), the iMac will open

To install America Online:

Go to the Applications folder.

Double-click the "Installers" folder.

Double-click "Install AOL for Mac OS X."

Follow the simple directions.

This is the Internet, vast and wild.

This is the online service. You can go out the back door of the service and get to the Internet.

Or you can go through an ISP.

the connection, log on, open your browser, and find the appropriate web page or information it needs. **But** if you have an America Online connection, you have to actually *sign on* to AOL yourself; the iMac cannot sign on for you automatically. Thus OS X cannot get connected and go where it wants to go. This will end up being very annoying.

EarthLink

EarthLink is a *national* ISP (Internet Service Provider), as opposed to a *local* ISP who would be physically located in your area. When you go through the iMac set-up process, you will have the option to choose EarthLink as your provider. Even though EarthLink is not local to most people, it provides local access numbers for most places. If there is no local number available for your area, EarthLink provides an 800 number (although the 800 number costs an *extra* $4.95 an hour). The current cost to connect to EarthLink is something like $19.95 a month, and it will be billed to your credit card automatically. If you choose to connect with EarthLink, you will be given an email address.

(If you are in Hawaii or Alaska, read the fine print for EarthLink service—they apply the foreign rate to most parts of those states, which is an *extra* charge per hour!)

You might choose EarthLink for any of these reasons:

1. You don't want to bother trying to find a local ISP and then gathering all the details to fill in the blanks as you go through the set-up process— you'd rather take advantage of the arrangement Apple and EarthLink have provided and let the software set up everything for you.

2. There is no local ISP in your area.

3. You travel a lot and you want to have a national ISP that can provide you with local numbers in many areas of the country.

    (America Online is also accessible all over the country, and in most places around the world.)

If you're not ready to make a decision to choose EarthLink during the iMac set-up process, you can always skip the connectivity part of the set-up and come back later. You have software on your iMac that will set you up with an EarthLink account at any time, and all it will take is a few minutes and a few clicks; see Chapter 15.

You need to choose: local or national ISP

Your iMac has an Internet Setup Assistant you will use, starting on the next page. It's going to ask whether you want to use a local ISP or a national one. You must know the answer before you start the set-up process.

If you already have a local provider, your decision is already made. If you don't have a local provider, you might want to use EarthLink for now because it's easy and you don't have to think hard to get connected. If you later decide you want to switch, you certainly can.

America Online and the iMac setup process

If you already use or plan to use America Online, **do not try to set up your iMac for the Internet** (as you'll see on page 15—choose "I'm not ready to connect to the Internet"). America Online connects you to both their internal service *and* to the Internet—**AOL will be your ISP.**

Using both AOL and an ISP

It is certainly possible to use both AOL and another ISP. In fact, your monthly bill from AOL is about half the regular monthly rate if you are connected to an ISP (although of course the ISP will also bill you monthly). Some people use both because someone in the house wants all the chats, clubs, organization, and structure of the AOL service, but someone else in the house wants the direct, clean connection to the Internet without AOL getting in the way. If this is your plan, **go ahead and do both**—connect with your ISP during the iMac set-up process, then install America Online and choose the option in AOL to "Bring Your Own Access."

Important note regarding credit cards: *If you plan to sign up with either EarthLink or America Online, you need a* **credit card** *to go through the set-up process because an Internet connection is not free. You will be asked to enter your credit card number. This is safe. Really. The information is highly encrypted (in secret code). It is much easier for someone to get your credit card number in a restaurant, over the telephone, through mail order, from a receipt dropped in the mall parking lot, etc., than it is to get it by hacking into a secure server. (And you're typically only liable for $50 if your credit card is used illegally anyway.)*

Start the computer

If you haven't turned on your iMac yet, do so now: press the Power button on the back, left side of the base, as pictured on page 5. The tone you hear means that the computer is starting. In a few seconds a computer "happy face" appears in the middle of the screen, indicating the iMac has found the operating system and can start up.

If this is your first time . . .

If this is the first time you have turned on your iMac, a series of welcome messages, set-up windows, and registration forms appear on your screen. These will help you set up your iMac so that you can be working or browsing the World Wide Web within a few minutes.

1. Welcome

The first thing you see is an animated "Welcome" message in various languages. Then a "Welcome" panel appears. Choose the county or region in which you're located (click on it with the mouse), then click the "Continue" button. **If you've never used a mouse before now,** read pages 26-27 and the description of "single-click," then come back to this page and begin.

Single-click on a country to select it. The selected (chosen) country is "highlighted" with a gray bar.

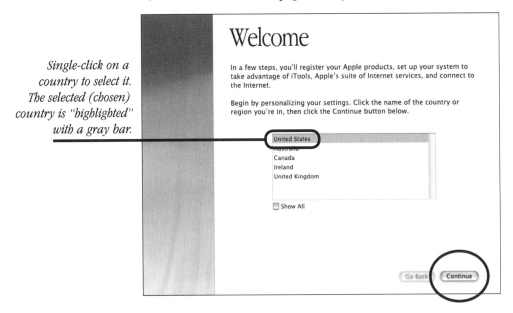

2. Personalize Your Settings

Choose a keyboard layout based on your country: Single-click on the name of the country you're in, then single-click the "Continue" button.

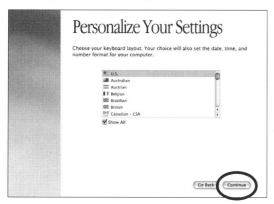

When you select a country, you also set the correct format for the date, time, and numbers for that country.

3. Registration information

Fill out the registration forms to register your iMac with Apple. After each "page," single-click the "Continue" button.

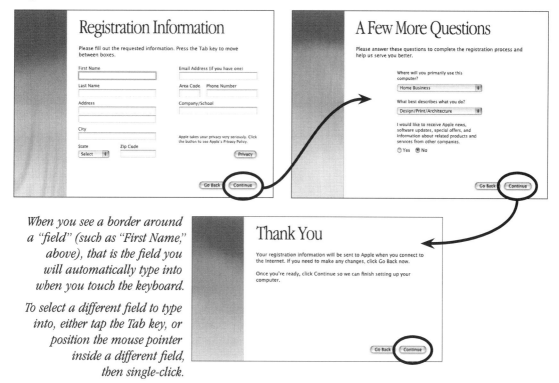

When you see a border around a "field" (such as "First Name," above), that is the field you will automatically type into when you touch the keyboard.

To select a different field to type into, either tap the Tab key, or position the mouse pointer inside a different field, then single-click.

4. Create Your iMac Account

Your iMac sets up a personal user "account" for you that contains folders in which to keep your documents, movies, and photos, and creates your own customized settings. Later, you can set up other "users," like your kids or grandkids, spouse, or co-workers; each user has his own account with his own settings, applications, documents, files, and folders.

For now, there are **two important things to know:**

a. The account name you fill in right now will be known as the **Administrator.** That might not seem important at the moment, but it will be. Only the Administrator can do certain things in Mac OS X; if the iMac ever asks you for the Administrator password, know that *you* are the Administrator and the iMac wants the password *you* enter in this set-up screen.

b. The **password** is extremely important—you will need it often. **Write it down somewhere. Don't forget it.** Type in a hint that will remind you what it is; if you do forget it, the iMac will give you this hint.

Fill in the text fields, then single-click the "Continue" button.

Create Your Account

With Mac OS X, everyone who uses the computer can have an account with their own settings and a place to keep their documents.

Set up your account now. You can add accounts for others later.

Name: `Robin Williams`
Example: Mary Jones

Short Name: `robin`
Example: mjones
An alternate name for your account, used by some network services. Enter 8 lowercase characters or fewer, with no spaces.

Password: `••••••`
The password for this account.

Verify: `••••••`
Enter your password again, exactly as you typed it.

Password Hint: `|`
(optional)
Enter something that will help you remember your password.

(Go Back) (Continue)

5. Get Internet Ready

This is where you have to make a decision about your Internet connection. If you have read pages 6–11, you might be ready to make a choice.

■ **If you do not want to set up an Internet connection just yet,***
or **if you have an AOL account** already or plan to get one, check the last option: "I'm not ready to connect to the Internet."

*If you want more time to think about your options, you can always sign up for any option later; when you're ready, use Chapter 15.

■ If you have not called an ISP (Internet Service Provider, as explained on pages 6–11) and set up an account with them, you can take the easy way out and **sign up with EarthLink.** Just click the first button (or the second button if you received a code for a special offer from EarthLink). Follow the simple step-by-step directions to get a free, thirty-day trial account. If you don't cancel your account at the end of thirty days, EarthLink will start billing you (about $21.95 a month for unlimited access).

At the moment, your EarthLink account will be a **dial-up** through the phone line you connected. If you want **broadband** from EarthLink (as explained on pages 6 and 7), sign up today through the dial-up, then go to their web site **(www.earthlink.com)**** and see if you can get a broadband connection in your area. They will send someone to your house with a special modem to get your iMac set up.

**If you don't know how to go to a web site, see Chapter 16.

■ **If you already have an account with an ISP** *(not including AOL),* click the third button, "I'll use my existing Internet service."

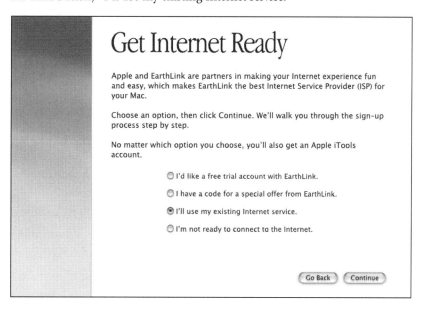

6. How Do You Connect?

Click the button that describes the type of Internet connection you have:

Just a reminder:
You did plug the telephone cable that came with your iMac into the computer and into a phone jack, yes? If not, do so now, unless you already have a broadband connection set up and working.

- If you have not made special arrangements for a high-speed broadband connection (such as DSL or cable modem) and you're not in a corporate office or large school, you probably use a **telephone modem.**

  If you sign up for **EarthLink's trial offer,** select the telephone modem.

- If you're in an office or school and plan to connect through a **network,** select "Local Area Network."

  Even if you have a small home/office network (a Local Area Network, also known as a LAN), such as a DSL or cable connection going through a switch or hub, choose this option instead of DSL or cable so the iMac will connect to your network.

- If you have already called a DSL or cable provider and they have already come to your home or office and set up the special modem and cables, and the cable from the modem goes directly into your iMac (not through another box called a hub or a switch), then choose **Cable modem** or **DSL (Digital Subscriber Line).** (If you have a small network in your home or office, see the note above.)

- If your iMac has an AirPort wireless card already installed and you plan to connect through an Airport Base Station, select **AirPort wireless.** Even if your AirPort Base Station is connected to a phone line or into a network, you still need to choose the "AirPort" option.

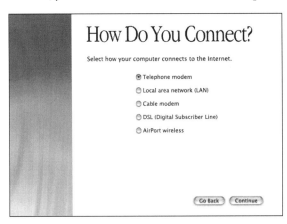

7. Telephone modem

If you already have or plan to have a dial-up account and so you clicked the "Telephone modem" option, you'll get the screens shown below.

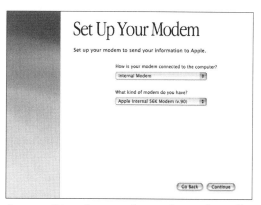

Enter the user name and password that your service provider gave you (not your email address nor your email password!). Enter the phone number the provider gave you that your modem *will dial, not the number* you *use to call the provider.*

On your iMac, these are the two choices that will automatically appear. These are correct, unless you have installed a different modem, which is unlikely.

Cable, DSL, LAN, or Wireless Service

You can choose only one of these options if the existing service is already up and running and you want to tap into it. You'll have to ask your cable or DSL provider to give you the information you need to enter into the appropriate fields, or the person called the "network administrator" for your corporation or school.

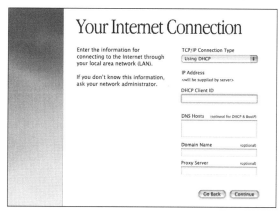

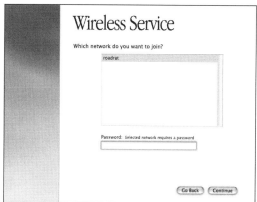

For a small network that is already established, you can usually choose "Using DHCP" and the iMac will go to the network and get the settings it needs.

If an AirPort Base Station is already set up and working, its name will appear in the larger box. You need to enter that station's password.

8. Get iTools

iTools is a suite of free services from Apple. You can get a "mac.com" email account, easily share files with people all over the world, and create a personal web site. If you plan to use iPhoto, you'll need an iTools account to take advantage of all the iPhoto features. Chapter 19 tells you all about iTools.

You can add an iTools account later, if you want to skip it now (see Chapter 19).

Even though iTools offers you a free email account, understand that **iTools is not an ISP**—you cannot get connected to the Internet through iTools or Apple. Even if you get free email account, you must still pay an ISP to connect you.

If you choose to sign up for an iTools account, you'll be asked for a "User Name." This will be the name on your mac.com email (such as robinw@mac.com), and when you make web sites with iTools or iPhoto, your web address will use this User Name (such as homepage.mac.com/robinw). You will also be asked to provide a password. Write that password down somewhere!!!

Tip: I have a special Rolodex on my desk that holds nothing but my passwords. I know you don't think you'll ever have that many passwords, but you will.

Apple also requires you to provide a "Password Question" and a "Password Answer" in case you lose your password. This should be a question only you know the answer to, such as "What is my true hair color?" If you forget your password when trying to *log in* to your iTools account, you'll see a little "link" to click that says something like, "Forgot your password?" Then you will see your Password Question, and if you answer it correctly, Apple will tell you the password you forgot.

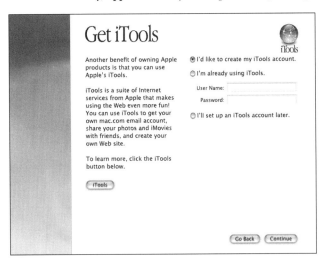

You can choose to set up an iTools account later, or not at all.
Click the "iTools" button to learn more about what iTools offers;
when you're done reading, click the button to come back to this page.

9. Now your iMac will connect to Apple

Single-click the "Continue" button on the previous screen; your iMac will connect to the Internet. It will create your Administrative user account on the computer, create your iTools account (if you chose to do so), and register this information with Apple. Even if you don't have an Internet Service Provider yet, the iMac will go out through the phone line you connected using a secret toll-free number to get straight to Apple, and it will register your iMac.

You only have one more step to go after this!

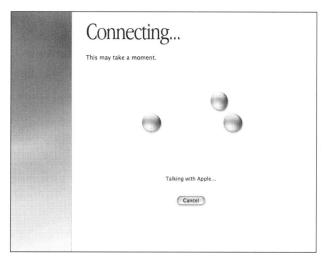

This bouncing bubble indicates your iMac is making an Internet connection.

10. Set Up Mail

"Mail" is the name of the email application that is installed on your iMac. Mac OS X automatically adds your new, free, iTools email information to this form. The Mail application, however, can check *all* of your existing email accounts, even though they are on different servers. It can even check your EarthLink account.

So if you have *another* email address that you want to add, select "Add my existing email account," and then fill in the information. If you don't know how to complete the "existing account" form (shown on the opposite page), call your Internet Service Provider and ask for the information (although they probably gave you a piece of paper with all that information written down).

If you don't have the information for the existing account right now, you can skip this part for the moment and fill it in later, directly in the Mail application (see Chapter 20).

If you click "Add my existing email account," you'll see the screen shown at the top of the following page.

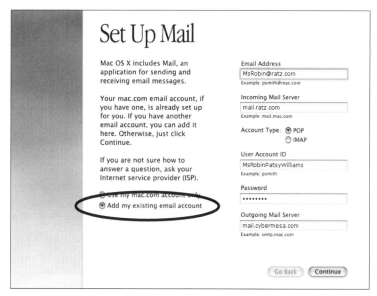

You only need to fill this out if you want Mail to check another email address.

- **Email Address:** Include the @ symbol and "domain name" (ratz.com, in the example above).

- **Incoming Mail Server:** This is usually the word "mail" in front of the domain name in your email account. For instance, if your email address is **john@dogfood.com,** your incoming mail server is probably **mail.dogfood.com.**

- **Account Type:** Your account is probably POP, unless you have been told otherwise. (iTools and America Online are IMAP servers.)

- **User Account ID:** This is the name the mail server knows you by. If this particular mail server is also your ISP, your User Account ID is probably the name you get billed under. It might be the first part of your email address, or it might be something altogether different! You might have to ask.

- **Password:** This is not the password to get your email! This is the password that goes with your User Account ID. It might be the same as your email password, but probably (hopefully) not.

- **Outgoing Mail Server:** This is also known as the SMTP server. This is always the name of your Internet Service Provider. For instance, I own the "domain" ratz.com and I get email at ratz.com. But my ISP is Cybermesa; that's who I pay every month for my Internet connection, so Cybermesa is my SMTP server. No matter where your *in*coming mail is from, everything you mail *out* goes out through your ISP. Usually you can just add "mail" to their name (or sometimes "smtp"), as shown in the example.

11. Select Time Zone

Single-click on your part of the world. Your time zone will appear in that pop-up menu just below the map. Click the "Continue" button.

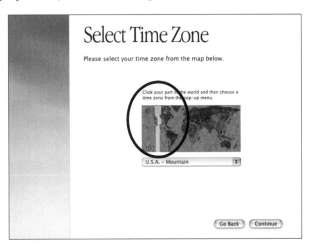

12. Thank You

Your iMac has now been registered and set up! Click "Go" to see your new Desktop and Dock, which are explained in detail in the next two chapters.

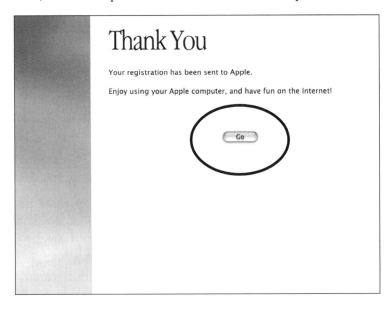

Mousing, Menus, and More

Now that you've got your brand-new iMac up and running, you're ready to roll. In this chapter, we'll talk about the wonderful world of the mouse, the Dock, toolbars, menus, windows, and so much more!

(After you're comfortable with the information in this chapter, if you still want to know more about these topics, *The Little Mac OS X Book* is a great resource.)

So, turn the page, and let the fun begin . . .

Start up

It takes a moment or two for your computer to turn itself on. This process used to be called "booting up" because the iMac is actually going inside of itself and pulling itself up by its own bootstraps, so to speak.

If you watch the screen (also called the monitor) while your computer starts up, you'll see a "happy Mac" icon, indicating that the computer has found what it needs to start up. A few moments later, you see a graphic that shows the operating system, Mac OS X, starting up. You may see another Mac OS graphic (9.2), and a panel with a progress bar that shows "Classic Environment starting from 'Macintosh HD." Your computer is loading some extra software that it may need, explained on the opposite page.

Software is the invisible programming code that makes things happen inside the computer. You can't touch the software itself. You can touch the disk that stores the software, but you can't touch the code.

*Your computer, however, is a piece of **hardware;** hardware is anything you can bump into.*

If you do not see the "Classic Environment" starting up at this time, don't worry. If you need it, it will start automatically.

*This colorful bar across the bottom of the screen is the **Dock.** See the end of this chapter for details about the Dock.*

Mac OS X (and OS 9)

The phrase "Mac OS X" is pronounced "Mac Oh Ess Ten." The OS stands for Operating System. Every computer has some sort of operating system that runs it. The Mac OS, of course, is the best, as evidenced by those who copy it.

Notice when your iMac starts up it says "Mac OS X." It displays the version of the operating system that your Mac is "running." The Mac's most recent OS before Mac OS X was OS 9. Because lots of people own lots of software that was designed to run using OS 9, Apple designed OS X to include something called the *Classic Environment,* as shown on the opposite page. Your computer will automatically switch to OS 9 whenever you use an application that needs it. You don't need to know anything about OS 9, and you may not even realize the computer has switched operating systems. To make this possible, the iMac already has both operating systems installed, Mac OS X and Mac OS 9.

This is the Mac OS X logo. The "X" is pronounced "ten."

If you know how to use your mouse and menus already, you can check to see which operating system any Macintosh is running: while you're at the Desktop, go to the Apple menu and choose "About This Mac." A panel will appear that tells you loud and clear which OS your particular machine is using. The small type below the words "Mac OS X" identifies the specific *version* of Mac OS X that's running. (See Chapter 13 on System Preferences to learn how to use "Software Update" to update your system when a new version becomes available.)

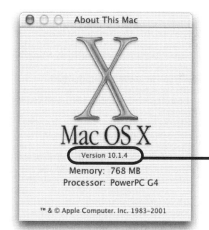

Click on this text to show the "Build" number (which you don't need to know). Click again to show the Serial Number of your Mac OS X software.

This is how your hand holds the iMac optical mouse:

*This is the **pointer:** You might also hear it referred to as a **cursor.***

The mouse

The first thing you need to become comfortable with is the **mouse.** You can plug it into either end of the keyboard, depending on whether you're right- or left-handed. It doesn't *have* to sit next to the keyboard—you can put it anywhere you can reach it easily. The mouse sits flat on the tabletop. The tail, I mean the cord, faces away from you.

Position your hand on the mouse so your index finger rests on the front of the mouse close to the end where the cord is attached. Place your thumb and middle fingers on the plastic finger rests on each side of the mouse. Press lightly with your index finger. It makes a clicking sound when you press, so we call this "clicking" the mouse. The optical mouse doesn't have an actual button to press. The entire mouse is, in effect, one big button. The closer to the front edge you press with your index finger, the easier it is to click.

Try it: Move the mouse around with your hand. Notice the *pointer* on the screen moves as you move the mouse on the desk—if you move the mouse to the right, the pointer moves to the right. Click the mouse button here and there, just don't click on a *picture* of anything yet!

How to use the mouse

You'll be using the mouse in four ways: *single-click, double-click, drag,* and something called *press-and-drag.* Each of these motions accomplishes different things, so it's very important to understand what each one does and when to do it. **Read** the stuff below, **read** the opposite page, **then** turn the page and experiment.

*The very **tip** of the **pointer** is the only part that does anything! Make sure the very **tip** is positioned where you need it before you click or drag.*

Single-click
Position the pointer, then click the mouse button *once.*

Double-click
Position the pointer, then click the mouse button *twice* very fast. You have to hold the mouse very still—if the mouse moves even a tiny bit between clicks, it won't work. If this happens to you, try again.

Drag (sometimes called click-and-drag)
Without holding the mouse button down, just drag the mouse. Usually you click something right before you drag (such as a menu), so it's often called **click-and-drag,** not to be confused with *press-and-drag* (as explained below).

Press-and-drag
Click and *hold the mouse button down,* then drag the mouse, keeping the button down. When you're done, let go of the button.

The mouse pad

You might already have a mouse pad, a thin pad of some sort that you place next to your computer and set your mouse upon. You don't *have* to have a mouse pad—there's nothing magical about the pad that makes the mouse work or not work. It's just a piece of plastic or heavy fabric that used to give better traction for your mouse back in the old days when a mouse had a rolling ball in it. The iMac mouse is an optical device that doesn't use a rolling ball, nor does it benefit from better traction. Even so, you may still want to use a mouse pad just to soften the feel of the mouse on the desk's surface and to mute the sound of plastic banging and rubbing against wood (or metal). The sounds of mouse clicks are more than enough, without adding clacking and scraping.

Running out of room on the mouse pad

When you're actually moving your mouse along a pad, you will come to the edge of it regularly. At first you might feel like the pad is much too small. But this is how to deal with it:

> If your finger is holding the mouse button down and you are about to fall off the pad while dragging, *keep your finger pressed down on the button and pick up the mouse.* Keep your finger holding down that button, and just pick up the mouse, put it anywhere you want on the pad, and continue dragging or whatever you were doing.

You will use this technique so much it will start to happen naturally and you won't even notice it.

So now let's go experiment with the mouse!

*This is a typical
sort of mouse pad.*

The windows

We're going to experiment with the mouse, using the **windows.** A window, as shown below, is one of the basic features of the Macintosh. (I know, you may have heard the term Windows, with a capital W, in reference to Microsoft and other computers besides Macintosh. Those other computers use technology, um, "inspired" by the Macintosh.)

You'll use windows at the Desktop, and you'll use them in every program you work in, including email and the Internet, so it's a good idea to get to know them pretty well. You're going to have to resize them, move them, put them away, and get them out again. You can do all of these things with the mouse.

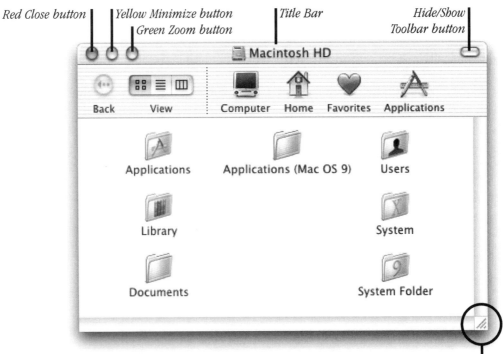

Red Close button | *Yellow Minimize button* | *Green Zoom button* | *Title Bar* | *Hide/Show Toolbar button*

Resize corner

Above is the window you probably see when you first turn on your iMac.

Macintosh HD

Double-click this icon to open your hard disk window.

If you don't see this window, *position the tip of your pointer over the little picture (the icon, as shown to the left) in the upper-right corner of the Desktop called "Macintosh HD."* ***Double-click*** *that icon and you will see this window (or one very similar).*

All of the icons (pictures) inside of this window represent folders that contain different files on your computer. We'll talk about them later.

Using your mouse, do these things:

Move the window

Position the tip of the pointer anywhere in the Title Bar (except on top of one of the buttons). Press the mouse button down *and hold it down; while the button is down,* drag the mouse (this is called **press-and-drag**). The window will move as you drag. Let go of the mouse when you've repositioned the window, and the window will stay in that spot.

Remember, the tip is the only part of the pointer that is "hot" (that does anything)! The rest of the pointer is just so you can see the darn thing.

Resize the window

Position the tip of the pointer on top of the **Resize corner** in the bottom-right corner of the window. **Press-and-drag—**don't let go! As you drag the mouse around, you see the window change size. When you let go, your window will stay that size until you change it again.

There's another way to resize a window very quickly: position the *tip* of the pointer on the green **Zoom button,** in the upper-left of the window (see the illustration below, right). **Single-click** right on that green button and the window will zoom larger or smaller, depending on whether it was smaller or larger before you resized it. After you've resized a window, the Zoom button toggles the window size between the last two window sizes (large and small).

If you clicked and your window disappeared, it's probably because you clicked the Close or Minimize button, which are both just to the left of the Zoom button! If so . . .

This is the Resize corner of the window.

Get your window back (if you lost it)

If your window disappeared, first look for it on the far-right end of the Dock (that bar across the bottom of your screen), which is where it went if you accidentally clicked the yellow Minimize button. If you see its tiny picture in the Dock, single-click on it and the window will reopen on the Desktop, as shown on the following page.

If there is no tiny picture of the window in the Dock, double-click the "Macintosh HD" icon that is sitting in the upper-right corner of your screen to reopen the window.

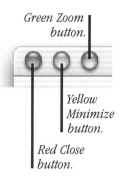

Green Zoom button.

Yellow Minimize button.

Red Close button.

Yellow Minimize button.

Minimize the window

Position the tip of the pointer on the yellow Minimize button in the upper-left corner of the window. **Single-click.** This sends your window down to the Dock as an icon (a small picture) which moves it out of your way and reduces the clutter on the Desktop.

To reopen the window, single-click its icon in the Dock.

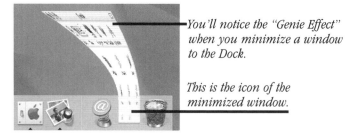

You'll notice the "Genie Effect" when you minimize a window to the Dock.

This is the icon of the minimized window.

Scroll with the scroll bars

Scroll bars (shown below) are along the right and bottom edges of every window and are very important features. You see, often there are so many items inside the window that they all can't be displayed at once, so the scroll bars make things "glide" past the window opening. It's sort of like sitting in a train and watching the scenery go by. Read about the scroll bars, below, then follow the steps on the next page to practice using your mouse and learn how to control the scroll bars at the same time.

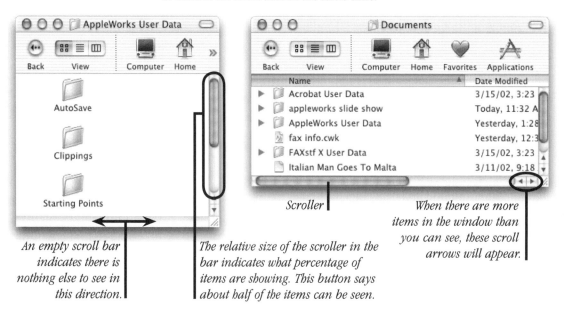

An empty scroll bar indicates there is nothing else to see in this direction.

Scroller

The relative size of the scroller in the bar indicates what percentage of items are showing. This button says about half of the items can be seen.

When there are more items in the window than you can see, these scroll arrows will appear.

Scroll bar and mouse practice

The scroll bars will be "empty" (no arrows and no blue scrollers) unless all of the items can't fit inside the window, so for this exercise you have to make sure the window is small enough that you can see the blue scrollers, as shown on the opposite page. To **resize** your window so it is fairly small, press on the Resize corner in the bottom-right corner, and drag diagonally up to the left until a scroller appears. Then do each of the following:

Single-click in any *empty* area of the scroll bar. Notice it pops the items in the window to one side or the other horizontally, or up and down vertically.

Notice on which end of the scroll bar the scroller is located (see opposite page). **Press** on one of the little *scroll arrows* that is pointing in the direction you want the scroller to move (don't worry, just press one or the other—you'll see). Watch as the contents of the window slide past. Notice that the scroller is a visual clue that tells you how close you are to one end or the other of the window.

I know the scrollers seem like they make things slide in the opposite direction than you expect. You'll eventually get used to it and will soon automatically choose the correct arrow to scroll in the direction you want.

Press-and-drag on the scroller itself to move it somewhere else along the scroll bar. Watch as the contents move.

Resize your window big enough so one or both of the scrollers disappear.

Pop quiz: *On first glance, the window below looks empty.*

a. *What are the two visual clues that tell you there actually is something in the window? I haven't explained one of them yet, so don't bother looking in the text. Take a close look at the window and find the clues.*

b. *Exactly how many files (items) are in this window? (That's a clue to the first answer.)*

c. *Name two ways to display the items (I did tell you these).*

Answers (printed upside-down):

a. *A scroll bar contains a scroller and scroll arrows; the Status Bar across the top of the window says there are "6 items" in this window.*

b. *The Status Bar across the top of the window says there are "6 items."*

c. *Click on the zoom button; drag the scroller to the opposite end of the scroll bar.*

The menu bar and menus

Let's use the mouse to see what's in the **menu bar** and how to use **menus.** The menu bar is the strip across the very top of the screen (shown below).

This is the Finder menu bar. You'll always see the menu bar, but it displays different items in different applications.

Each word and icon in this menu bar has a menu of commands to make the computer do something. A typical menu looks like this one on the right:

To drop down a menu, position the tip of the pointer on any word or icon in the menu bar, then **single-click** on it. The menu appears. Go through the menu bar and read the lists of options. Don't forget to check the Apple menu as well, under the Apple icon on the far left.

To choose an item in the menu, drag the mouse down the menu. As you pass over each item with the pointer, it "highlights," or changes color. That means that item is *selected.* If you **single-click** on a *selected* menu item, that command is executed. Be careful! There are a number of commands you don't want to execute right now!

I used the pointer to select the command "Empty Trash."

The menu will disappear after a few seconds if you don't click on anything. If you want to **make it go away** *instantly,* just click anywhere on the Desktop.

You've probably noticed that many **menu items are gray** instead of black, and they don't highlight as you slide your pointer over them. When an item is gray, it means that particular command or item is not available at the moment. For instance, the command "Empty Trash" in *your* Finder menu might be gray, right? (Check to see.) The gray command indicates there is no trash in your Trash basket to be emptied so you can't use that command.

Select something from a menu

First of all, make sure there is a window open because the command you are going to choose will affect the open window. If you have been following along, there should be a window open.

Macintosh HD
This is the icon that represents your hard disk.

If you don't see an open window:

1. Position the tip of your pointer directly over the icon of your hard disk, which is in the upper-right corner of the screen, below the menu bar, and is called "Macintosh HD."

2. Double-click the icon. It will open to a window.

If you still don't see a window, you may have moved the mouse between the two clicks and it didn't work. Try again.

Okay. Whew. We've all got an open window on the screen. Unless you changed things yourself, your window probably looks something like the one shown below, right? Now let's change the way the files are displayed, called the window View (next page).

This window is currently in Icon view, indicated by the highlighted Icon view button.

If you don't see the Toolbar, click this button.

I'll tell you more about these different "views" right after the menu exercises!

You're looking at a window full of **icons,** which are small pictures that represent the various files stored on your computer. These icons give you clues as to what kinds of files they are (we'll talk about that later). But some people prefer to view the files in a list of names, instead of looking at all the picutures. Let's change this window to a **List View,** using the menu.

This is how the window looks in Icon View. Notice the "Icon View" button in the Toolbar is highlighted.

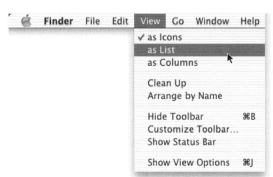

To change a window to a **List View,** go to the "View" menu, then choose "as List" (shown on the left). The window changes to show all the items in a list, as shown below. Practice using the menu with this folder—choose every other item in the View menu and experiment!

This is how the window looks after switching to List View. Notice the "List View" button in the Toolbar is highlighted.

Click-and-drag vs. press-and-drag

On the oppposite page you used the mouse movement called **click-and-drag,** where you click once to bring the menu up, then you drag the mouse down the list *without holding the button down,* and click again. You can also use a **press-and-drag** in a menu to do the same thing, where you press, *hold the mouse button down,* then let go on the selected item.

It's a good thing to be conscious of the difference between click-and-drag and press-and-drag because sometimes you *must* use a press-and-drag because the click-and-drag doesn't work. (Also, if you ever work on an older Macintosh, you'll find that the only way to select items from menus is to press-and-drag.)

So let's change the window view again using **press-and-drag.** Make sure you are conscious of the difference. It will make everything easier as you learn to use the rest of the iMac features.

1. **Single-click** anywhere on the hard disk window, in any blank area. This selects the window and makes sure the command you are about to choose does its business to *this* window.

2. In the menu bar across the top of the screen, position the tip of the pointer on the menu called "View." **Press** on the word, *and hold the mouse button down.* The menu will drop down.

3. *Keep holding the mouse button down,* and **drag** the pointer down to the choice "as List" (or "as Icons," whichever one does *not* have the checkmark next to it). The choice will highlight, or turn dark, and when it is dark, **let go.** Don't try to click! Just let go.

I recommend you switch views several more times and make sure you are conscious of using either the *click*-and-drag technique or the *press*-and-drag technique. You will feel more in control of your computer if you can recognize the difference.

Unfortunately, many technical writers use the term "click-and-drag" when they really mean "press-and-drag." If click-and-drag doesn't work, try press-and-drag.

So are you starting to feel more comfortable with the mouse? Let's do one more useful exercise with the mouse. Along the way you'll use the **Apple menu** and take a look at what are called "hierarchical menus."

Hierarchical menus

Some menus need to contain many more choices than a single menu can accommodate. Hierarchical menus organize items into appropriate groups so that many menu options can be hidden under a single heading. To demonstrate, go to the Apple menu.

1. On the far-left end of the menu bar is a tiny icon of the Apple logo. This is actually a menu, called the Apple menu! **Single-click** on the Apple to drop down the menu.

2. Find the menu item called "Dock." Notice it has a little triangle pointing to the right. The triangle is a visual clue that indicates if you select that item, another menu will pop out to the right, as shown below. This is called a "hierarchical menu," or "h-menu."

3. So point to "Dock" to display the submenu, *slide across the highlighted bar to the submenu list,* then click on "Position on Left." The Dock changes from a horizontal Dock at the bottom of your screen to a vertical Dock on the left side of the screen.

   To revert back to a bottom Dock position, repeat these three steps, but choose the "Position on Bottom" option in the submenu.

Click here to get the Apple menu.

So this is an h-menu. You'll find them all over your iMac. H-menus can be a little tricky to maneuver in, so don't get upset if they disappear on you now and then. The trick is to follow the highlighted bar horizontally, then slide right down the h-menu. In this case, when "Position on Left" highlights, click on it.

If you're really studious, try using the **press-and-drag** technique on an h-menu, as opposed to the click-and-drag.

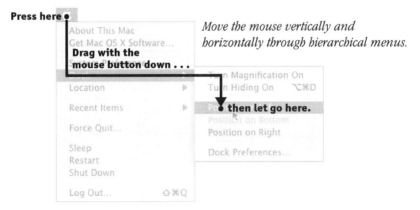

Move the mouse vertically and horizontally through hierarchical menus.

Remember, if you run out of mouse pad space, just pick up the mouse and move it. If your finger was holding the mouse button down to get the menu (pressing), keep it down while you move the mouse.

It can sometimes be a little tricky to grab an item on an h-menu. If the menu disappears or if a different one pops up, just slide the pointer back to the item you want ("Dock," in this case), then slide directly across the highlighted bar to the right, then down the h-menu. Below are some other examples.

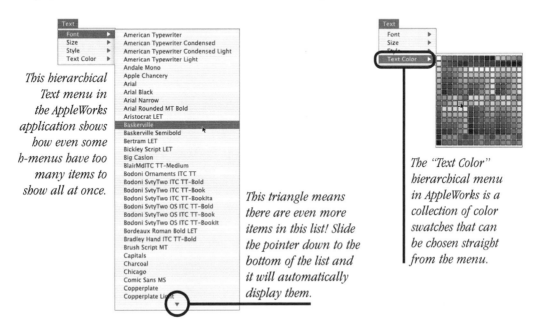

This hierarchical Text menu in the AppleWorks application shows how even some h-menus have too many items to show all at once.

This triangle means there are even more items in this list! Slide the pointer down to the bottom of the list and it will automatically display them.

The "Text Color" hierarchical menu in AppleWorks is a collection of color swatches that can be chosen straight from the menu.

The window views

Several pages ago you used the menu to change views. Now let's change the window views using a button and talk about the different views.

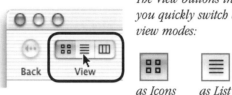

The View buttons in the window Toolbar let you quickly switch between the three different view modes:

as Icons   *as List*   *as Columns*

To change to the List view:

Position the tip of the pointer on the "List View" button in the Toolbar and **single-click** on the button.

So now your window is displaying all of the items as a list, right? It should look similar to the example below.

The nicest thing about the List View is that you can see the contents of a number of folders in the same window, as shown on the opposite page. This will come in handy when you start making a lot of files and want to find them or move them.

Below is another example of a window in the List View, as well as callouts to the many ways you can customize your window. Many people prefer to see their files as a list of names instead of all the icons. It's entirely up to you!

*Single-click any one of these column headings to **organize,** or **sort,** your files by that heading. How can you tell that the files shown below are sorted by "Name"?*

*You can **resize the columns.** Just position your pointer directly on the dividing line between two column headings; the pointer will turn into a double-headed arrow:* ✛. *With that arrow, just press-and-drag to the left or right.*

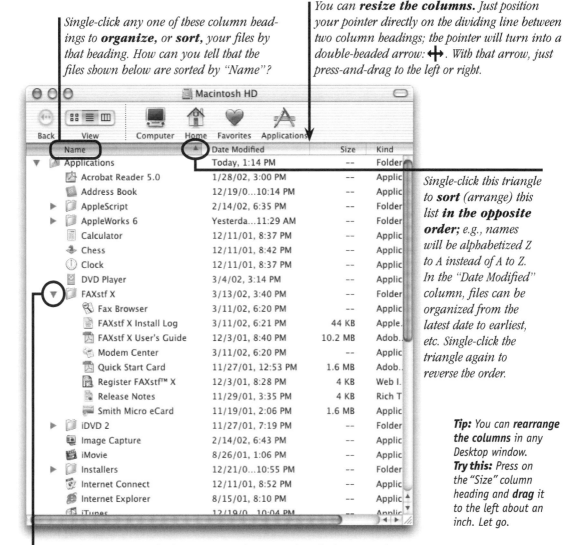

*Single-click this triangle to **sort** (arrange) this list **in the opposite order;** e.g., names will be alphabetized Z to A instead of A to Z. In the "Date Modified" column, files can be organized from the latest date to earliest, etc. Single-click the triangle again to reverse the order.*

Tip: You can **rearrange the columns** in any Desktop window. **Try this:** Press on the "Size" column heading and **drag** it to the left about an inch. Let go.

Single-click any tiny "disclosure" triangle to see a list of what is inside that folder. Single-click again to close it up. Try it.

Clicking that triangle to see the files stored inside is called "expanding" a folder. All of the files you see indented under the folder name are actually stored inside that folder.

In the List View, you can also **double-click any tiny folder icon** to open it up in its own window, the same as if it were a large folder icon in the Icon View.

If you are looking at your "Macintosh HD" window in List View, as shown below, double-click on the tiny "Applications" folder icon. The new window that opens *replaces* the current window; that is, you now see the contents of the "Applications" folder instead of the "Macintosh HD."

To return to the previous window (which in the example shown below would be "Macintosh HD"), click the "Back" button in the Toolbar.

*Double-click a folder icon to open that folder as its own window, as shown to the right. The contents of this newly opened folder **replace** the contents of the previous window.*

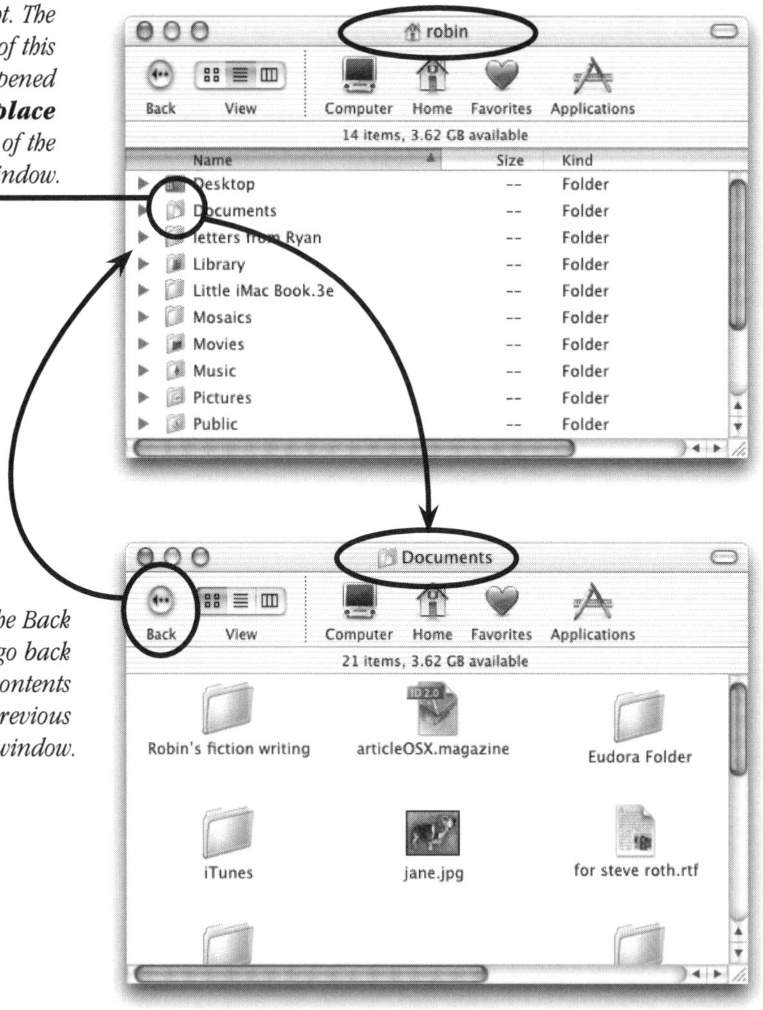

Click the Back button to go back to the contents of the previous window.

To change to the Column View:

Position the tip of the pointer on the "Column View" button in the Toolbar and **single-click** on the button.

Tip: When you Save or Open a document, you'll find the Column View in the dialog box, so it's good to understand how it works.

So now your window displays the contents of a folder in relation to the organizational structure on your computer. Take a look:

Folders have small triangles on the right, pointing to their contents in the next column.

Follow the highlighted items and you can see that the disk named "Macintosh HD" is showing its contents in the column to its right. The "Applications" folder is showing its contents in the column to its right. If you were to click on the AppleWorks 6 folder, another column would appear to the right, showing you the contents of the AppleWorks folder.

If you see the far-right column of Column View, you can always go back in the other direction: press the blue scroller at the bottom of the window and drag it to the left—you'll see the columns that are temporarily out of sight.

Below, if you start in the far-right column, you see the contents of the "Documents" folder, which is in the "robin" home folder, which is in the "Users" folder, which is stored on the "Macintosh HD."

The title bar says "Documents" because the Documents folder is actually selected, as shown by the darker highlight.

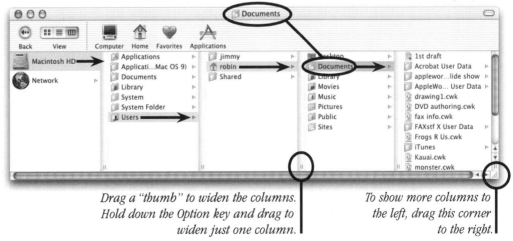

Drag a "thumb" to widen the columns. Hold down the Option key and drag to widen just one column.

To show more columns to the left, drag this corner to the right.

The Dock

The **Dock** is that strip across the bottom of your screen that contains a number of icons. Apple has put those icons in the Dock for your use, but you can customize it endlessly, as explained on the following pages. You can add folders, applications, web sites, documents, windows, or just about anything else to the Dock. Once an item is in the Dock, you just single-click to open it. You can delete items, rearrange items, move the Dock to the left or right of your screen, enlarge it, reduce it, hide it, and more.

Below is a typical Dock with brief explanations of what each item does and where you can find more information about it.

Items marked with asterisks (∗) will **automatically** attempt to connect your iMac to the Internet when you click them.

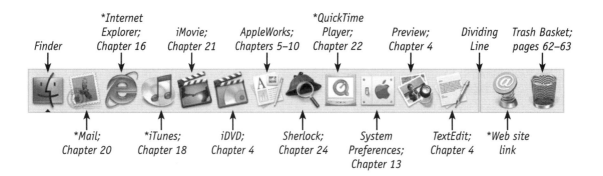

Finder   **Internet Explorer; Chapter 16*   *iMovie; Chapter 21*   *AppleWorks; Chapters 5–10*   **QuickTime Player; Chapter 22*   *Preview; Chapter 4*   *Dividing Line*   *Trash Basket; pages 62–63*

*Mail; Chapter 20   **iTunes; Chapter 18*   *iDVD; Chapter 4*   *Sherlock; Chapter 24*   *System Preferences; Chapter 13*   *TextEdit; Chapter 4*   **Web site link*

Position your mouse over a Dock item (don't click or press), and a "Help tag" appears to tell you what that item is.

After you open an application, its icon appears in the Dock (if it wasn't already) and a small triangle is your visual clue that the application is still open. How many applications are open at the moment, according to the Dock above?

Add items to the Dock

You can **add** anything you want to the Dock. Typically, you'll add files and folders that you want easy access to, as well as new applications you acquire. You'll notice when you add *applications,* they go on the *left* side of the dividing line. All other files must stay to the *right* of the dividing line.

To add a file: Find its icon (folder, application icon, document icon, etc.), then simply drag that icon down to the Dock and let go. You are not actually *moving* the file—you are simply adding an "alias" of it to the Dock (an alias goes and gets the real file; see Chapter 23 about aliases).

To add an *open* application: While the application is open and active, you will see its icon in the Dock. Press on that icon and you'll get a pop-up menu; choose "Keep In Dock" (shown to the right).

To add a web site: Using Internet Explorer, go to the web site you like. In the Address bar, drag the little @ symbol in the Address bar (circled, below) down to the Dock. If you are using Netscape, drag the Bookmark icon (next to the Location box) first to the Desktop, let go, then drag that icon into the Dock.

After you add a folder (just drag the folder to the Dock), you can *single-click* its icon in the Dock to open the folder window, or *press* its icon to pop-up a menu listing every item in the folder (shown below, right). Slide up the list to choose an item and that particular file will open. If you have folders inside this folder, you will get a submenu showing the items in that subfolder. Notice, however, that the folder icon in the Dock gives you no visual clue as to *which* folder it is. You can customize its icon, if you like (see page 407), so you can identify individual folders without having to mouse-over each one and wait for the Help tag.

Rearrange items in the Dock

To move the positions of items in the Dock, simply press-and-drag them. Only *application* icons are allowed to sit to the left of the dividing line (shown on the opposite page), however; everything else must stay to the right.

Remove items from the Dock

This is the "poof" that appears when you remove something from the Dock.

To remove items from the Dock, simply press-and-drag them off the Dock and drop them anywhere on the Desktop. A cute little "poof" will appear. Don't worry, you won't destroy the original files. All you remove is an icon from the Dock—you won't hurt the original application, folder, file, web site, or anything else. (You cannot remove the Trash basket or the Finder icon, though.)

Dock Preferences

When you're ready, you can customize several aspects of the Dock using the **Dock preferences.** To open the Dock preferences, as shown below, go to the Apple menu and choose "Dock...." You can either change several settings using that menu, or choose "Dock Preferences..." to get the preferences "pane" shown below.

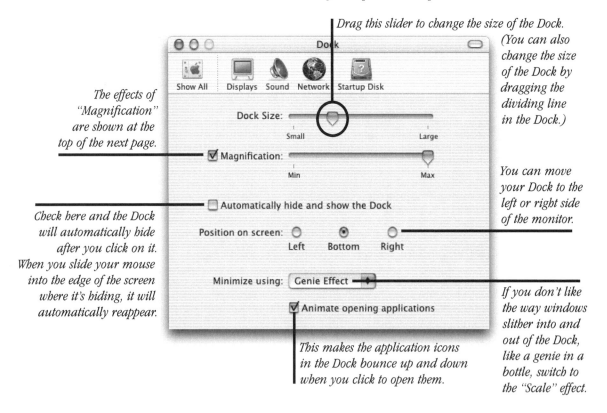

Drag this slider to change the size of the Dock. (You can also change the size of the Dock by dragging the dividing line in the Dock.)

The effects of "Magnification" are shown at the top of the next page.

You can move your Dock to the left or right side of the monitor.

Check here and the Dock will automatically hide after you click on it. When you slide your mouse into the edge of the screen where it's hiding, it will automatically reappear.

This makes the application icons in the Dock bounce up and down when you click to open them.

If you don't like the way windows slither into and out of the Dock, like a genie in a bottle, switch to the "Scale" effect.

*There is a **shortcut** to get the Dock preferences: Control-click (which means to hold down the Control key while you click) on the divider line in the Dock and change your preferences from the pop-up menu.*

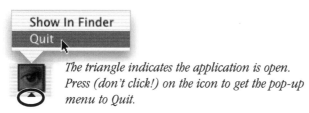

When "Magnification" is checked in the Dock preferences, as shown on the opposite page, the Dock icons grow as you run your mouse over them. How large they grow depends on where you set the Magnification slider.

Quit an application from the Dock

If you need to **quit an application,** just press on its icon in the Dock, and in the pop-up menu, choose Quit.

The triangle indicates the application is open. Press (don't click!) on the icon to get the pop-up menu to Quit.

Missing icons in the Dock

Every now and then one of your Dock icons might turn into a question mark or a generic Mac OS X icon, both shown to the right.

Question mark   *Generic icon*

Drag the **question mark** out of the Dock to get rid of it, then replace it: Find the icon in your window (probably in your Applications window), and drag it to the Dock.

The **generic icon** is okay. It still works just the same, and next time you restart your iMac, your real icon will probably come back.

Mouse preferences

Let's do one more thing to help make you feel comfortable using the mouse. Apple provides many ways for you to customize your iMac so it suits the way you work. One way it does this is through small programs called "System Preferences." I'm going to show you how a couple of the System Preferences work, and you can open up any others you want and tweak the obvious things. Most of them are very self-explanatory. Chapter 13 explains the ones you'll use most often.

To open the System Preferences, find the System Preferences icon in the Dock (circled below) and single-click it.

This is the System Preferences icon.

In the System Preferences window, single-click the **Mouse** icon.

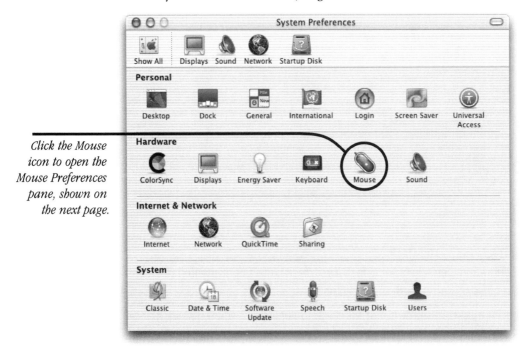

Click the Mouse icon to open the Mouse Preferences pane, shown on the next page.

Shown below is the **Mouse preferences pane.** It has two settings labeled "Tracking Speed" and "Double-Click Speed." First let's adjust the "Tracking Speed" of the mouse you are using.

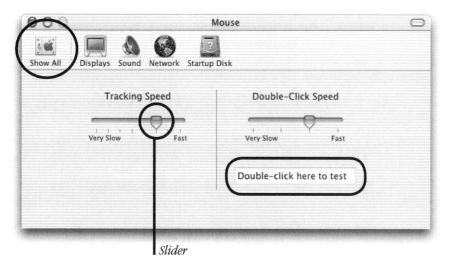

Slider

Tip: *Click the 'Show All" button when you want to return to the System Preferences main window.*

If you move the **Tracking Speed** slider to a "Fast" setting, it doesn't mean the *mouse* actually moves any *faster*—it means you don't have to move the mouse so far across the mouse pad to make the pointer travel across the screen.

> **Try it:** Move the "Tracking Speed" slider toward the "Very Slow" setting and see how far you have to move your hand and the mouse to make the pointer move across the screen. Then move the slider toward the "Fast" setting and see how the pointer moves. I set my tracking speed on "Fast," but many designers and illustrators like to set their speed to "Slow" so they have more control in the painting programs, moving the mouse dot by dot.

You can also change the **Double-Click Speed** of the mouse. If you choose the "Very Slow" setting, your iMac may interpret two separate clicks as a double-click (if you make the second click too soon after the first). After moving the slider to a setting, double-click in the middle of any word in the text field (circled, above) to test the effect of your setting—a proper double-click will highlight the word you double-click on.

To put the Mouse preferences away, single-click the red Close button in the upper-left corner (just like you put away windows, right?). The settings you made will now be in effect everywhere on your iMac.

Another useful tip

You can put files or folders in the Toolbar that you use often so you can open them easily. Any item you put in a Toolbar will appear in every window's Toolbar, giving you access to it at all times.

To place an item in the Toolbar:

Press on a folder or file that you want to put in the Toolbar, then drag it to the Toolbar and let go.

Try it: Drag the Documents folder to the Toolbar. Now, from any Finder window, click on the Documents icon in the Toolbar to open the Documents folder.

To remove an item from the Toolbar:

Removing something from the Toolbar does not affect the original file!

- *If the item is an existing Toolbar item or a "fancy" folder created by Mac OS X (like the Documents folder),* **Command-drag** the item out of the Toolbar (hold down the Command key while you drag) and drop it on the Desktop. It will disappear in a puff of white smoke.

- *If the item is a folder or file that you created,* just **drag** it out of the Toolbar, drop it on the Desktop, and watch it disappear in a puff of smoke.

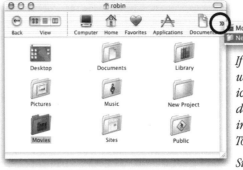

If your window view is not wide enough to show all the icons in the Toolbar, a small double arrow (shown circled) indicates there are more Toolbar icons available.

Single-click the double arrow; from the pop-up list, choose a Toolbar item.

If you widen the window, all the Toolbar icons will be visible.

Working at Your Desktop

3

By now you should feel pretty comfortable using the mouse and menus. In the section following this one, you're going to open an application and write a letter, but first I want you to understand how to work at the Desktop. Lots of computer users know how to open an application and work in it, but don't know how to manage the Desktop. In this chapter, we're going to look at the important things the icons are telling you, what those icons are in the Toolbar, how to make new folders and put *files* in them, how to use keyboard shortcuts, how to throw away stuff you don't want anymore, how to make copies of things, how to put a CD or DVD in and take it out, and how to shut down when you're done for the day. Along the way you'll learn lots of little tidbits about working on your computer. **However,** feel free to skip this chapter, go right into your application, and come back later when you realize you need to know this information!

file: This is a generic term for anything on your computer. On the iMac, every file is represented by an icon. Even a folder is technically a file. Applications, documents—everything you see on your iMac is a file.

Icons

One of the original features of the Macintosh that made it famous was its use of **icons,** or little pictures, to represent every file in the computer so you can just double-click to open a document, instead of having to dig up the file by typing in awful codes.

Because all the visual stuff on an iMac screen can be so overwhelming, new users often don't notice that icons provide very useful clues.

The three most important icons you'll work with are these:

Folders

Research

A typical folder icon.

Macintosh *folders*, whose icons look just like real manila folders, are as important to your organization on the computer as manila folders are to your organization in an office. You must learn how to make new ones, put files inside them, empty them out, rearrange them, throw them away, etc. We'll do all that in a minute. For now, just look on your iMac and find the folders. (Open your hard disk window, if it isn't already.)

Movies

Some special folders have fancy graphics.

When you **double-click** a folder, the current window changes to show the *contents* of this folder, and the name in the window's title bar changes to show the *name* of this folder. (The only other icons that open to *windows* on your Desktop are icons of *disks,* such as hard disks or CDs.)

Applications

AppleWorks 6

Applications are the programs you will be working in to create your own documents. Their icons are typically "fancier" than anything else, and there's no consistent pattern to them except they usually give a visual clue as to what they do. Take a look at the ones to the left. iMovie, for instance, is an application that creates movies from your digital video camera.

iMovie

When you **double-click** an application, the iMac opens the application and usually puts a blank *application window* on the screen for you to work in.

TextEdit

These are application icons.

(Some applications, such as AppleWorks, open up but don't create a new and blank window for you until you first tell it what sort of document you want. After you choose, then you get a new, clean window to work in, as you'll see in the next chapter.)

Documents

When you work in an application and create a document, you *save* it onto your hard disk (see page 124). When you save it, the iMac creates a document file for you and gives it an icon. A document icon always has the *upper-right corner* turned down (as shown to the right).

A document icon almost always matches the icon of the application it was created in. Take a look at the three icons to the right, and take a look at the three application icons on the bottom-left of the opposite page. Match each document to its application.

When you **double-click** a document, the iMac finds the application you used to create the document, then opens that application and puts your document on the screen.

Documents folder: Don't confuse a document you created with the *Documents folder* on your hard disk. The Documents folder is meant to *store* documents you create (although you *can* store a document almost anywhere, in any folder, depending on how you want to organize your file storage).

These are document icons. Notice the upper-right corners.

Kauai.cwk

1st draft

A Movie

The icons in the Finder window Toolbar

You can customize your Toolbar to include other tools, or to exclude any of the default tools; see pages 398–399.

Every Finder window has a **Toolbar.** The buttons and icons in the Toolbar make it easy to change window views, or to move to folders on your computer that you use most often. Following is a brief description of each of the Toolbar items.

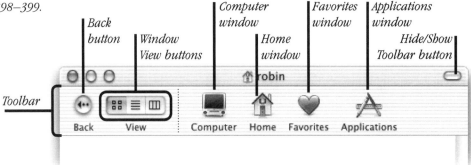

Back button: When you click a Toolbar icon to view its contents or when you double-click a folder in a window, the contents of the new folder *replace* what was already in the window.

To go back to the contents you previously saw *in this particular window,* click the Back button.

View buttons: Click one of these three buttons to change how the contents of the window are displayed. **Icon View** (left-most button) shows a window's contents as *icons.* **List View** (center button) displays a *list* of file names. **Column View** (right-most button) changes the view to *columns* that show the organization of folders and files.

Hide/Show Toolbar button: Click this button to Hide or Show the Toolbar. If the Toolbar is *hidden* when you double-click a folder, a new and *separate* window opens to show the folder's contents (instead of replacing the existing contents).

*Here, the Toolbar is hidden. If you double-click any folder in this window, it will open to another window so you'll have **two** windows open on the screen. This makes it easier to move files from one folder to another.*

Computer: The Computer window shows the icon of your hard disk and any other disks that are in your iMac, such as CDs or another computer that may be connected to your iMac over a network. Unless you are on a corporate network, this "Network" icon is useless to you. The disk icons you see in this window are the same ones you see on the right side of your screen.

Home: When you first set up your iMac, you assigned a name and password for yourself to create a "user" account. Each user has her own "Home" window, with her own folders and files. Click the Home icon to show the contents of *your* Home window. ***Do not rename or remove any of the folders in this window!*** Every one of them will come in handy later. For instance, the "Public" folder is where you can put files you want to share with other users on your iMac; see pages 222–224 about other users.

Favorites: "Favorites" can be folders, documents, web site addresses, or any other files that you want easy access to. To make an item a Favorite, drop it right on top of the Favorites icon in the Toolbar. **Or** select a folder or file, then from the File menu, choose "Add to Favorites." Both of these methods put an "alias" (see pages 394–397) of that item in this folder. In the "Open" and "Save As" dialog boxes, every folder in this Favorites window will appear in the drop-down menu so you can easily find files to open and find folders to store documents into.

Applications: This button displays the Mac OS X applications. Icons for some of these applications appear in the Dock, but there are many others in this folder. See Chapter 4 for an overview of every program, with references to tutorials for many of the applications.

Folders

Research
Get used to working with folders!

Folders are great. Folders are indispensable. Can you imagine having a large filing cabinet in your office and putting all the papers into that filing cabinet without using manila folders? What a mess! Yet that's what some people do on their computers. Before we get into organizing things with folders, let's get used to making, moving, and deleting them, as well as putting things inside.

Follow these instructions carefully. I don't want to you move or throw away anything important, so please follow along and *don't do anything I don't tell you to do.*

1. Make a new folder

a. You can put a new folder directly onto the Desktop or into any existing folder/window. For right now, let's put one in your "Macintosh HD" window. To do that, we need to make sure the hard disk window is open and is the *active* window, which is always the window on top; see Step b.

active window:
The window that is in use at the moment. You can always tell which window is active because it is the only one whose title bar is not grayed out. Only one window can ever be active at a time, whether you are at the Desktop or in an application.

b. So open your hard disk window by double-clicking on the hard disk icon ("Macintosh HD"). The window should look something like the one shown below. If you don't see icons in your window, click the Icon View button in the Toolbar.

Title bar and Toolbar of an active window.

Title bar and Toolbar of a window that is not active.

*The window on the left is the **active window**. You can tell by the brightly colored buttons in the title bar (shown above, left). The non-active window's buttons, title bar, and Toolbar are gray like a ghost (shown above, right).*

All of the commands at the Desktop and in any application always apply to the active window. *That is, if you choose the "Close Window" command from the File menu, it will close the **active** window; if you choose the "New Folder" command, the new folder will appear in the active window.*

c. While this window is *active,* go to the File menu and choose "New Folder." Instantly a new folder appears in the *active* window. You should see this:

Here is your new, untitled folder.

d. Notice the new folder is named "untitled folder" and has a **border** around its name and the name is highlighted. This border and the highlight are visual clues that indicate you can type and replace the existing name. All you need to do is type. Really. Just put those fingers to the keyboard and rename this folder "Toss This Folder" so you know it's practice.

> (If the folder doesn't have a border around the name because you accidentally clicked somewhere else and the border disappeared, don't worry, do this: Click directly on the *name* of the folder, not on the *picture* of the folder. Wait for the border to appear. Then type.)

e. When you've **finished** renaming the folder, click anywhere outside of the folder or hit the Enter key; the border will disappear and the name will be set.

If you decide you want to **rename** the folder, just click on the name, wait until the border and the highlight appear, then type.

Here is the folder with its new name. Click anywhere (except on the folder itself) and the border will disappear.

untitled folder

*If you click anywhere else before you follow the directions in Step d, you will lose the border around the name! If so, click on the **name** once more to select it again.*

2. Move the folder

Okay, so now you have a new folder in your hard disk window. Let's **move the folder icon** into a more convenient location—into your Home window. Using Mac OS X, many people can use the same iMac and everyone has their own private space, including a **Home window,** a private Desktop, Trash basket, Documents folder, etc. The *Home* button you see in the Toolbar is the personal space that was created for you when you first set up your computer.

Make sure you don't accidentally drop folders inside of other folders! To prevent that from happening, don't let go of a folder you are dragging when the pointer is positioned over another folder.

Tip: *If you accidentally drop one folder inside of another, see page 60, "Take something out of a folder."*

a. To move a folder to your Home area, just press-and-drag: position the tip of the pointer on the folder itself, *press and hold the mouse button down,* then *drag* the folder (still holding the button down) to the Home button in the Toolbar, as shown below.

b. When the Home button highlights (turns dark), let go of the mouse button. The new folder is now in your Home folder.

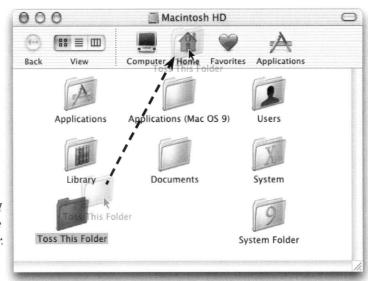

The folder has a ghosted look as you drag it to the Home icon in the Toolbar.

To look in your Home window (shown below), single-click the "Home" icon. Notice the window's title bar now contains the Home icon and the "User name" you assigned yourself during the initial setup of your computer. The window now shows the contents of your Home folder, including the folder you just made named "Toss This Folder." (If you don't see your folder, enlarge the window by dragging its bottom-right corner.) Within your Home window (or any window) you can press-and-drag any folder to any position.

This is the Home folder, as you can tell by the name and the house icon in the title bar. Notice the new folder, "Toss This Folder," is safely inside this window.

3. Put something into a folder

You will be putting things inside of folders and taking them out constantly. Now let's put something *into* a folder.

a. First of all, make yourself a new folder so you'll have two of them. Name the new folder "Toss This Too."

After you name the newest folder, click anywhere *or* hit Enter to set the name.

Enlarge the window if necessary so you can see both new folders ("Toss This Folder" and "Toss This Too").

b. Now put one folder inside of the other folder: *Drag* the folder named "Toss This Too," and *drop* it directly onto the folder named "Toss This Folder." Remember, the **tip** of the pointer is the hot spot, so the tip of the pointer must be positioned directly over the folder "Toss This Folder." The folder you are putting something *into* will "highlight," or turn dark, when it is ready to take the item, as shown below.

c. After you drop the file into the folder, open the folder "Toss This Folder" (double-click it) and see the other folder inside.

*The folder on the right is highlighted because I pressed my mouse on it. Then, still holding the mouse button down, I dragged that folder over to the folder on the left, indicated by the shadow. The left folder, "Toss This Folder," is also now highlighted, which means if I let go of the mouse button, the first folder will drop inside "Toss This Folder." Notice where the tip of the pointer is located—**on the left-hand folder.***

Tip: You can also drag an item into a window (which is, of course, an open folder) from another window or the Desktop. Just drag the item and drop it on any blank area in the window.

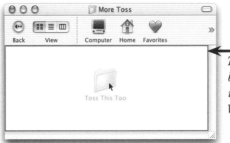

The window displays a gray border around the inside edge when you drag an item into it. Watch for it.

4. Duplicate a folder (or any file)

You can make a duplicate of any file on your hard disk. Let's duplicate one of the folders you just made to see how it works.

a. *Select* the folder named "Toss This Too" (or any file you want to duplicate) by clicking **once** on it.

b. From the File menu, choose "Duplicate." This will duplicate any *selected* file. If the selected file is a folder, *it will duplicate the entire contents of the folder.*

c. Drag the new, duplicated folder away from the original (but leave it in the same folder, ready for the next exercise). You'll know which one is the duplicate because it has the word "copy" at the end of its name.

The duplicate is sitting on top of the original file, so just drag one away to the side to separate them.

Toss Thi
Toss This Too copy

The duplicate file is automatically named the same as the first one, but with the word "copy" added because you cannot put two files of the same name in the same folder, nor can you have two folders with the same name.

d. If you're following along with these exercises, click the "Back" button in the Toolbar in preparation for the next exercise. This should take you back to the Home window.

5. Take something out of a folder

To take a file out of a folder on your iMac, you must first open its window. Consider this action just like taking a file out of a manila folder in your filing cabinet—first you have to find and open the folder.

Use your practice folder for now ("Toss This Folder"); later, follow these directions for any file.

a. Double-click the folder named "Toss This Folder" to open its window and display its contents.

b. Simply drag the item you want *out* of the window and drop it onto the Desktop.

Later, when necessary, you can drag any file out of a folder window and drop it on the Desktop, into another window (if another window is open), or on top of another folder to put the item inside that other folder.

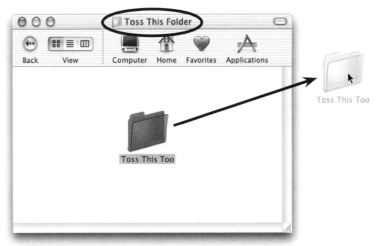

*To **move** any file or folder from one place to another, press-and-drag the file to another location.*

This is an advanced trick—feel free to skip this until the day you need it.

6. Copy a file to another folder (don't just move it)

When you drag a file from one place to another, you *move* the *original* file. But sometimes you don't want to *move* the original file—sometimes you want a *copy* of that same file in another folder. The technique below makes a *copy* of a file as you drag it from one place to another. This is essentially the same as making a duplicate (as described on the previous pages), but it's a shortcut.

You can surprise your Mac-user friends by knowing this trick—they might not know it!

a. Select the file you want to copy. If you're continuing from Step 5, select "Toss This Too" which is probably on the Desktop.

b. Hold down the Option key (on the bottom row of the keyboard, either side of the Spacebar). *With the Option key held down,* press-and-drag the selected file from one place to another (from a window to the Desktop, the Desktop to a window, or into another folder).

As you drag, notice the pointer arrow now includes a "plus" sign. This is a visual clue that you are in the process of *copying* the selected file.

When you've dragged the file to its destination, let go of the file and the Option key.

c. Open the folder you dragged the file into and you'll notice the new, copied file is named exactly the same as the original one, without "copy" at the end. You can change its name.

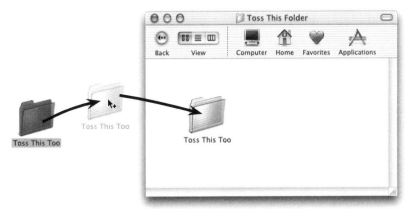

Don't worry— on the next page I'll show you how to throw away these extra folders.

*When you Option-drag a file, the iMac makes a **copy** of the file and the original stays right where it was.*

The Trash basket and throwing things away

You've surely noticed the Trash basket sitting in the right corner of your Dock. Looks like the kind of basket in which you throw things away, doesn't it? It is.

Which Trash is full and needs to be emptied?

Throw something in the Trash

1. Just drag any item you don't want (like one of those practice folders you made) down to the Trash.

2. Make sure the *tip of the pointer* highlights the basket, then let go and the item will drop in. The icon changes to look like it's got stuff in it.

Empty the Trash

1. What you put in the Trash will stay there, even if you turn off your iMac, until you go to the Finder menu and choose "Empty Trash...."

2. When you choose "Empty Trash," you will get a message asking if you really want to throw it away. If you do, click "OK."

You must empty the Trash before garbage will really go away.

Tip: You can also press (don't click) on the Trash basket to pop up the "Empty Trash" command. Slide the pointer up to the command and let go.

Take something out of the Trash

1. Single-click the Trash basket in the Dock; it opens to display a window.

2. Drag the item out of the Trash window and drop it in your hard disk window, in a folder, or on the Desktop.

Use the menu or a keyboard shortcut to Trash an item

I explain keyboard shortcuts in detail on pages 66–67.

1. **Single-click** on the item you want to eliminate.

2. From the File menu, choose "Move to Trash."

   Or use the keyboard shortcut that you see in the menu: Those two symbols for the "Move to Trash" command indicate the Command key and the Delete key. So do this: While the file is selected, *hold down* the Command key and *tap* the Delete key once. The file will instantly move to the Trash.

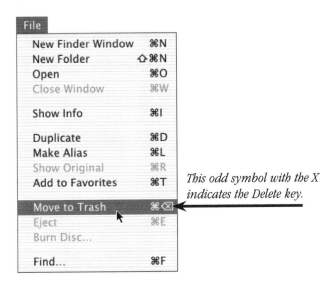

This odd symbol with the X indicates the Delete key.

Select more than one item or folder in Icon View

If you're following along with these exercises, you might want to skip this one for now and come back to it when you actually need to do it, which might not be for a while.

This technique explains how to move, duplicate, or throw away more than one item at a time. To do that, you need to *select* more than one at a time.

1. To select more than one item in Icon View, hold down the **Shift key** or the **Command key** (the Command key is the one with the apple on it). Each item you select *with the Shift or Command key down* will be added to the selection. (This is a *Shift-click* or *Command-click.*)

   To **deselect** one of the items in the selected group, hold the **Shift key** down (or the **Command key**) and click on it. You see, the Shift key or Command key will do whatever it needs to—it will *add* an item to the group, or it will *remove* an item from the group. Try it.

2. Now **to move the entire group of selected files,**
   let go of the Shift key,
   press on any one of the *selected* items,
   and drag away.
   All of the selected items will come along with the one
   you are actually dragging.

   Drop the selected files onto the Desktop, into another window, in the Trash, or on a folder. Remember, it is the *tip* of the pointer that's the boss—all of the selected items will drop wherever you position the *tip* of the pointer and let go.

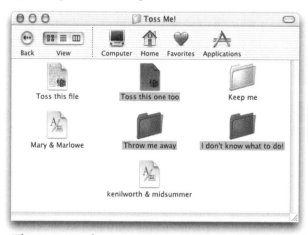

When you select a folder, you select every item inside the folder as well.

*When your window is in Icon View, you can Shift-click or Command-click to select more than one item. Just make sure before you drag that you **let go** of the Shift key and drag a **highlighted** item.*

*And remember, the files will move to wherever **the tip of the pointer is** when you let go.*

Select more than one item or folder in List View

When selecting more than one item in a List View, **Shift-click** and **Command-click** have different effects.

To select *contiguous* items (items that are next to each other) in a List View, hold down the **Shift key** as you click on multiple items.

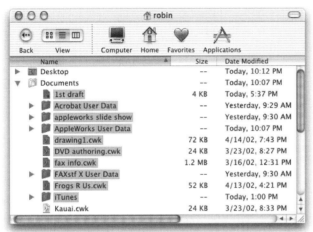

*Click once (don't press) on the **first** item you want to select. Move your mouse down to the **last** item you want to select and Shift-click on it (hold down the Shift key and click). The first and last items **and all items between them** in the list are instantly selected.*

To select *non-contiguous* items (items that are *not* next to each other) in a List View, hold down the **Command key** as you click on items throughout the list.

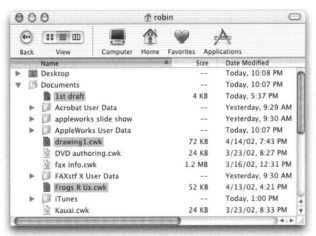

Command-click lets you select individual files that are not next to each other. In a List View, they don't even have to be in the same folder.

Note: In **Column View,** you can select multiple items as in List View, but only in one column at a time.

Keyboard shortcuts

The iMac lets you do a lot of things using the keyboard without having to pick up the mouse. These are called **keyboard shortcuts.** Once you get used to using keyboard shortcuts, you'll start looking for them.

Modifier keys

Keyboard shortcuts always use "modifier keys," which are those keys that don't do anything when you press them by themselves. For instance, the Shift key is a modifier key—if you press it, nothing happens. Something only happens when you press the Shift key *in combination with* another key, as you do when you want to make capital letters. Each modifier key is represented in the menu by a symbol, shown to the left of the explanations below. The modifier keys are:

Spacebar:
The Spacebar is not a modifier key because it does something (it makes spaces between words). The Spacebar is the long, blank key at the very bottom of the keyboard.

⇧ **Shift key,** labeled "shift" on your keyboard.

⌥ **Option key,** labeled "option" on your keyboard.

⌘ **Command key,** which has the Apple on it, plus the symbol that looks like a freeway interchange. (This is sometimes, not often, and don't you do it, referred to as the "Apple key." To a Mac user, calling the Command key the "Apple key" is like calling San Francisco "Frisco" to a native Californian. Gag me.)

⌃ **Control key,** labeled "control." Don't get the Control key mixed up with the Command key! Take a look at your keyboard and make sure you know which is which.

F3 **Fkeys** are those keys across the very top of the keyboard, the ones labeled from F1 through F15. You might see them in some keyboard shortcuts.

esc **Escape key** is at the very top-left of your keyboard. You won't need it very often.

+ *add*
- *subtract*
* *multiply*
/ *divide*

Use these keys as math operators. Most of the time you can use either the symbol on the keypad or the one on the keyboard.

See the opposite page for instructions on how to use keyboard shortcuts. Once you start using them, you'll feel good and you'll get things done more efficiently.

Numeric keypad

You have **numerals** across the top of the keyboard, and you also have a **numeric keypad** at the right end of the keyboard. Sometimes in a keyboard shortcut it makes a difference which ones you use: If the numeric keypad doesn't work, try the keyboard.

How to use shortcuts

To use a shortcut, first look in the menu to see what it is. For instance, in the File menu (shown at right) you see the command "Open." You also see an odd symbol combination next to "Open," which is the shortcut you can use *instead* of using the mouse and going to the File menu. This Open shortcut is ⌘**O**. This means *hold down* the Command key and *tap* the letter key *once* (O for open, not zero).

Walk through the following exercises to learn how to use keyboard shortcuts, then look for them in your applications.

Use a shortcut to open a folder

1. **Single-click** on a folder to select it.

2. Press Command O (*hold down* the Command key, then *tap* the letter O).

3. Can you **close** this window, using a keyboard shortcut? Try it:

   Take a look at the File menu and find the shortcut combination;
   click once on the Desktop to make the menu go away;
   click once in the open window to make sure the window is selected.
   Now use the keyboard shortcut to close that window.

A selected folder is highlighted, or dark, like this.

Make a new folder

1. **Single-click** in the window in which you want the new folder to appear. (You can only create new folders in *open* windows or directly on the Desktop. To select the Desktop, single-click on any empty space on the Desktop.)

2. Take a peek at the File menu and see what the keyboard shortcut is to create a new folder. (Notice it's Shift Command N, like N for New.) Then ignore the File menu.

3. Hold down both the Shift and Command keys, then tap the N once.

When you make a new folder, it is named "untitled folder." The blue border around the folder name means that the name is currently selected. Replace "untitled folder" by typing a new name.

Reminder: One of the rules on the iMac is to **select first, then do it to it.** That is, if you want a new folder to appear inside of an open window, you must **first select the open window.** If you want to open a folder, you must **first select the folder.**

The Media Eject key opens and closes the optical drive tray that holds your CDs and DVDs.

Inserting and removing discs

You will probably use CDs often. All major software you buy, including games, will arrive on a CD. Your iMac came with a number of CDs, and you'll enjoy playing music CDs and creating your own music collection. If your iMac has a "Combo" drive you can play CDs, create your own CDs, and also play DVDs. If you have a "SuperDrive," you can do all of that, *plus* create your own DVDs. See Chapter 12 for information about creating your own CDs and DVDs.

Insert a disc

1. Open the drive tray by pressing the Media Eject key on the upper-right corner of the keyboard (shown circled, above left). If you have a smaller keyboard that doesn't have a Media Eject key, hold down the F12 key until the tray opens.

2. Put a disc (a CD or DVD) in the tray, shiny side down, label up.

3. Press the Media Eject key to close the tray (or F12 on a smaller keyboard).

4. If the disc you insert is a **data CD** (as opposed to music), the icon for the disc will appear on the Desktop (it might take several seconds). If the CD doesn't open by itself to display its window, double-click the CD icon (it isn't always a round icon).

   If the disc is an **audio CD** (music), iTunes will automatically open to play the music tracks from the CD. See Chapter 18 for more about iTunes.

   If you insert a **movie DVD,** the DVD player will automatically start up and begin playing. If it's a **data DVD** (a DVD disc for storing files), the disc's icon will appear on the Desktop.

Unmount:
When a disk is working and the computer knows it is there, the disk is considered "mounted." Some disks must be "unmounted" before you can remove them (drag its icon to the Trash to unmount).

Remove a disc

1. To start with, close all the windows that belong to anything on the CD and **quit all applications** that you used from it. If an application on the disc is in use, you won't be able to eject it.

2. Press the Media Eject key to unmount the disc and open the tray.

   Or drag the disc to the Trash basket. Really. This will never remove any data from the disc. The Trash icon will change into an "Eject" icon, as shown to the left, and the tray will slide out so you can get the disc.

The Trash icon turns into an "Eject" icon when you drag a disc to the Trash.

Play a music CD!

You can play any music CD right on your iMac.

The iTunes application plays your music CDs.

1. Insert a music CD as you would any other CD (see opposite page).

2. iTunes, an application for playing music CDs, should open automatically. If not, click once on the iTunes icon in the Dock.

   If you have an active Internet connection, iTunes automatically connects to a CD database online, collects all the names and information for the songs on your CD, and displays the song titles and other information in its window. Amazing.

3. Click on the CD icon in the "Source pane" (circled, below) to see the music tracks (song titles) in the main window. Then double-click a track in the "Song" list.

4. Use the controls just like you would the controls on your own CD player. You can close the player and continue working while your music plays.

   Or click the green Zoom button to reduce the player size, but keep it available on the screen.

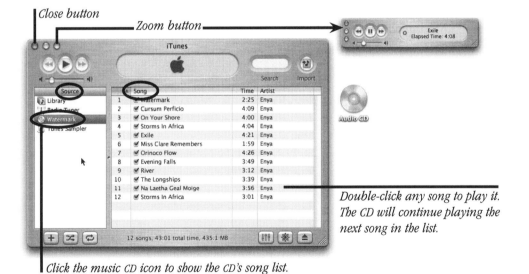

Close button

Zoom button

Double-click any song to play it. The CD will continue playing the next song in the list.

Click the music CD icon to show the CD's song list.

iTunes can do much more than just play music CDs. It can copy songs from a CD and convert them to other formats for use on the computer. It lets you organize your music files into "Playlists" to create your own customized CDs. iTunes can connect to dozens of Internet radio stations. It contains an equalizer to control the audio, and you can even watch a dazzling, live, visual-effects show that's synchronized with the music. Learn lots more about iTunes in Chapter 18.

Volume

You can use your keyboard to make the sound louder or softer. The sound keys are across the top of the numeric keypad on the far right of your keyboard, the keys with the speaker symbols. The first key makes the sound softer, the second key makes it louder, and the third key mutes the sound.

Headphones and speakers

You can plug headphones into the Headphones port on the back of the iMac so you won't bother anyone else, or connect external speakers for better sound. The Apple Pro Speakers designed especially for the iMac plug into a special port on the back of the computer, while other speakers might use a USB cable and plug into a USB port (see Chapter 25).

Connect your headphones or analog speakers here.

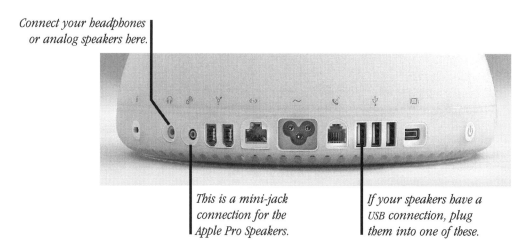

This is a mini-jack connection for the Apple Pro Speakers.

If your speakers have a USB connection, plug them into one of these.

Put your computer to sleep

Your iMac will probably fall asleep if you go away and leave it alone for a while. The screen (display) turns dark and the hard disk "spins down." **To wake it up,** just tap any key at all on the keyboard, or click the mouse.

You can control how long your iMac waits before it goes to sleep by using the Energy Saver preferences:

1. Click once on the System Preferences icon in the Dock, then click once on the Energy Saver icon (both shown to the right). You'll see the panel below:

System Preferences

Energy Saver

Energy Saver

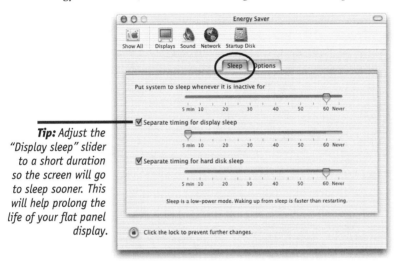

Tip: *Adjust the "Display sleep" slider to a short duration so the screen will go to sleep sooner. This will help prolong the life of your flat panel display.*

2. Click the "Sleep" tab to make sure you see the Sleep pane.

   Set the top slider to how long you want the entire system (hard disk and screen display) to idle before it goes to sleep.

   To set separate settings for "display sleep" (the monitor) and "hard disk sleep," click the checkboxes of the two bottom sliders, then adjust their settings. (Neither of these separate settings can be set to a longer time than the top slider.)

The Power button is also a Sleep button

To put the computer to sleep manually, press the Power button for **one** second on the back-left side of the base. If the Power button is hard to reach, use the "Sleep" command in the Apple menu, as shown to the right. (If you hold the Power button in for **five** seconds, it will turn off your iMac *without saving your files.*)

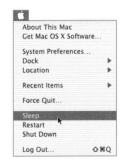

To instantly put the computer to sleep, go to the Apple menu and choose "Sleep."

Shut Down

When you have finished working on your computer for the day, you may want to shut down. Years ago, people said it was best to leave a computer on all the time, rather than turn it off and back on again, but today it's unnecessary. You will outgrow your computer long before you will turn it on and off too many times.

Tip: If you prefer, you can leave your iMac on for long periods of time. Make sure the Energy Saver preferences are set to your liking (see the previous page), then let the Energy Saver take care of putting your computer to sleep.

To prolong the life of your flat-panel display, though, set the dislay to sleep when you're not at the computer.

If the computer has been asleep a long time, it may take a little longer to wake than usual, but it will start faster than it would if the computer had been turned off. (My iMac has been on for a couple of months without a problem.)

It's a good habit to quit all of your applications before you shut down, although the iMac will quit them for you if you forget. I explain about opening and quitting applications in Chapter 4, but if you've been following along in this book, you don't have any applications open at the moment.

To shut down:

Go to the Apple menu and choose "Shut Down." Your iMac will safely shut down immediately (after making sure you have no unsaved documents still open).

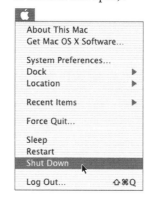

It's possible to turn off your iMac by pressing the Power button on the left-back side on the iMac base and holding it down for five seconds, but this method is more like pulling the plug—it doesn't save any unsaved documents or go through the Quit process in any open applications. It just shuts off, so only use this technique if something has gone wrong and your iMac won't turn off any other way.

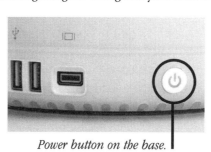

Power button on the base.

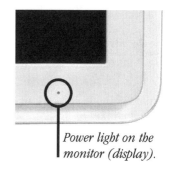

Power light on the monitor (display).

Things to Do with Your iMac

Your iMac is loaded with a number of software *applications,* which are programs you use to get work done, like write letters, pay bills, create flyers, and more. This section explains what those applications are and what to do with them. I can't give you a full tutorial on each separate item, but I can tell you what each one does so you can make decisions about which applications you want to ignore, and which ones you want to use and learn more about. And I'll tell you where you can learn more when you're ready.

Many people buy an iMac so they can use the **Internet.** You'll find all the Internet and World Wide Web information in the Internet section in Chapters 14 through 16.

"I thought it was a machine, then
I realized it's actually a Muse."

John Tollett, digital artist

First, an Overview of Applications

Your iMac is filled with all sorts of *programming,* which is the code written by humans that makes the computer work. Different kinds of programming create different kinds of software, such as games, operating systems, utilities, and *applications.* Applications (which are often just called "programs") are written specifically for *you* to create things in, or to work productively in, as opposed to other programs that enable the *computer* to make things happen.

Apple has provided you with many really great applications already installed on your computer. In this chapter, you'll read brief explanations of what you have. Some of the applications have entire chapters devoted to them, so if any of these overviews interest you, read the appropriate chapter for tutorials on how to get started using that application.

Applications on your iMac

There are many great applications already installed on your iMac. Below is a picture of the Applications folder on iMacs that are running Mac OS X. To open this folder, single-click the "Applications" icon in the Toolbar, or go to the Go menu and choose "Applications."

Most of the smaller applications are described in the following pages. The more complex applications are discussed in the chapters indicated.

iPhoto:
See Chapter 17 for an iPhoto tutorial.

*If you don't see the **FAXstf X** folder (top gray arrow), it's because you haven't installed it. Look for the "FAXstf X Installer" in the **Installers** folder (bottom gray arrow).*

Chapter 20
Chapter 15
Chapter 21
Chapter 20
Chapter 18
Chapter 24
Chapter 13
Chapters 5–10
Chapter 11
Chapter 23

Acrobat Reader

This is the Reader. It's free so everyone can read Acrobat files.

Adobe Acrobat Reader isn't an application you will be *creating* anything in; it's an application you need to *read* and print documents that someone else wrote. Sometimes files, such as software manuals, are saved in a format called PDF (Portable Document Format). This PDF file can be opened and read on any computer (Mac or otherwise), and the pages are fully formatted just as they would look in a printed book. You can choose to read on the screen just the parts of the manual you need, or you can print up individual pages or the entire document.

Acrobat Reader menu and toolbar

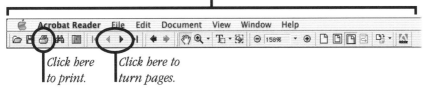

Click here to print. *Click here to turn pages.*

Tip: *Hover your mouse over any item in the toolbar to reveal a description of the tool's function.*

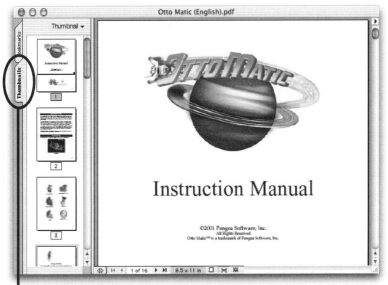

The Thumbnail pane lets you navigate directly to any page of a multiple-page PDF document.

Otto Matic (English).pdf
This is an example of a "PDF," an Acrobat file, that you can read with the Acrobat Reader. Just double-click this icon to open the document in the Reader, as shown on the left.

Address Book

The **Address Book** works with the Mail application (as well as an independent application) to create Address Cards that store contact information for individuals or groups. See Chapter 20 for the Address Book and Mail tutorials.

AppleWorks

AppleWorks is one of the main software applications on your iMac. It's called an "integrated software package" because it contains a variety of applications rolled into one. Each one of the next six applications listed here is actually one module of AppleWorks. Because AppleWorks is so useful, I've provided a separate tutorial for each of the modules (see Chapters 5 through 10). But you can read through this information first and decide which modules might be the most practical (or fun) to learn to use.

Word Processing

Word processing

A word processor is the most basic and useful application on any computer—it's a really fancy typewriter. Even the simplest word processor today is more powerful and easier to use than any professional typewriter or typesetting machine in history.

Use a word processor to write letters, reports, manuscripts, memos, simple newsletters, and anything else you would have used a typewriter for. See Chapter 5 to learn how to create a word processing document and *format* your text.

Database

Database

A database is like an address book or a recipe box, but you can find and use information much more quickly and powerfully in a computerized database than you can in a paper address book. Let's say you make a contact list in your database that includes checkboxes for whether people are family members, whether you sent them holiday cards, and whether they work at your company or not. And you also create places (called "fields") where you can type in birthdates, anniversaries, and the names of their children.

data: This simply means "information."

In a paper address book with the same data, you would have to flip through all the pages to find the people who have birthdays in October. Using your database, you can click a button to see a list of all the people who have birthdays in October. In fact, you can click a button to find all the people who have birthdays in October who also work at your company, live in the neighboring town, and have a child named Ryan.

A database is surprisingly easy to create and work with. **Use a database** to make address books with mailing lists, keep track of business contacts, membership rosters and dues, household or business inventory, or customer information. I guarantee that once you start working with a database you'll find more and more reasons to use it, and you'll be delighted with how easy it is. See Chapter 6 for a quick and easy tutorial on putting together a simple database.

Spreadsheet

Spreadsheet

A spreadsheet is mostly used for number-crunching and "what-if" scenarios. For instance, you can create a spreadsheet that works out mortgage payments, then change specific data (information) to see what happens if the interest rate goes up or down, if you pay it off in 20 years instead of 30, or if you apply a bigger down payment. You change the data and the spreadsheet instantly and automatically recalculates everything for you.

You can also *enter* text in spreadsheets, not just numbers. For instance, you can set up an invoice for your small business that includes your logo, address, contact information, etc., plus an itemized list of your products or services. When you enter the quantity of each item sold, the spreadsheet calculates the total cost, including the appropriate tax, exactly the way you need it for your particular invoice.

enter: Another computer jargon term; this one basically means "type."

You can tell a spreadsheet to look something up. For instance, if you offer a discount on certain quantities, the spreadsheet can look up the correct discount for the number of items you enter, then apply the discount to the total. Of course, the spreadsheet does this "automatically" after you have set it up.

You can produce all sorts of charts and graphs out of your data. You create the spreadsheet and fill in the data, then click a few buttons and make a variety of visual representations out of all the data or just selected parts of it.

Even if you don't love numbers, there are lots of things you can do with a spreadsheet. In addition to simple and complex invoices, use a spreadsheet to create school grading sheets that automatically calculate grades, percentages, and graphs of results; make proposals for clients that display how the variables affect the final estimate; create charts that compare price quotes, etc.

Another great use of a spreadsheet is to make forms, forms of all sorts, even if you never use a number. It's the easiest program in which to make lines, boxes, columns, borders, etc., and you can color in rows, columns, or boxes easily. You can format the text larger, smaller, or use different typefaces. See Chapter 7 for a short tutorial on how to use a spreadsheet.

Painting

A paint program lets you "paint" right on the screen. You get to choose from a variety of tools, such as various paintbrushes, pens, a pencil, airbrush, and others. You choose the colors or patterns to paint with and the thickness of the stroke or the style of brush. You can even "pour" paint right from the "can" into a shape, and erase your mistakes. It's too much fun.

Use a paint program to decorate holiday cards, make birthday invitations, entertain your grandchildren, illustrate a story, or anything you would use a paintbrush for in the first place. Don't worry if you don't consider yourself an "artist"—you'll be amazed at what you can do on a computer when you have the power to revise on a whim. See Chapter 8 for an unintimidating exercise in using a paint program.

Drawing

A draw program is similar to a paint program in that you are creating artwork of some sort, but a draw program works with hard-edged "objects" instead of with paintbrushes and airbrushes. In a paint program, once you use a brush to paint a color, that's the size and the color it is unless you paint directly over it, just as if you painted it on a wall at home. In a draw program, however, after you draw a shape you can change your mind a million times and replace the color or pattern inside the shape, replace the thickness and color of the border surrounding the shape, and even re-form the shape. You can put shapes in front or in back of each other, and then change the order of the various layers. Rather than painting on a wall, a draw program is more like cutting shapes out of paper and layering them one on top of another.

You can also use text in a draw program and it looks just as good as if you did it in a word processor, plus you can edit (change) it later, just like you can in a word processor. (You can use text in the paint program, but it doesn't look very good when you print it. The only way to change the text is to erase it and type it over again.) See Chapter 9 for a silly exercise in using a draw program.

Paint vs. draw

So a paint program gives you the flexibility to throw paint around in a very freeform way, and a draw program gives you more flexibility in changing everything, including the size of the finished piece. Walk through the simple tutorials in Chapter 8 (paint) and Chapter 9 (draw) and you'll soon see the difference, and then you can make your own decision about which is the best application to use for a particular project.

Presentation

This module makes it easy and fun to create professional-looking slide show presentations. Make slide shows for your family and friends, for school, or for work. Then present the slide shows on a computer or print them onto transparencies so you can display them on an overhead projector. If you make your presentation on a computer, you can include movies, sounds, and visual transitions between slides. To aid you in giving your presentation, print a copy of the slide show and include notes to yourself.

Presentation

A note about AppleWorks

Besides providing so many different applications in one package, AppleWorks makes it so easy to **integrate the various elements.** For instance, you can write a letter in the word processor that prints out with different names and addresses on each page, the names and addresses coming from your database. You can create a memo for your boss in the word processor with a spreadsheet pie chart directly on the memo. You can create a spreadsheet form and draw your own logo at the top of it using the draw program. Oh, there's so much to do.

All of the applications I've described (word processing, database, spreadsheet, painting, drawing, and presentation) are rolled into the one application called AppleWorks on your iMac. However, you *can* buy a single application that is nothing but a very powerful word processor, and you *can* buy a single application that is nothing but a database, spreadsheet, a paint or draw program, or a presentation program. Each individual application, of course, is much more powerful than the one in AppleWorks, but even though the ones you have on your iMac may not be quite as powerful as the "dedicated" programs (dedicated to one function), AppleWorks will take you a very long way. When you get to a point where you want more than the applications in AppleWorks can give you, invest in the next level up. You will be able to take all of your data from AppleWorks and put it in the new application. For now, I think you'll probably be happy for a long while with what you have.

AppleWorks provides various *templates* to keep track of things like collections, family and friends, medical records, and all your music tapes, CDs, and videos, as well as a file to help you plan and keep track of a party or wedding. Also available are templates to track investments, analyze mortgages, budget events, maintain gradebooks, and much more.

The templates are in a "Templates" folder: In the AppleWorks 6 folder, open the Starting Points folder, then open the Templates folder.

Tip: When you're ready, go to the Apple web site for lots of tips, techniques, templates, tutorials, free stuff, and other resources for AppleWorks. It's a wonderful gift.
www.apple.com/appleworks

template: *A file that is designed and formatted already and is waiting for you to customize it to suit your own needs.*

Script Editor   Script Runner

AppleScript

An **AppleScript** is an advanced feature that is a series of commands written in the AppleScript language that tells your Mac to do something for you. AppleScripts can perform repetitive tasks for you, such as change all of your .tiff file names to .tif, or number all of the items in a folder. Or let's say you get lots of files from PC users who name files with all caps and it makes you crazy—you can write a script that will change all of the file names to lowercase. Once you write the script (or find it, like in your "Example Scripts" folder), you can run it anytime.

To get help specific for AppleScript, open the Script Editor and then go to the Help menu. To learn how to write AppleScripts, go to Apple's site and use their tutorial **(www.apple.com/applescripts).** Or if you want detailed information, check out *AppleScript for Applications: Visual QuickStart Guide* by Ethan Wilde.

Calculator

The **Calculator** is a handy little device for making basic mathematical calculations. The asterisk (*) is the multiplication symbol, and the slash (/) is the division symbol. Use the numeric keypad on the right side of your keyboard to enter data, or use the mouse to click on the Calculator's numeric keys.

You can copy and paste numbers into the Calculator from another application, or copy a number from the Calculator and paste it into another program. Read about the "copy and paste" technique on page 122.

For a more robust Calculator that even gives you a printable tape, see PCalc on page 95.

Chess

Chess is an electronic chess game between you and the computer. Or you can watch the computer play against itself. You can choose to play on a three-dimensional or two-dimensional board. To get details on how to play, double-click the Chess icon to open the game, then go to the Help menu and choose "Chess Help."

Clock

If you want to display a clock in the Dock or as a floating window on your Desktop, use the **Clock** application. Double-click the Clock icon to open it, then from the Clock menu, choose "Preferences…" so you can customize its appearance and behavior. You can choose to display an analog or digital clock, as shown below, with some variations in the digital version. If you display the clock in a floating window, you can adjust its transparency. Even if you choose to see the clock as a floating window, it will still appear in your Dock.

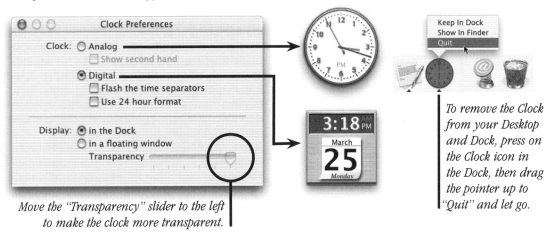

To remove the Clock from your Desktop and Dock, press on the Clock icon in the Dock, then drag the pointer up to "Quit" and let go.

Move the "Transparency" slider to the left to make the clock more transparent.

DVD Player

The **DVD Player** plays DVD (Digital Versatile Disc) movies on your computer. The Player includes a Viewer (a window in which a movie plays) and a Controller (the device that lets you control the video and audio).

To play a DVD, insert a DVD into your computer's CD/DVD drive, press the Media Eject key (upper-left on your keyboard) to open the tray. Insert the DVD, label-side up, then press the Media Eject key to close the tray, and the Player will automatically open. You'll see something like the example below.

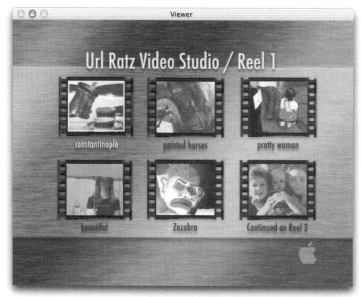

The DVD Player plays commercial DVDs and home-movie DVDs, such as this one created with Apple's iDVD 2 software.

Note: Only iMacs that have a Combo Drive or a SuperDrive can play DVDs. If a drive can "read" a disc, that means it can play it (as a movie) or that you can see the information stored on it. If a drive can "write" a disc, that means you create your own disc by storing (burning) information or movies on it yourself.

CD-RW drive: Cannot read or write DVDs.

Combo Drive: Can read DVDs.

SuperDrive: Can read and write DVDs.

Every one of the new iMacs with the flat-panel displays can read and write CDs.

You can use the **Controller** in either a horizontal or vertical position:

From the Controls menu, choose "Controller Type,"
then choose "Horizontal" or "Vertical."

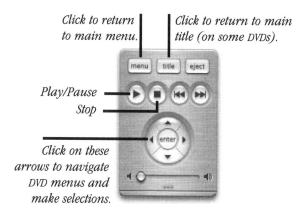

Click to return to main menu.

Click to return to main title (on some DVDs).

Play/Pause

Stop

Click on these arrows to navigate DVD menus and make selections.

Click to go to Previous or Next Chapter.

Press the buttons circled above to forward or reverse the DVD.

To set the default speed at which the DVD fast forwards or reverses, go to the Controls menu in the menu bar across the top of the screen: From Controls, choose "Scan Rate," then choose 2x, 4x, or 8x.

While a DVD movie is playing, you can **hide or show the Controller:**

Move your mouse all the way to the top of the screen until it bumps into the top edge. The DVD Player menu bar will appear. From the Window menu, choose "Hide Controller" or "Show Controller."

For more details about the Controller, please see the following page.

Click the small bumps near the edge of the Controller to reveal a number of **additional controls,** as shown below.

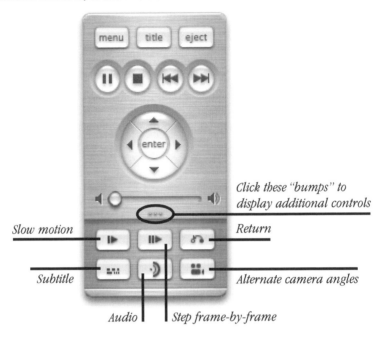

Click these "bumps" to display additional controls

Slow motion   *Return*

Subtitle   *Alternate camera angles*

Audio   *Step frame-by-frame*

Tip: Hover the pointer over a button and a "help tag" appears to tell you the name of the control.

Slow motion: Click to cycle through slow ($1/2$ speed), slower ($1/4$ speed), and slowest ($1/8$ speed). Click the "Play" button to resume normal playback speed, *or* tap the Spacebar.

Step frame-by-frame: Click to advance the playback one frame at a time. Click the "Play" button to resume normal playback, *or* tap the Spacebar.

Return: Click to return to a previous DVD menu. The DVD that you play may have a different function applied to this button, or none at all.

Subtitle: Click to turn subtitles on or off. Language settings for subtitles can usually be set in the DVD movie's menu or in the Preferences, as explained on the following page.

Audio: Some DVD videos (not all) include additional audio tracks, such as director's comments, that you can select with this button. You can also use this button to switch to alternate languages.

Angle: Some DVDs have alternate scenes that were filmed from different angles. If so, the "Angle" button lets you select these alternate angles.

You can **customize** some of the Player and Disc settings. From the DVD application menu, choose "Preferences…." The Player pane and the Disc pane show the options available.

The options in **Full Screen Mode** are self-explanatory.

In the **Windows** section, check "Display Controller Help Tags" to turn on the feature that makes descriptive names pop-up when you hold your mouse over a button or icon, as shown on the opposite page.

Check "Display Status Window" to show which commands you've chosen, such as "Stop," "Pause," or "Chapter 3." They will display in the upper-left corner of the Viewer.

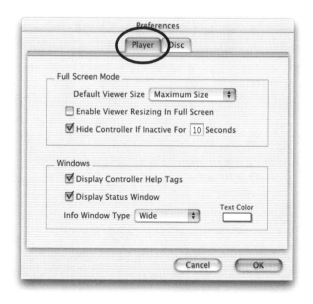

The **Disc** pane is rather self-explanatory:

Under **Default Language Settings,** set your language preferences. If you turn on "Subtitle," and the subtitles don't appear, click the "Subtitle" button, one of the additional controls hidden in the Controller, as shown on the previous page.

In the **Features** section, check "Enable DVD@ccess Web Links" to activate an advanced feature that lets some DVDs display "hot spot" links that connect to web sites, right in a movie.

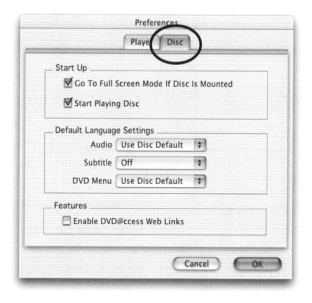

iDVD 2

If your iMac has a SuperDrive (a CD/DVD drive that can write DVDs), you can use **iDVD 2** to author original DVDs using your edited iMovies as content. For instructions, open iDVD 2, then from the Help menu, choose "iDVD Help." Or, for complete details, get the book *The Little iDVD Book*, by Bob Levitus.

Image Capture

Image Capture transfers (*downloads*) images from most digital cameras to your computer. You can choose to download all photos in the camera, or just selected photos. Image Capture can build preview sheets in different size formats so you can print them on your printer, and it can build a web page that you can publish on the World Wide Web. Image Capture can also download video clips and MP3 audio files from your camera (if the camera can create those types of files).

Note: iPhoto now does just about everything Image Capture does—and does it better. If you have iPhoto, you might want to skip Image Cature. See Chapter 17.

Application settings

Read this before you connect your camera! When you connect your camera to the iMac with the USB cable and then turn on the camera, Image Capture automatically downloads your images from the camera to the "Pictures" folder on your iMac. Because Image Capture settings determine what happens during this process, you should open Image Capture and select your settings *before* you connect your camera to the computer for the first time! After customizing the settings, you won't need to manually open Image Capture the next time you download images.

To open Image Capture and change the settings, double-click the "Image Capture" icon (it's in your Applications folder).

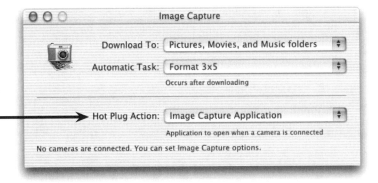

Hot Plug Action: Select the application you want to use to open images when a camera is connected. It's easiest to use the default setting of "Image Capture Application."

Download To: From this pop-up menu, select a folder that you want your pictures stored in. The option "Pictures, Movies, and Music folders" means Image Capture will put the *pictures* from your camera in the *Pictures* folder; if you have *movies* on the same camera, those will go in the *Movies* folder; and any *MP3 files* on the camera will end up in the *Music* folder.

Build Web Page: Choose this option from the "Automatic Task" menu and Image Capture will automatically build a web site with a home page of "thumbnail" versions of your photos, plus a separate web page for each full-sized photo. The page design is stark, but it works. If you're familiar with web design and HTML, you can open the files and make changes, or at least change the names beneath the photos. (All the photos and web pages are put in the Pictures folder, in a folder named "Index.")

To avoid building a web page with a photo that needs to be rotated, as shown here, see "Automatically download all items" on the next page.

Format: Choose one of the "Format" options (3 x 5, 4 x 6, 5 x 7, or 8 x 10) to automatically create image preview pages that open in Internet Explorer for viewing and/or printing.

In this example, Image Capture created three HTML pages (each HTML page is a web page):

     3x5index02.html
     3x5index01.html
     3x5 tips.html

Two of these HTML pages show the eight photos that were downloaded from the camera (four per page), and they are in a format that will print on most printers. The third page ("3 x 5 tips.html") is not for printing or viewing on the Internet—it's for you to read because it contains tips for printing the other HTML pages.

The photo preview pages open automatically in your Internet Explorer browser as soon as Image Capture creates them. To open the pages again later, double-click the HTML file icons (you'll find them in your "Sites" folder).

Now you should set the **Image Capture Preferences.** The "Download Options" and "View Options" directly affect how the camera downloads your photos. **To open the preferences,** go to the Image Capture menu and choose "Preferences…." Click the "Download Options" tab (if it isn't already showing).

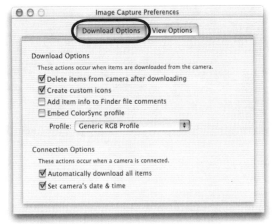

Delete items from camera after downloading: This erases all items from the camera's storage as soon as they are transferred to your iMac. Uncheck this option if you want to keep the current images on the camera.

Create custom icons: Creates an icon for each image that looks like the photo, rather than a generic icon.

Add item info to Finder file comments: Adds information about a photo to the Comments section of the photo's Show Info window (as explained on page 392), such as size measurements and image resolution.

Embed ColorSync profile: This is generally of interest only to professional photographers. To attach "color profile" information to an image file for color management, choose a profile from the "Profile" pop-up menu. Color management strives to accurately capture, display, and output color by using standard color protocols. Located in System Preferences, Apple's ColorSync lets you set profiles for Input, Display, Output, and Proof devices.

Automatically download all items: This downloads items from the camera without giving you a chance to preview them. If you want to preview items so you can delete or rotate some images *before* downloading them, *un*check this box. I prefer to uncheck this option so I can see an immediate preview window of the images, then select and download only the images that look good. See the following page for more details.

Set camera's date & time: If you set the date and time in your camera *before* you took the photos, the date and time will be shown in the camera preview window. See the following pages.

Tip: When you download photos from your camera, keep the camera plugged into its AC adapter so you'll have plenty of power for the download and won't use up all the battery juice.

The **View Options** pane has settings for an "Icon View" and a "List View"—these settings do not apply to the regular Finder window, but to a special camera preview window, as explained below.

In the "Download Options" pane (as described on the previous page), you could choose to have the camera "Automatically download all items." If you did *not* choose this, when you plug in your camera to the iMac a window opens that lets you choose to either "Download Some..." or "Download All" of the images in the camera.

If you chose **Download Some...,** a camera preview window opens in which you can preview images in the camera before they're downloaded, as shown on the following page. The window's title bar will show the name of the attached camera.

In the camera preview window (next page), click the "Icon View" or "List View" button. That special window is where you'll see the effects of the View Options settings shown below.

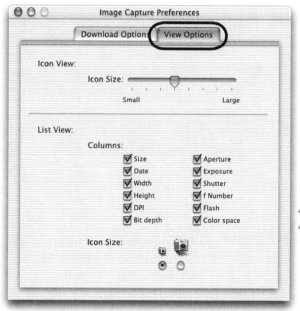

Icon View: *Use the "Icon Size" slider to determine the size that an icon will appear in the camera preview window when "Icon View" is active.*

List View: *From the "Columns" list, choose which columns of information you want to see in the camera preview window when "List View" is selected. Also choose an "Icon Size" to display.*

*These first two examples show the **Icon View** with two different icon sizes chosen.*

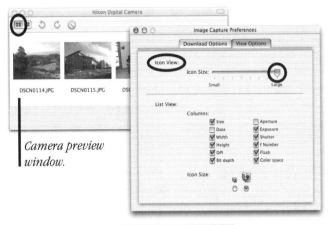

Camera preview window.

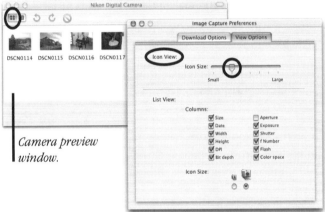

Camera preview window.

These two examples show the List View with different options selected.

Single-click an image to select it, then use these buttons to rotate the image or delete it.

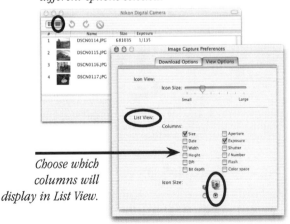

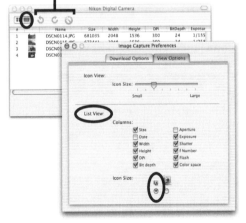

Choose which columns will display in List View.

iMovie

If you have a digital video camera with a FireWire connection, with **iMovie** you can digitize and edit your movies, complete with sound tracks, transitions between scenes, special effects, and customized titles. See Chapter 21 for a detailed look

Internet Connect

Internet Connect is the program that will connect you to the Internet using the iMac's internal modem. See Chapter 15 for more information.

Installers

The **Installers** folder contains two installers and a folder of Developer Tools.

> The **AOL** installer installs America Online. See Chapters 1 and 16 for information about AOL.

Install AOL for Mac OS X

> The **FAXstf X** installer installs a program that will let you send and receive faxes right from your iMac. See Chapter 11 for FAXstf X instructions.

FAXstf X 10.0 Installer

> The **Developer Tools** folder contains tools, documentation, and software for developers who want to create applications for Mac OS X. Ignore this folder (or throw it away) unless you plan to be a software developer.

Developer Tools

Internet Explorer

To view web pages you need a program called a "browser." **Internet Explorer** is the browser that came with your iMac. A browser tutorial is in Chapter 16.

iPhoto

iPhoto is a powerful application for organizing and sharing your digital photos. If iPhoto is not already on your iMac, you probably have an iPhoto CD; use this CD to install iPhoto, or download it from Apple's web site. See Chapter 17.

iTunes

iTunes plays music CDs, converts songs from CDs to the popular MP3 format, plays Internet radio stations, organizes your song files into Playlists, and burns CDs of your Playlists. iTunes also creates a dazzling light show that pulsates with the beat of the music. See Chapter 18 for a wealth of information about iTunes.

Mail

Mail is an email program that sends and receives your email messages. There's lots of information about Mail in Chapter 20.

Otto Matic

Otto Matic is a fun, challenging, 3D game from Pangea Software—you play the part of Otto Matic, a fearless robot from 1957 whose quest is to save humans from abduction by evil aliens. Otto's plan is to transport Earthlings to his rocket as he travels to strange and exotic planets. If you advance far enough into the game's ten different levels, you eventually have to face the ultimate alien leader, the Great Brain from Planet X. But don't worry, you have seven types of space-age weapons.

On the way to Planet X you'll visit Earth, Snoth, Knarr, Rennie, Sulak, Deniz, and Shebanek.

Otto Matic (English).pdf

Double-click this PDF file, located in the Instructions folder, to learn the basics of how to play **Otto Matic.**

On Planet Earth, the first level of the game, you'll have to deal with killer vegetables and an evil tractor. From there it gets stranger as you ski on toxic ooze and ride soap bubbles across lakes of slime. Good luck getting any more work done.

Unless you're an expert gamer obsessed with conquering Otto Matic by yourself, you'll want to read the instructions. Inside the Otto Matic folder, open the "Instructions" folder, then look for the PDF file in the language of your choice.

Scroll through the Otto Matic manual using the scroller. Or click the Thumbnails tab and quickly move to any page by clicking on a thumbnail.

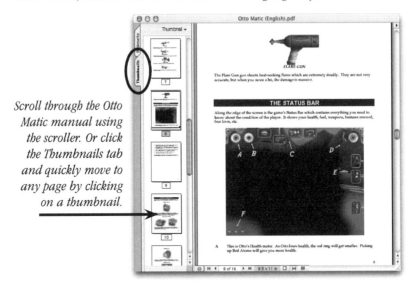

You can also access "The Otto Matic Strategy Guide" on the MacCentral.com web site at **http://maccentral.macworld.com/news/0202/ottomatic/index.php**. The Strategy Guide provides maps of the different game levels, tips and tricks for making it through each level, and clues about obstacles and the twenty-five different alien species you'll encounter along the way.

PCalc 2

PCalc is a scientific calculator that has many more features than the regular Calculator (also in the Applications window), including automatic conversions of measures, volumes, weights, and temperatures. There's a "tape" function that makes a list of your calculations, and lots of functions that only mathematicians and scientists will need. To open multiple calculators, use the "New" command in the File menu.

Tips: To shrink the calculator down to just the LCD display, click the green Zoom button in the upper-left corner of PCalc. PCalc will still respond to the numeric keypad and to keyboard shortcuts.

To see a list of keyboard shortcuts, from the Help menu, choose "PCalc Help."

To make PCalc remember its contents when you quit, *from the PCalc menu choose "Preferences...," then uncheck the option "Clear calculators at startup."*

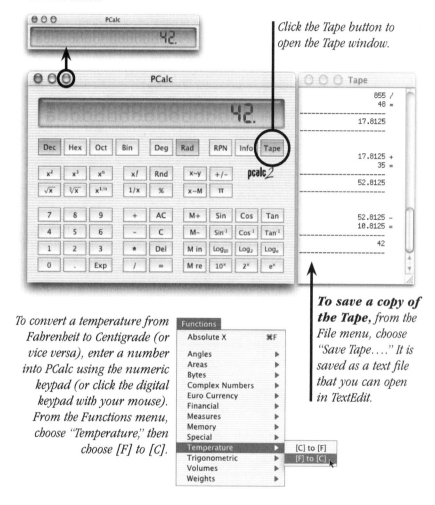

Click the Tape button to open the Tape window.

To save a copy of the Tape, from the File menu, choose "Save Tape...." It is saved as a text file that you can open in TextEdit.

To convert a temperature from Fahrenheit to Centigrade (or vice versa), enter a number into PCalc using the numeric keypad (or click the digital keypad with your mouse). From the Functions menu, choose "Temperature," then choose [F] to [C].

From the Constants menu, which contains a list of numbers used often in mathematical and scientific calculations, you can enter a complex number into PCalc automatically. You can edit the list to include any special numbers that you use often. My personal favorite is Ultimate Answer (according to the Douglas Adams book, *The Hitchhiker's Guide to the Galaxy,* the ultimate answer is "42").

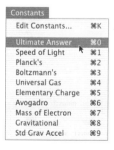

Preview

Preview is a little application that displays your photos and PDF files. You've probably already noticed that when you double-click on many photos and other images, they automatically open in Preview, as shown below. You can zoom in on an image (enlarge it) and zoom out. You can flip it vertically or horizontally and then save it in that new rotation. Just check the menus.

jane.jpg

This is the icon that indicates a file will automatically open in Preview when you double-click on it.

This is an open Preview window.

Quicken Deluxe

Quicken Deluxe is personal finance software for managing and keeping track of your money. Quicken makes it easy to balance a checkbook, plan budgets, and generate reports of all kinds. It also provides little movie tutorials, a 600-page manual in the Quicken folder, and lots of online Help files.

QuickTime Player

The **QuickTime Player** can open image files, but its main job is to play multimedia files that have been saved as QuickTime movies. The QuickTime Player includes links to QuickTime "channels" on the Internet that provide multimedia content such as news, sports, movie trailers, weather, and music videos. Details about QuickTime are in Chapter 22.

Sherlock

Sherlock searches for files, both on your computer and on the Internet. It can even search the contents of some files. If you're connected to the Internet, Sherlock can find shopping bargains, old friends, the latest news, and almost anything else. See Chapter 24.

Stickies

The **Stickies** application can be very useful. Use it to leave notes to yourself or to others who might use your iMac; the notes appear right on your screen. Create your shopping list, notes on your upcoming presentation, gossip, snippets for poems you will write later, tidbits to add to your research, interesting stuff from web pages, etc. Below are examples of Stickies and the sorts of things you can do with them.

From the File menu, you can **import** text directly into a Stickie note, or **export** text from the active Stickie so you can use it in other applications. You can **print** the active note (the one in front with the title bar visible) or all of the open notes.

From the Edit menu, you can **find** certain words that might appear in any of the open notes. You can run the **spell checker** (the "Spelling…" command) on *all* open notes, or ask to **check the spelling** of just the *active* note, in which case each time you choose the command ("Check Spelling") or press Command Semicolon (;), a misspelled word is underlined with dots.

From the Note menu, you can **change the typeface** of selected text, or **change the style** (bold or italic if one is designed into the font). You can **copy the font,** size, and color of a word (*click* inside the typeface example in the note; *do not* select the word; choose "Copy Font"), then select a word in another note (or the same note) and **"Paste Font."** The selected word will take on the typeface, color, and size of the word you copied from.

If you've created a style of note that you like, with the font, size, and color of note, you can make this note's formatting your **default** so every new note you create will have this same font, size, and color. Just create a note with the formatting you like (only one style of text will apply), then from the Note menu, choose **"Use as Default."** The color of the text will not apply to the default.

Drag a **graphic** from any folder and drop it into a Stickie note.

—continued

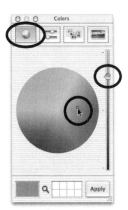

Drag the tiny square around the circle to choose a color, and use the slider bar to make the color darker or lighter.

You can **change the color of selected text**—select the text (drag over certain words or press Command A to select all), then choose "Text Colors…" from the Note menu. In the Colors panel that appears, drag the little square around until you find a color you like, then drag the slider bar up or down to make the color darker or lighter.

The Color menu **changes the color of the note,** not the text.

"Note Info" will tell you the date the note was created and modified.

Use the Window menu to **close the active note, miniaturize it,** as shown below, or **deminiaturize** it. Or use the keyboard shortcut Command M or double-click the title bar to miniaturize and deminiaturize a note ("deminiaturize" is not in my dictionary, and the spell checker in Stickies flags the word as a misspelling). You can choose to neatly arrange your notes (choose **"Arrange in Front"**) whether they are miniaturized or not.

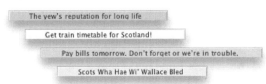

These four notes are miniaturized and arranged in front. Double-click the title bar of any note to open it.

You can use **Services** to do a number of things with the selected text in a Stickie. For instance, select the text, go to the Stickies menu, and from the Services submenu, choose "Mail" and "Mail Text," as shown below. This will automatically copy the text from the Sticky, open the Mail program, open an email form, and paste this text into the form, ready for you to add the email address and send it.

Use Services to email the text in a Sticky to someone.

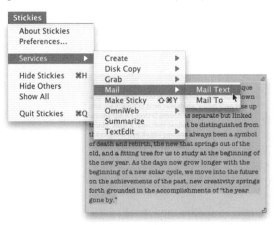

And from any other OS X application, even from a browser, you can select text, then go to the Application menu and **use Services to make a Sticky** of your selected text.

System Preferences

The **System Preferences** let you customize the settings that affect many aspects of how your computer looks and behaves.

The System Preferences icon is located in the Dock for quick and easy access. Click once on it to open the System Preferences pane, shown below, which displays all the different features you can customize.

Single-click an icon (such as "Dock") and that item's preferences pane will replace the existing one. Single-click the icon "Show All" in the upper-left corner to return to the pane that displays *all* the preferences.

With System Preferences you can adjust the time that appears in your menu bar, change the picture on your Desktop, choose a language for your menus and dialog boxes, enter the networking and Internet settings, and much more. The System Preferences you will probably use most often are discussed in Chapter 13. All of the System Preferences are covered in detail in *The Little Mac OS X Book*.

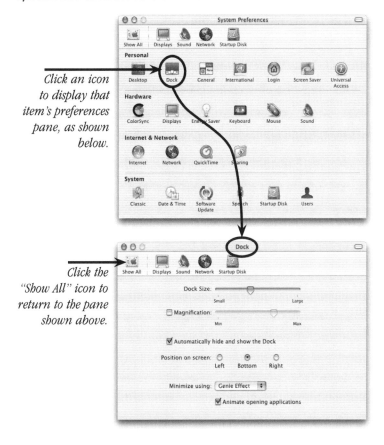

Click an icon to display that item's preferences pane, as shown below.

Click the "Show All" icon to return to the pane shown above.

TextEdit

The application **TextEdit** is a small word processor. It can do some surprising things, but is missing enough serious features that you might not want to use it as your only word processor. But here is what it can do:

From the File menu, you can **"Open Recent"** files. This is nice so you don't have to go scrounging around in your hard disk looking for that file you created several days ago.

From the Edit menu, you can do all the basic stuff like **cut, copy, paste, delete** (clear), **undo,** and **select all.** If you don't know how to use those features, please see Chapter 5.

The **Find** command has some fairly robust features. You can *find* words or phrases, and you can *replace* found words or phrases with entirely new words or phrases. For instance, you might have written a novel with a main character named "Peter," then you decide, after 173 pages, that you want his name to be "John." Use the Find panel to "Find: Peter" and "Replace with: John," then click the "Replace All" button. Instantly, your hero has a new name.

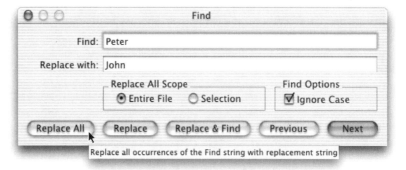

*Position your pointer over a button and wait a second or two—
a Help tag appears to tell you what that button will do.*

The **Spelling** command gives you three options. "Spelling…" brings up the spell checker for the active document. "Check Spelling" will point out your misspelled words in the active document one at a time; press Command Semicolon (;) to find the next misspelled word. The option to "Check Spelling As You Type" will underline words with red dots as you misspell them.

Use the **Speech** command to hear your text read out loud (it will be read by the voice you choose in the Speech preferences pane of System Preferences). If text is selected, that is what will be read. If nothing is selected, the reader will start at the beginning.

From the **Format** menu, use the **Font** and **Text** submenus to format your text, most of which is explained in Chapter 5.

The command to **"Make Plain Text"** will turn your document into a "text-only" or ASCII file, which removes all font choices, styles, underlines, etc., and takes the text down to its most basic form. This file is then safe to send through the Internet to any other computer user, regardless of the kind of computer or applications she has on her machine.

If you choose **"Make Read Only,"** TextEdit will lock the file so it can be read by others, but no one can make changes to it or delete it. Well, they could if they went up to the Format menu and chose "Make Editable," so it's not a very safe way to protect your document. This command is only meant to prevent accidental damage to the file.

"Wrap to Page" will display the printing guidelines in the window. You can't change the margins—they are stuck at one inch all the way around. But in "Wrap to Page" you are guaranteed that what you see on the screen is what will print, as opposed to "Wrap to Window," explained below.

While in **"Wrap to Window,"** the lines of type stretch to fill the space as wide as you drag your window. When you print, the printer will try to match your line endings, but if your window is wide, it may have to reduce the size of the type to fit your sentences on the same lines of the page that you have on the screen. So if your page of text prints too small, reduce the size of your window and print again, or choose "Wrap to Page."

"Allow Hyphenation" does just what it says—it will allow words to be hyphenated at the ends of lines.

Be sure to go to the TextEdit menu and check out the **"Preferences...."** They are self-explanatory. The "New Document Font" lets you choose a default font and size so every time you open a new document in TextEdit, you will automatically start to type with your choice of font.

You can drag **pictures** into your TextEdit documents:

1. On your Desktop, position your *open* Pictures folder (or whichever folder you store your pictures in) on the *right* side of your screen.

2. In TextEdit, position your page on the *left* side of the screen.

3. From the Pictures folder, press-and-drag an image to your TextEdit document—watch carefully to see the insertion point move around the page as you drag the image around! (See Chapter 5 if you're not clear on what the insertion point is and why it is so important.)

4. When the insertion point is flashing in the position you want the image, as shown below, drop it on the page (just let go of the mouse button). The picture will insert itself where the insertion point was flashing.

5. To make more space *above* the picture, position your insertion point to the left of the photo and hit a Return.

To make more space *after* the picture, position your insertion point to the right of the image and hit a Return.

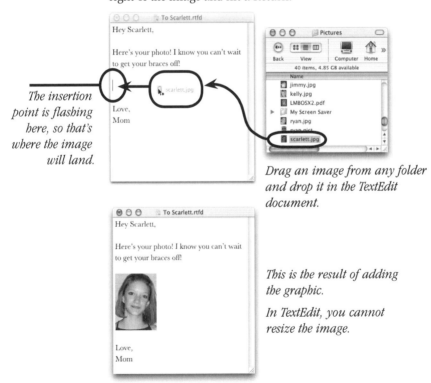

The insertion point is flashing here, so that's where the image will land.

Drag an image from any folder and drop it in the TextEdit document.

This is the result of adding the graphic.

In TextEdit, you cannot resize the image.

When you **save** a text document in TextEdit, it creates what is called a Rich Text Format file with a file name extension of **.rtf**. "Rich Text" means it can include fonts, styles, different point sizes, and other formatting (as opposed to "Plain Text" which removes styles and formatting from text).

If you insert a photo or other graphic into a TextEdit document, it will become a "Rich Text Format with Attachments" file and must be saved with an extension of **.rtfd** (the "d" stands for "directory" because an .rtfd file is actually a folder, or directory, that bundles the text with the graphics). Don't worry about remembering that—as soon as you try to save a document that has an image in it, the iMac will tell you that you have to change the extension and will actually do it for you.

Tip: You can go to the Print dialog box and click the "Preview" button. This will make a PDF preview of your document which will open in the application Preview. From there, you can save the document as a PDF file so you can email it to anyone in the world and they can see it just like you created it.

You can also save any file as a PDF: In the Print dialog box, choose the "Output Options." Check the box to "Save as File," then choose the PDF format.

You'll get this message when you try to save a TextEdit document with a graphic in it.

TextEdit does not have a feature that automatically creates real **apostrophes** and **quotation marks,** so you have to learn to type them yourself. Don't ever print your work with typewriter apostrophes and quotation marks—it looks stupid. This is what the marks look like and how to type real ones:

Typewriter apostrophe:	It's Mary's turn.
Typewriter quotation marks:	"Go get 'em, Mary." *(Oooh, these are so nasty.)*
Typesetter's apostrophe:	It's Mary's turn.
Typesetter's quotation marks:	"Go get 'em, Mary."

To type true typesetter's apostrophe and quotation marks:

apostrophe	'	Shift Option]
opening quotation mark	"	Option [
closing quotation mark	"	Shift Option [

Utilities

Utilities

The **Utilities** folder contains a large collection of useful *utilities,* which are small applications that perform special functions. Although many of these utilities are self-explanatory (and others may not be useful until you're more advanced), I'll describe some of them in Chapter 23. For a more complete description of all the items in the Utilities folder, refer to *The Little Mac OS X Book*.

World Book folder

World Book

The **World Book** application is a digital encyclopedia. It includes a search feature; a dictionary; sticky notes and a highlighter for research; and an Atlas and distance calculator that also gives the latitude and longitude of selected locations. You'll also find several "wizards," which are utilities that take you step-by-step through procedures for creating timelines, reports, charts, or quizzes.

This is the World Book "Home Screen" that provides links to its main features. Subsequent pages provide these same links (plus several other tools) in a Toolbar, as shown on the opposite page.

To access some World Book material, you have to insert the World Book CD that came with your iMac. You'll see a blue "CD" icon and a message when it's necessary to insert the CD.

The World Book Toolbar contains nine tools, as well as links to the seven major areas in the encyclopedia. Also, from the Tools menu, you can open the World Book Notepad, a simple word processing application that allows you to create documents using text and graphics from World Book (page 110).

The appearance of either of these CD icons on your screen indicates that additional content is available on the World Book CD that came with your iMac.

Tools; see pages 106–107.

From this Tools menu, you can open World Book Notepad; see page 110.

World Book Areas; see pages 107–110

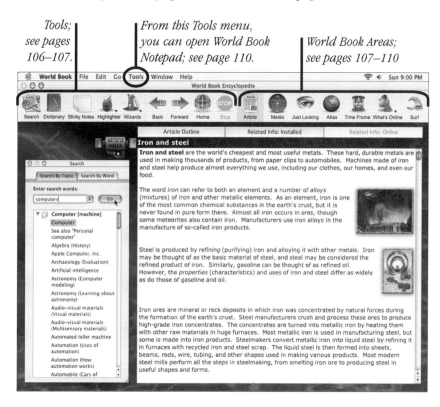

—continued

The **tools** on the left side of the Toolbar include the following items.

Search

Search: Single-click the "Search" button on the Toolbar, *or* single-click the "Topics" button on the World Book Home Screen to open the Search window. The Search window contains "Search by Topic" and "Search by Word" options. Select and drag any *word* or *phrase* from a World Book screen onto the Search entry field to display related matches.

Dictionary

Dictionary: Look up the definition of any word. Type a word in the Dictionary text field, *or* drag a selected word to the text field or onto the Dictionary icon in the Toolbar. You can also double-click any word in an article to open the Dictionary at that word.

Sticky Notes

Stickie Notes: Use Stickie Notes to mark information and to add comments or reminders. Single-click in the article where you want to place a Stickie Note, then single-click the "Stickie Notes" icon in the Toolbar. A Stickie Note will open, titled with the name of the current article. Type any comments you wish, then click the Stickie Note's Close box. A small marker will appear in the article. Drag the marker or the Stickie Note to reposition it.

To see a list of all Stickie Notes, go to the Tools menu and choose "Stickie Notes List." In the list, double-click the note that you want to open.

To open an existing Stickie Note within an article, click once on it.

Highlighter

Highlighter: Single-click the "Highlighter" button in the Toolbar, then drag across selections of text to highlight that text. To choose from four highlighter colors, press the Tab key. *Or* press-and-hold the Highlighter button in the Toolbar, then choose a color from the pop-up menu.

To erase your highlights from the current article or from the entire World Book, go to the Edit menu and choose either "Clear Current Article Highlights" or "Clear Highlights From All Articles."

Wizards

The **Wizards** button takes you to four applications that help you write reports and guide you through the creation of charts, timelines, and quizzes, as described on the opposite page.

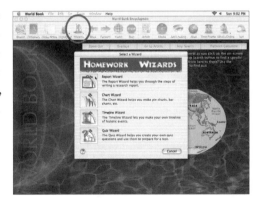

Report Wizard guides you through the process of writing a report, including topic selection, scheduling, research, notecards, writing a thesis statement, outlining, first draft, visuals, revisions, bibliography, and preparing the final paper.

Chart Wizard creates charts and graphs for reports or presentations.

Timeline Wizard creates timelines that contain events and dates. You can choose to make horizontal or vertical timelines. Timelines can include pictures and can be placed in reports or presentations.

Quiz Wizard makes it easy to create quizzes, just for fun or to practice for a test. Choose between True/False, Flash Card, or Mathematics formats.

The **Back** and **Forward** buttons navigate through the pages.

The **Home** button is a link to the World Book Home Screen.

Click the **Stop** button to stop a video or animation from playing.

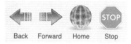

The **Area** buttons on the right side of the Toolbar link to the various sections of the World Book Encyclopedia.

Article: This opens the "Article Display" area on the World Book Home Screen; you can also click the "Topics button" to get here. From this area you can access all of World Book's features.

At the top-left of an article you'll see the **Article Media canister.** Click the canister body (or click the tab beneath the canister) to roll down a filmstrip of all media (a video, sound, or picture) related to the current article. Single-click one of the thumbnail frames in the filmstrip to jump to the page containing that thumbnail, *or* double-click the thumbnail in the filmstrip to immediately open the media file.

The Up and Down arrows on each side of the canister show and hide the filmstrip one frame at a time. **To close the canister,** single-click the canister body *or* click the tab at the bottom of the filmstrip.

Media opens the Media Center window where you can search or browse through lists of available media files (videos, sound files, pictures, maps). There are three different lists: World Book media files for the current topic, all World Book media files that are installed on your computer, or all media files that are on the World Book CD.

—*continued*

Just Looking lets you search for graphics and articles by category, content, media type, document type, content, or randomly. Single-click this icon and the screen will fill with a random selection of topics, pictures, and the "Just Looking" panel.

Single-click on a topic or picture that interests you, *or* click the Random button in the middle of the "Just Looking" panel to fill the screen with a new random collection of topics. This is a fun way to explore World Book. Of course, you can also search using the pop-up menus and entering keywords into the text entry field.

Click the "Random" button to reload the screen with new choices.

Click on a picture or a text box to open it in the Media Center or Article Viewer.

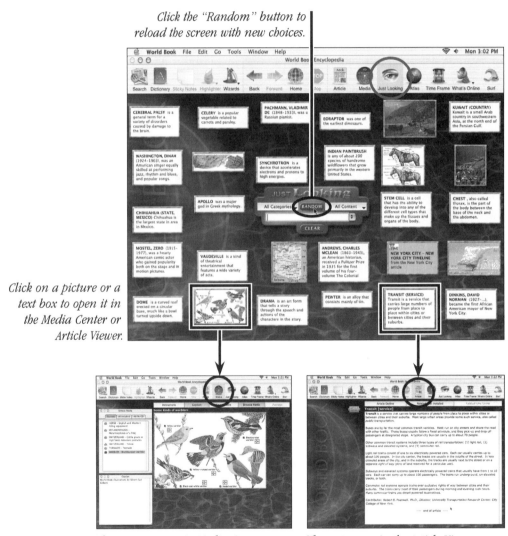

The picture opens in Media Center. Note the audio file icons next to the birds.

The text opens in the Article Viewer.

Atlas is the map-viewing area of the World Book. As you move your mouse over the names of continents (or countries, states, or cities), the pointer turns into a magnifying glass, indicating a "hotspot." Click on a hotspot **to zoom in** on that area and display a more detailed map. Continue clicking to open progressively more detailed maps. **To zoom out** and view a larger map area, click the "Zoom Out" button.

The Map Search button opens a window in which you can type the name of a location. As you type, a matching item in the list is highlighted. Single-click on the highlighted name in the list to display that map.

Zoom Out   *Map Search*   *Distance Calculator*

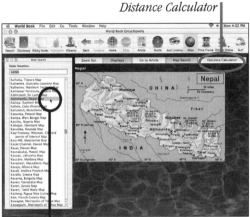

Click on a name in the Map Search window to display that map.

Click the "Distance Calculator" button to open the window shown below. You can find the approximate distance between two points that you specify, as well as latitude and longitude information for each location.

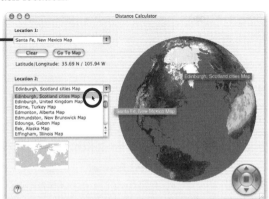

To enter a location in the Distance Calculator, start typing a location name into the Location 1 entry field. As you type, a list pops up that matches what you've typed (as shown in Location 2). Click on a location in the pop-up list to enter it into the Location field.

Repeat the procedure for the Location 2 field.

—continued

Time Frame: You can make a chronological search for information related to a specific year, decade, century, millennium, or era. Click the "Time Frame" button in the Toolbar to open the "New Time Frame" control box and use the pop-up menus to search for a time period. Or move your mouse over any date in an article; when the pointer changes to an hourglass, click to see that date's time-related details.

What's Online: Explore online features of World Book, and get World Book updates and special reports downloaded from the Internet.

Surf connects to "Surf the Millennium" where you view simulated web sites for a historically accurate look at the past 1000 years, with each century represented by its own home page that links to imaginary web sites from that period. This is a creative and imaginative romp through history, presenting what some web news sites might have been like if the World Wide Web had existed for the past 1000 years.

World Book Notepad is a small word processor that makes it easy to create reports or presentations. You can drag text and pictures from World Book directly into an Open Notepad document.

Click the World Book icon in Notepad's corner to return to World Book.

To switch back to Notepad, press Command N.

Tip: For more World Book instructions, open the World Book folder. Double-click the PDF file named "User Guide.pdf."

You can save Notepad documents in three different formats:

World Book Text Format (.wbt) is for simple text-only documents without styles or formatting.

Rich Text Format (.rtf) is for documents in which you want to retain text formatting, such as bold and italic characters.

World Book Notepad Format (.wbn) is for documents that contain both text and pictures.

Typing (also called Word Processing) and More*

Typing is one of the basic things you'll be doing on your iMac. In addition to information about typing, this chapter also contains stuff you need to know to work in every application on the iMac. No matter what you plan to use your computer for, you should work through this "Typing" chapter because all of the things you learn here will apply to everything you'll ever do on the iMac.

These next six chapters are short tutorials to teach you the basics of many of the software applications on your iMac. If you took a break from the first part of the book and turned off your computer, then of course you must now turn it back on. In this chapter, open **AppleWorks** and make a new word processing document. You'll change the typeface, the type size, the indents, and more. And you'll save the document, print it, close it, and quit the application. It's not an entire tutorial for using a word processor, but it's what you need to get started using any application on your iMac.

*This is the most important chapter in this book! Please read it!

111

Open the AppleWorks application

To create a word processing document, you have to open the application AppleWorks because the word processor is one of its components.

1. To open AppleWorks, single-click on the "AppleWorks 6" icon in the Dock.

   Or open the Applications folder (single-click the Applications icon in any Finder window Toolbar), open the AppleWorks folder (double-click on it), *then* open the AppleWorks application (double-click on the icon).

2. The first thing you see when you "launch" (that is, "open") AppleWorks is the "Starting Points" palette because AppleWorks integrates several applications into one and you have to choose which one you want.

3. For this exercise, single-click the "Word Processing" icon.

Single-click the "Word Processing" icon.

Click the other tabs to see what they display, but make sure this "Basic" tab is chosen when you want to start a new, blank word processing document.

The **tabs** on the bottom of this palette provide easy access to other panes of the "Starting Points" palette:

Assistants: Contains small utilities that guide you through creating various kinds of files.

Templates: Contains pre-designed templates that you can modify for your own use.

Web: Has several links to web sites.

Recent Items: Holds files that you've worked on recently.

Plus symbol: Lets you add custom panes to the "Starting Points" palette.

Create a new page

So here you are at a blank page! Whenever you create a "new" document on the Macintosh, you will get a clean, blank page, just waiting for you to do something creative to it.

Notice there is a little, flashing vertical bar at the top of the page (circled, below); that's called the **insertion point,** and you will see it everywhere on the iMac. The insertion point is your visual clue that you are in typing mode. When you touch the keys on the keyboard, *the text will appear wherever that insertion point is flashing.* That's a very important guideline to remember because you'll see the insertion point in every application and in many other places on the iMac.

Open: When you choose the command "Open," it means you want to open a document that has already been created! That is very different from creating a new, untitled, clean page, as we're doing now.

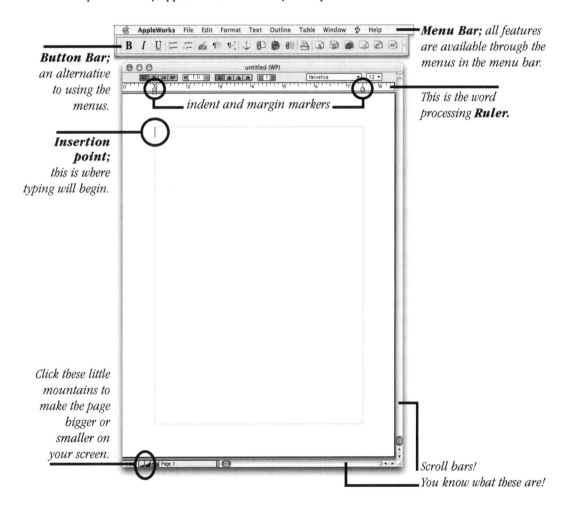

Menu Bar; *all features are available through the menus in the menu bar.*

This is the word processing **Ruler.**

Button Bar; *an alternative to using the menus.*

indent and margin markers

Insertion point; *this is where typing will begin.*

Click these little mountains to make the page bigger or smaller on your screen.

Scroll bars! You know what these are!

Type some text!

Type one space after periods. This is professional-level type you are creating, not typewriter-level. Read The Mac is not a typewriter.

Just go ahead and type. When you get to the end of the line, ***do not hit the Return key!*** Just let the type bump into the right edge; it will "wrap" itself onto the next line all by itself. (That's called "word wrap.")

After you have typed a *paragraph,* go ahead and hit the Return key. In fact, you can hit it twice if you want more space between the paragraphs.

To fix typos along the way: If you made a typo just a character or so ago, hit the "Delete" key, found in the upper-right of the main section of keys (where the Backspace key is found on typewriters). This will move the insertion point to the left and ***backspace*** over the characters, ***deleting*** them. Make the change and continue typing.

To fix typos somewhere else on the page: If the typo is farther back in the line or in another paragraph, of course you don't have to delete all of the characters up to that point! That would be really boring. This is what you do:

1. Put your hand on the mouse and move the pointer around on the page (don't click the button!). You'll see that the pointer turns into what's called an **I-beam** when it's positioned over text: ⌶ .

   cursor: A general term for the thing on the screen that moves when you move the mouse, whether it appears as a pointer, I-beam, crossbar, or anything else.

   Notice that if you drag the mouse so this I-beam "cursor" is outside of the text area, it turns into a pointer again. Inside the text, it's an I-beam.

2. Okay. So in the text, position that I-beam directly to the *right* of the character you want to delete, right between it and the next character, like this:

   serem⌶dipity

3. **Click** the mouse button right there. *This moves the insertion point from wherever it was and positions it where you click.* You can't see the insertion point, though, until you move the I-beam out of the way. So go ahead and push the mouse to the side (*don't* hold the button down) so the I-beam floats around somewhere else. What you need is that **insertion point.** It should look like this:

   serem|dipity

   ☛*The flashing insertion point is the important item now, not the I-beam or any other cursor!*

114

4. Now that the insertion point is in position, hit the Delete key to remove the wrong character (the one to the *left* of the insertion point), then type the correct character in its place:

`serendipity`

5. To put your insertion point back at the end of your document so you can continue typing (or to put it somewhere else to correct another typo):

   a. Use the **mouse** to position the I-beam where you want it.

   b. **Single-click.**

   c. **Move** the I-beam out of the way. Typing starts at the insertion point, not at the I-beam!

   Note: if you like to keep your hands on the keyboard, you can also use the **arrow keys** on your keyboard to move the *insertion point* around (not the I-beam). Try it.

So type a page. *If you want to remove everything you've done so far and start over,* go to the Edit menu and choose "Select All," then hit Delete.

Try this: Type a headline, then hit two Returns. Type a few paragraphs like the ones shown below. Type a byline at the end ("by" you). Fix your typos. Enjoy yourself. When you've got a few paragraphs, turn the page (of this book) and we'll *format* the text (change the size, the typeface, indents, etc.).

Doll Tearsheet's Answer

Charge me! I scorn you, scurvy companion. What! You poor, base, rascally, cheating, lack-linen mate! Away, you mouldy rogue, away! Away, you cut-purse rascal! You filthy bung, away!

By this swine I'll thrust my knife in your mouldy chaps, an you play the saucy cuttle with me. Away, you bottle-ale rascal! You basket-hilt stale juggler, you!

He, a captain! Hang him, rogue! He lives upon mouldy stewed prunes and dried cakes. A captain! For God's sake, thrust him down stairs; I cannot endure such a fustian rascal.

Doll Tearsheet, from King Henry IV
by William Shakespeare

This is an example of text typed in the word processor of AppleWorks. Yours will look a little different, of course.

Formatting in general

Once you understand the basic rule of changing anything on the Macintosh, you can bumble your way through any program. This is the rule:

Select first. Then do it to it.

That is, the trick is to *select* what you want to change, and *then* go to the menu and make a formatting choice, otherwise the computer doesn't know what you want to change.

In a word processor, select text by pressing-and-dragging over the text:

Tip: If you miss the last character or two while selecting text, hold down the Shift key, then press-and-drag or tap the arrow keys to select more (or to select less).

Position the I-beam at one end of what you want to select, then press the mouse button down, hold it down, and drag to the other end. The text will "highlight," like this sentence.

Many changes can be made right from the Button Bar (shown below) or from the "Ruler," that strip across the top of the page (shown on the opposite page). You can also choose formatting commands from the menu.

*This is the **Button Bar** in AppleWorks, and you see the Help tag displayed for the B button.*

Format the text using the Button Bar

The Button Bar, above, might look rather intimidating, but it will eventually grow useful to you. Many of the commands from the menus are represented by these little buttons so you can click a button instead of having to go to the menu. For instance, which button could you click to make selected text **bold?**

As you position your mouse over a button, AppleWorks shows a "Help tag," which is a pop-up message that tells you what that button will do, as shown in the example above.

To use the Button Bar, first select the text you want to change, then click a button. Try making some text bold and some other text italic.

Many of the buttons in the Button Bar will change when you switch to different modules in AppleWorks. If you want to customize this bar, see page 121.

Format the text using the Ruler

Follow the directions below to use the Ruler to change some of the text.

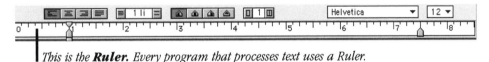

*This is the **Ruler**. Every program that processes text uses a Ruler.*

Center the headline

Select the headline, then click in the tiny icon on the Ruler that indicates a *centered* alignment: ⊟. (Don't ever center a headline by spacing over with the Spacebar—this is not a typewriter!!)

Justify the rest of the text

Select the rest of the text and click the tiny icon on the Ruler that indicates a *justified* alignment: ☰ (aligned on both the left and right sides).

Indent one of the paragraphs

Select a paragraph (click in it). In the Ruler, position the very tip of the pointer on the tiny *rectangular* part of the marker on the left of the Ruler (shown below, left). Drag that marker to the *right* to create the indent.

*Tip: To make changes to a **paragraph** from the ruler, you don't actually have to select all the characters. Just click once anywhere in the paragraph you want to change.*

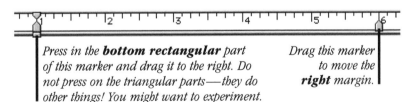

*Press in the **bottom rectangular** part of this marker and drag it to the right. Do not press on the triangular parts—they do other things! You might want to experiment.*

*Drag this marker to move the **right** margin.*

117

Make text bold or italic using the menus

Select the text. Then from the Text menu, choose "Style," then "Bold" or "Italic."

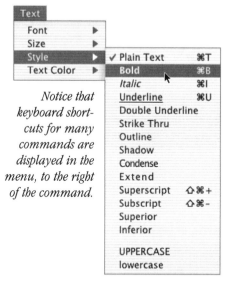

Notice that keyboard short-cuts for many commands are displayed in the menu, to the right of the command.

Or *select the text* and use the keyboard shortcut. What is the shortcut for the bold style? For the italic style?

Or *select the text* and use the buttons on the Button Bar.

Change the size of text

Select the text you want to change. From the Text menu, choose "Size." The current size of the text is indicated by the checkmark. Select a size from this menu.

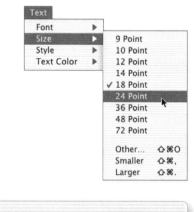

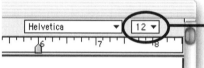

Or *select the text* and choose a size from the Size pop-up menu in the toolbar that is just above the Ruler.

Change the typeface

Select the text you want to change. From the Text menu, choose "Font" (the current font is indicated in the menu by a checkmark). Select the font you want to use.

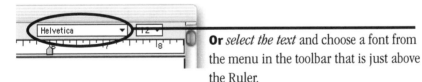

Or *select the text* and choose a font from the menu in the toolbar that is just above the Ruler.

Color the text

Select the text you want to color. Then, from the Text menu, choose "Text Color."

Choose a color from the palette that appears. You can customize the Button Bar and place a "Text Color" button in the Bar if you want to make it even easier to select text colors; see page 121.

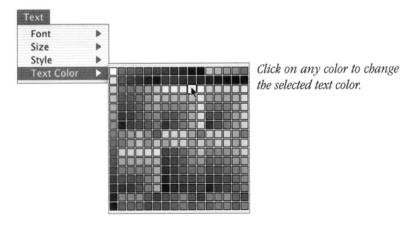

Click on any color to change the selected text color.

Unformat the text

To remove bold, italic, or any other formatting, *select the text* and choose the same formatting again. This is called a *toggle* command, where the same command turns things either on or off.

Or select the text and choose "Plain Text" from the Text menu to remove all formatting. (What is the keyboard shortcut to change selected characters to Plain Text?)

Example of formatted text

So play around and learn a lot. Below is an example of the same copy you saw on page 121, but with simple formatting applied (the headline is red). If you feel comfortable using a word processor, you will feel comfortable anywhere on your computer.

Doll Tearsheet's Answer

Charge me! I scorn you, scurvy companion. What! **You poor, base, rascally, cheating, lack-linen mate!** Away, you mouldy rogue, away! Away, you cut-purse rascal! You filthy bung, away!

By this swine I'll thrust my knife in your mouldy chaps, an you play the saucy cuttle with me. Away, you bottle-ale rascal! You basket-hilt stale juggler, you!

He, a captain! Hang him, rogue! He lives upon mouldy stewed prunes and dried cakes. A captain! For God's sake, thrust him down stairs; **I cannot endure such a fustian rascal.**

Doll Tearsheet, from King Henry IV
by William Shakespeare

Advanced exercise *(skip this if you want!)*

The Button Bar is **customizable.** You can add preconfigured buttons to the Bar or you can create buttons for specific tasks and name them whatever you want.

1. From the AppleWorks menu, choose "Preferences...," then choose "Button Bar..." to open the "Customize Button Bar" window.

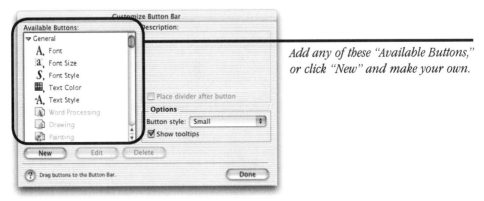

Add any of these "Available Buttons," or click "New" and make your own.

2. Double-click a button in the list of "Available Buttons" to add it to the Button Bar, or drag it from this window and drop it on the Button Bar in the position you want it.

3. To remove a button, drag it from the Button Bar to the Trash basket icon in the Dock.

You can also **create a whole new button:** Click the "New" button you see in the dialog box above; you'll get the dialog box shown below.

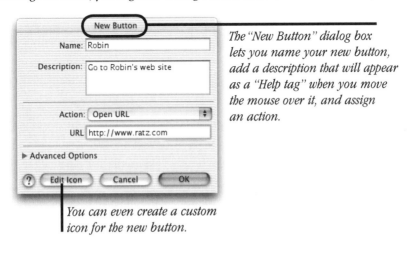

The "New Button" dialog box lets you name your new button, add a description that will appear as a "Help tag" when you move the mouse over it, and assign an action.

You can even create a custom icon for the new button.

121

Cut, Copy, and Paste

One of the most exciting features of working in a word processor is editing. Never again do you have to retype a whole page just to change one paragraph. You can **cut** (remove) text from one place and put it someplace else, or copy a favorite sentence and insert it in the middle of another page (or even in another document), etc. It's too much fun. Makes you want to write books or somethin'.

Cut

The cut feature **removes** selected text from the page, just as if you took some scissors and cut it out (except there won't be a hole in the paper).

Copy

The copy feature makes a **copy** of the selected text, and leaves the original text intact.

Paste

The paste feature will **insert** onto the page whatever text you *previously* cut or copied. The text will be inserted *wherever the insertion point is flashing*.

Try it!

Click the button shown below in the Button Bar to make a new, blank word processing page.

So these are the steps to edit your page. Practice on the text you already have on your page, or create a new document (just click on the tiny page icon in the Button Bar at the top of the screen).

Cut text from one place

1. *Select the text* by dragging across it (as explained on page 116).
2. From the Edit menu, choose "Cut." Notice the keyboard shortcut is Command X (like Xing or crossing something out).

Copy text

1. *Select the text* by dragging across it (as explained on page 116).
2. From the Edit menu, choose "Copy." Notice the keyboard shortcut is Command C (C for copy).

Paste text somewhere else

1. Single-click to set the insertion point (as explained on pages 114–115) at the spot where you want to paste the text into.
2. From the Edit menu, choose "Paste." Notice the keyboard shortcut is Command V (like the caret ^ for inserting something).

Tip: If the Cut, Copy, or Clear commands in the Edit menu are gray, that's because nothing is selected at the moment! Remember, select first, then do it.

Clear and Delete

So have you practiced cutting, copying, and pasting? Let me explain what you did. When you cut or copy, the iMac puts the text (or graphic) into an invisible place called the Clipboard. The Clipboard can only hold one item at a time, so as soon as you copy something else, whatever was in the Clipboard disappears. When you paste, you are actually pasting whatever was on the Clipboard. For instance, if you *cut* three separate pieces of text and then you *paste,* you will paste the *last* item that you cut.

You can paste items forever (well, until you turn off the computer). Whatever you cut or copied will stay in the Clipboard even when you change to a different program or come back in several hours. As soon as the power is turned off, though, whatever was in the Clipboard disappears.

The **Clear** command from the Edit menu, as well as the **Delete** key, will get rid of whatever you had *selected,* but it does *not* go to the Clipboard! Think about this for a minute. Let's say you have a photo of your daughter in the Clipboard because you copied it from one document, and you are pasting it into several different letters. If you want to get rid of some text now, use the Delete key instead of the Cut command so your daughter's photo stays in the Clipboard, ready to paste again.

Tip: If you want to see what is currently stored in the Clipboard, go to the Edit menu and choose "Show Clipboard." When you're done, close the Clipboard just like you close any window.

Undo

The Undo command is one of the most important things you can learn. Most of the time you can undo the very last thing you did by going to the Edit menu and choosing "Undo." Let's say you wrote a whole letter and then you selected all the text because you wanted to change the typeface. But before you could choose a new typeface, you leaned on the keyboard and all of the selected text turned into "vnm;id." Before you scream, choose Undo from the Edit menu. Memorize the keyboard shortcut: Command Z. Just undo it.

Practice using Undo: Select some text, cut it, then undo it. Paste some text, then undo it.

Save the document

Rule Number One:
SOS: Save Often
Sweetheart.

You must "save" every document you create on your computer (unless you never want to see it again). Saving it means you store a copy onto the hard disk. After you save a document, you can open it again, make changes, make a copy, add to it, delete from it, etc. You need to save a document as soon as you begin, and then you need to save changes every couple of minutes as you work. Why every couple of minutes? Because as you work, all of your changes are being held in "memory," which is a temporary storage space. So temporary, in fact, that if the power in your home or office flickers or goes out, or your computer crashes or freezes up, or the cat chews your power cord, everything you had not saved will disappear. Nothing can get it back.

Unfortunately, humans seem to learn best through catastrophes. I can almost guarantee that you won't bother saving often until one very late night when you lose the last two hours worth of work on a report that is due first thing in the morning.

To save your document:

1. With your document open on the screen, go to the File menu and choose "Save As...." You will get the dialog box shown below.

2. Name your document! Name it something you will remember and something that gives you a clue as to what this document is about.

3. Single-click the "Save" button (or hit Return).

4. Your documents will be automatically saved into the folder called "Documents," which you'll find in your Home window.

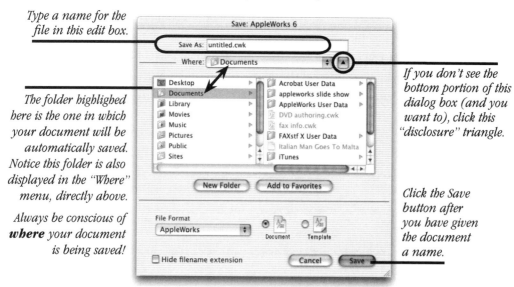

Type a name for the file in this edit box.

The folder highlighed here is the one in which your document will be automatically saved. Notice this folder is also displayed in the "Where" menu, directly above.

*Always be conscious of **where** your document is being saved!*

If you don't see the bottom portion of this dialog box (and you want to), click this "disclosure" triangle.

Click the Save button after you have given the document a name.

Print the document

You will most likely want to print your documents. First, of course, you must have a printer, and it must be plugged into the iMac and plugged into the wall. Turn on your printer and wait until it stops making noise.

If you or someone else already hooked up your printer and got your iMac ready to print, then all you have to do is choose "Print..." from the File menu. You will get a dialog box similar to the one shown below that asks you a few questions. You can ignore everything in that dialog box for now and just click the "Print" button. When you feel like it, go back to this dialog box and poke around, looking at the various options.

Make sure your printer is selected in the Printer pop-up menu. If you do not see your printer here, you can add it to the list, as shown on the next page.

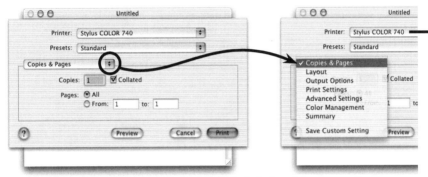

Click the "Copies & Pages" menu (circled above) to choose other panes of the Print window. These various panes provide different settings that affect how your document prints.

Printer: The name you gave your printer should show here. If some other name appears (such as "Apple Internal Modem"), click on the menu and choose your printer's name.

Presets: You can customize any of the settings found in the Print window and then save the settings as a "preset." The Presets pop-up menu shows the saved customized settings as "Custom."

Copies: To print more than one copy, type the amount in here.

Pages: If you want to print all pages in the document, click "All." If you want to print just a couple of the pages in your document, click "From" and type the page numbers in the text fields. For instance, you might want to print only pages 5 through 8. Or, if you want to print just page 5, enter 5 in both boxes.

Add your printer to the Printer List

If your printer doesn't automatically appear in the "Printer" menu, you can add it. If you have a document open on your screen, follow the directions below. Or open the Print Center directly as explained in the sidebar, then skip to Step 3.

You can open the Print Center directly:

Open the Applications folder.

Open the Utilities folder.

Double-click the "Print Center" icon.

From the Printers menu, choose "View Printer List."

1. Turn on the printer(s) you want to add to the List. Wait until it is fully warmed up.

2. While your document is open, go to the File menu and choose "Print." In the Print dialog box, click the "Printer" menu and choose "Edit Printer List...," as shown below.

3. This will open the Printer List, as shown below. This list shows you the printers the Mac knows about already. The printer with the gray dot to the left of its name is the "default" printer (the one that will automatically appear in the Printer menu to print to).

   To add another printer to the list, click "Add Printer...."

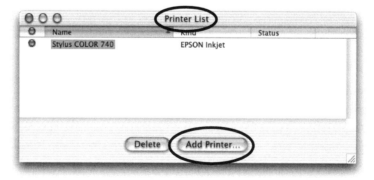

4. A dialog "sheet" will slip down from the title bar, as shown below. Click on the menu circled below to see your options.

To add a USB printer to the list, choose "USB" from the menu. (If you have an inexpensive color printer, like less than $2,000, it's USB.)

To add an AppleTalk printer, which is probably on a local network and connected with an Ethernet cable, to the list, choose "AppleTalk." (If your printer is a PostScript laser printer, it is probably on an AppleTalk network whether you realize it or not.)

If your computer is at home or in a small office, you won't use Directory Services.

If you are in a large corporation or school with a large network, talk to your network administrator about Directory Services.

5. If you chose "AppleTalk," you might get a message that you have to turn AppleTalk on — if you don't get this message, skip this step. If the message shown below appears, go ahead and click the button, "Open Network Preferences."

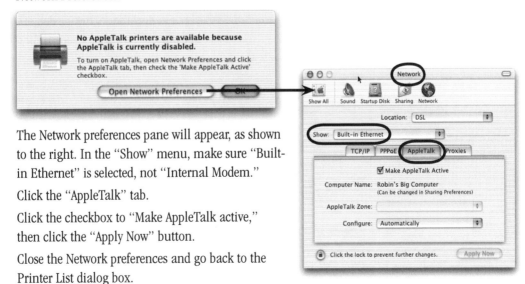

The Network preferences pane will appear, as shown to the right. In the "Show" menu, make sure "Built-in Ethernet" is selected, not "Internal Modem."

Click the "AppleTalk" tab.

Click the checkbox to "Make AppleTalk active," then click the "Apply Now" button.

Close the Network preferences and go back to the Printer List dialog box.

6. After you choose the type of printer, you will get a list of those printers *that are turned on* and available for you to use.

If you don't see your printer in the list, click on the "Printer Model" menu and choose the model you know is attached and turned on. This should make it appear.

Tip: If your printer is turned on and properly connected and still doesn't show up in the list, the most likely reason is either a bad cable or the wrong cable attaching the printer to the iMac.

Or you might have a loose connection. Unplug both ends and plug them back in again.

7. Click on the printer name in the list, then click the "Add" button.

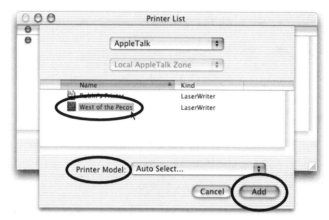

8. This will take you back to the Printer List, which can be confusing because it makes you think you should click the "Add Printer..." button again—don't. (Well, you can if you want, but it will just take you back to the dialog box above.)

Click the red Close button in the upper-left corner of the window. That printer is now added to the list and you will be able to choose it in the main Print dialog box.

Close this window with this button.

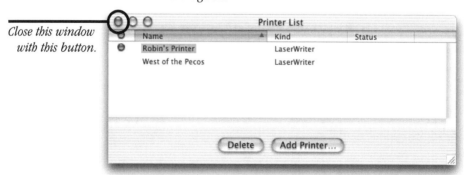

*The **default printer** (the automatic choice) has a **gray button** to its left. If you have more than one printer in this list and you want a different printer to be the default, do this: Single-click on the printer name, go to the Printers menu, and choose "Make Default."*

Close the document

When you are finished working on a document, you "close" it, which is like removing the page (the document) from the typewriter (the word processor) and putting the page in a filing cabinet.

1. Click the red Close button, just as you would to close any window.
    Or go to the File menu and choose "Close."
    Or use the keyboard shortcut, Command W.

2. If you didn't save the document at the last minute, you will get a dialog box asking if you want to save it or not.

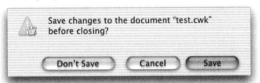

Create another document, or open an existing document

1. If you want to **create another document,** single-click on the word processing icon in the Button Bar.

2. If you want to **open a document** you already created, go to the File menu, choose "Open…," and you should see the document's name in the list. Double-click the name. (Or check the "Recent Items" tab in the "Starting Points palette, as shown on page 112.)

Tip: You don't have to close one document before you open another! You can have dozens of documents open at the same time. They will all be listed in the Window menu in AppleWorks.

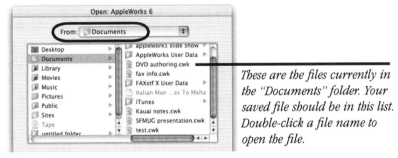

These are the files currently in the "Documents" folder. Your saved file should be in this list. Double-click a file name to open the file.

If you made a terrible mistake

If you did something terrible to the document, like perhaps you selected everything and accidentally deleted it, do this:

From the File menu, choose "Revert." This will revert the document *back to the way it was the last time you saved it*. That means if you didn't save the document recently, you are out of luck. Save often, sweetie.

Quit the application

You don't have to quit right now, if you want to continue on with the exercises in this section! Or you might want to practice quitting, then you'll just reopen AppleWorks when you are ready to read the next chapter.

It's important to understand exactly what happens when you **quit.** You see, when you **close** the document, you are essentially putting that one piece of paper away, but the word processor itself (the typewriter) is still on the desk. Now, it might *look* like you put the word processor away because when you close the document, you see the Desktop, as if nothing is there. But trust me, that typewriter, I mean word processor, is still sitting in the Macintosh memory (desk), taking up space. It does not go away until you **quit.**

To quit the application:

Go to the File menu and choose "Quit."

Or use the keyboard shortcut, Command Q.

Or press and hold the AppleWorks icon in the Dock, then choose "Quit" from the menu that pops up.

While an application is open, a small black triangle appears beneath its icon in the Dock.

To know whether an application is still open or whether you really did quit, check the **Dock.** If it shows a small black triangle beneath the icon, then you didn't quit and the word processor is still open. If you see the triangle, press (don't click) the icon in the Dock, then choose Quit from the menu.

On the Desktop, find the document you just created

So you saved and closed the document, and you quit AppleWorks, and now it is the next day and you want to read that letter again or maybe make some changes to it. Where is it? Well, it should be in the Documents folder in your Home window, where everything goes by default. This is a good thing for a while, because you can always go there and find whatever it was you created. Later, when you feel more comfortable working with your iMac, you will want to start creating different folders for different projects and saving your documents directly into those specific folders.

To find your document all you have to do is look inside the Documents folder. Look for it in your hard disk window.

Documents

This is what the Documents folder looks like. It's in your Home window.

If you can't find your document, see Chapter 24 to use Sherlock to find it for you.

To open the Documents folder:

1. Open your hard disk window.

2. Single-click the "Home" button in the open window's Toolbar. The window will change to show the contents of your Home folder. One of the items in your Home folder is the Documents folder which contains icons of every document you've made so far, as well as folders.

3. Double-click the Documents folder to see its contents, as shown below.

4. If you prefer to see a *list* of the documents in this window instead of the icons, click the List View button in the window's Toolbar, as circled below, left.

Click here to change from Icon View to List View.

Click the triangle to alphabetize the files backwards or forwards. Click again to alphabetize them in the other direction.

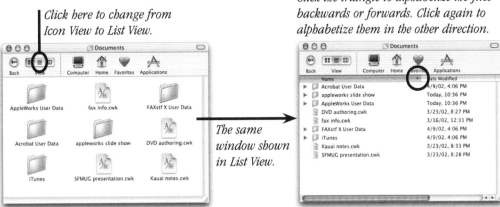

The same window shown in List View.

Here you see several documents (and other folders) inside the Documents folder.

A few guidelines from Robin
for creating professional-level text

Here are some basic rules for creating type on your iMac. Your iMac is not a type-writer. You have to let go of the rules you either learned from a typing teacher or from someone who grew up on a typewriter—it's different when you are setting professional-level type on a Macintosh computer. Trust me. I was trained as a medical secretary and I was trained as a typographer, so I am well aware of the differences between the two.

- One space after periods. Really.

- One space after colons, semicolons, question marks, exclamation points, and all other punctuation.

- Periods and commas always go inside of quotation marks. Always. (In America.)

- Question marks and exclamation points go inside or outside quotation marks depending on whether or not they belong to the phrase inside the quotes.

- Professional type does not use the half-inch or five-space indent that we used on typewriters. The correct space is equivalent to about two spaces.

- Use an indent for new paragraphs, **or** use space between the paragraphs, but not both.

- Learn to use your software to set about a half-line space between paragraphs, instead of hitting two Returns.

- Read *The Mac is not a typewriter.*

- If you discover you like this typesetting stuff and want to learn much more about how to make your type beautiful and sophisticated, read *The Non-Designer's Type Book,* by me.

Make a Simple Database

A **database** is like a really fancy recipe card box, like the kind in which you might store recipes, addresses, baseball cards, or dues-paying membership information. But in a database you can do a lot more with the information than you can with the recipe cards.

In this chapter we're going to create a new, blank database to serve as an address book. Just follow the steps in this chapter and in a couple of minutes you'll have an address book you can use for years. If you like working in a database, there are entire books that will teach you much more, and you can build directly on the database you create right here. Even without reading anything else, you'll be able to make another database for any other collection of information you happen to have, such as research data, personal possessions, scout troop members, etc.

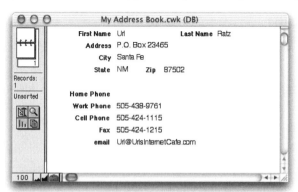

This is a very simple database that took about five minutes to build. You can add to it, change it, rearrange the layout, search it, print labels with it, and much more.

Get ready to make a database

Now, you might be in one of four different situations, depending on whether you've been following along or not. Choose the situation you're in and follow the directions:

A. You just finished the word processing exercise and the letter is still on your screen.

1. Save this letter once again: press Command S.

2. Click the red Close button in the upper-left corner, *or* use the keyboard shortcut Command W (W for Window).

B. You finished the word processing exercise, saved and closed it, and didn't quit AppleWorks. In the far-left corner of the menu bar, it says AppleWorks (to the right of the blue Apple logo).

✪ You are exactly where you need to be! Don't touch anything. Go to the top of the next page (in this book).

C. You finished the word processing exercise, saved and closed it, and didn't quit AppleWorks. BUT in the far-left corner of the menu bar (to the right of the Apple logo), you see the name of some other application.

1. In the Dock, find the AppleWorks icon. Single-click it.

2. After you click the AppleWorks icon, the "Starting Points" palette and the Button Bar should appear at the top of the screen. Go to the next page (in this book).

D. You skipped the word processing exercise, or you turned off your computer and came back later, and AppleWorks is not open on your iMac.

1. Open AppleWorks just like you did the first time: Single-click its icon in the Dock.

   (*Or* go to the Applications folder, then open the AppleWorks folder. The AppleWorks *application* is inside the AppleWorks *folder!* Double-click the AppleWorks *application* icon.)

2. Click the "Database" icon in the "Starting Points" window.

3. Go to the next page (of this book), but *skip the first step* because you just started a new document.

Create a new database document

1. If you do not yet have the beginning of a database on your screen (as shown below, under Step 3), single-click the Database button in the Button Bar (circled, below).

AppleWorks Button Bar

2. When you start a new database, the first thing you see is the "Define Database Fields" window (shown below).

   A database is filled with "fields" in which you will (later) enter information. What you need to do here is *name* the fields that you plan to include in your address book, such as First Name, Last Name, Address, City, State, etc. When you're done, each of these "Field Names" will have a space in which to enter the appropriate information.

3. So type "First Name" in the Field Name edit box, as you see in the example circled below.

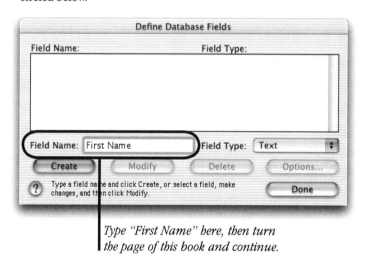

Type "First Name" here, then turn the page of this book and continue.

—continued

4. Click the "Create" button. This puts the field name in the list (shown below), and AppleWorks automatically asks what you want the name of the next field to be. In the next one, type "Last Name," then click "Create."

   Tip: You always want to have separate fields for first names and last names because the computer alphabetizes by the *first letter* in the field. If you have both first and last names in one field (such as "Robert Burns"), you'll get an alphabetized list by first names, which isn't useful very often. If you enter the last name, comma, first name ("Burns, Robert") then your mailing labels will print exactly that, which is kind of dorky.

   So always set up one field for first names and one field for last names.

5. Continue adding fields until you have all the ones you need for an address book, *until you get to the zip code.*

6. When you get to the zip code, do an extra step:

   Notice to the right of the "Field Name" is "Field Type" (circled, below). A field type will help you automatically format the data stored in that field. For instance, if you were to choose the field type "Time," the database would automatically enter the time, and it would be formatted to specifications that you can set up.

   So for the zip code field, press on the "Field Type" menu (where it currently says "Text") and you'll get the pop-up menu shown below. Choose "Number," since a zip code is always a number.

Tip: Set the phone number Field Type as "Text." If you set it as "Number," you won't be able to use hyphens to separate the numbers. The database software considers hyphens as text.

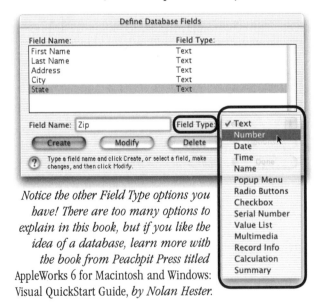

Notice the other Field Type options you have! There are too many options to explain in this book, but if you like the idea of a database, learn more with the book from Peachpit Press titled AppleWorks 6 for Macintosh and Windows: Visual QuickStart Guide, *by Nolan Hester.*

7. Continue to add any other fields you might want in your address book.
   Make sure you change the "Field Type" back to Text (or whatever type you need) for any additions after "zip code."

8. When you have added all the fields you need, click the "Done" button.
   (You can always add, delete, or modify fields at any time, even after you save the database.)

   After you click "Done," you will see the database. It looks like this:

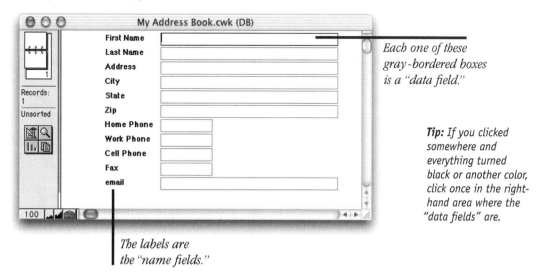

Each one of these gray-bordered boxes is a "data field."

Tip: *If you clicked somewhere and everything turned black or another color, click once in the right-hand area where the "data fields" are.*

The labels are the "name fields."

9. Before you start entering data (typing information), save this document!
   Go to the File menu, choose "Save As…," and name this database.

10. Now turn the page of this book and start entering data.

Enter data into the database

Your next task in a database is to "enter data," which means to type in the information. It's so easy.

To enter the first address:

1. Click in the "First Name" *field.* You should see the insertion point flashing, which is your visual clue that the computer is ready for you to type. So type the *first name* of the person whose information you want in your database.

*Tip: If you accidentally hit the Tab key too many times, **hold down** the Shift key and tap the Tab key; it will move the insertion point **upward** through the fields.*

2. Now, you *could* pick up the mouse and click in the next field, the one for "Last Name." But the *easier* thing to do is hit the Tab key, which will send the insertion point to the next field.

   So hit the Tab key, type the *last name,* then hit the Tab key again.

3. Continue through the rest of the fields, typing and tabbing. If you don't have information for one of the fields, just skip it (Tab twice). You can always come back next week and fill it in, or change or delete any information.

   After everything is filled in, your database should look something like this:

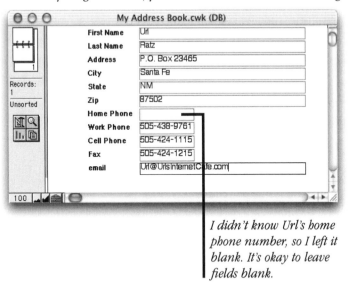

I didn't know Url's home phone number, so I left it blank. It's okay to leave fields blank.

Make more records

This one collection of fields for one person is called a "record." Your database can have hundreds or thousands of records in it. Each individual record is sort of like one recipe card.

To make another record:

1. Go to the Edit menu and choose "New Record," **or** press Command R.

2. The new record will be added directly after the record you are currently in.

Format the fields

You can change the typeface, size, placement, etc., of any field name or of the data in any individual field. This is called "formatting."

To format the name fields:

1. From the Layout menu, choose "Layout."

2. In the record, click on a field *name,* such as "City."

3. To select the rest of the names, hold down the Shift key and click on any of the other name fields that you want to have the same typeface and size. When you've selected all, let go of the Shift key, but don't click anywhere!

4. From the Format menu, slide down to "Font," then out to the side and pick a font (typeface) you like.

5. Click anywhere to *deselect* the name fields.
   To enter more data, go back to the Layout menu and choose "Browse."

*This is what a **name field** looks like when you select it.*

To format the data fields:

1. Follow the same directions as above (choose "Layout" from the Layout menu), but this time select the fields themselves: Click on the field *data,* the box where you actually type the text.

2. Hold down the Shift key and click on any of the other data fields that you want to have the same typeface and size. When you have them all selected, let go of the Shift key, but don't click anywhere!

3. Use the Format menu again to format the information.

4. Click anywhere to *deselect* the data fields.

*This is what the **data field** looks like when you select it.*

To enter more data:

Go back to the Layout menu and choose "Browse."

Change the layout

You can rearrange the name and data fields, and you can resize them.

1. From the Layout menu, choose "Layout."

2. Press in the *middle* of any field (name or data), and drag it to a **different position.** You can hold the Shift key down and click on more than one field to select a group, then *let go* of the Shift key and move the entire group.

 Press-and-drag in the **middle** of a field to move it.

3. **Resize any field:** Click once on it, then position the *tip* of the pointer in one of the tiny, square handles that appears. Press-and-drag any handle to resize the field. Try it.

 Press-and-drag the **handle** of a field to resize it.

Rearrange your database into a more pleasing and sensible order.

This is the "Layout" view.

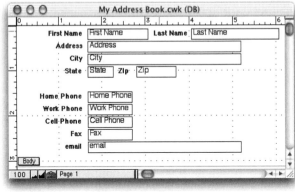

From the Layout menu, choose "Layout" to format text or to rearrange data fields and name fields.

This is the "Browse" view.

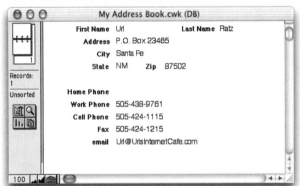

This is a more logical placement of fields than what automatically appears (as shown on page 138).

Make a list of the records

I find it helpful to view the records as a list. That way I can see a whole collection at a glance. You can enter data while it is in a list view.

1. From the Layout menu, choose "List."

2. **To rearrange the columns,** press-and-drag any column heading to the left or right, then let go.

3. **To resize the width of any column,** position the cursor directly on the dotted line between two column headings (as shown below). The cursor turns into a two-headed arrow. With this cursor, ✛ press-and-drag to the left or right to widen or narrow a column.

*Press-and-drag in the **middle** of any column heading to move the column.*

*Press-and-drag **between** columns to resize them.*

The field names become the column headings.

Sort the information in your database

Tip: *If you don't enter
data exactly the same
way every time, then
your sort won't work
very well. For instance,
if you enter McCoy (no
space) or Mc Coy (with
a space), the name
with the space will
be sorted before the
name with no space
(in computerized
alphabetizing, spaces
come before letters).*

*Capital letters are
sorted differently from
lowercase, also, so
Penelope **v**onSchnitzel
would come before
Abigail **V**onSchnitzel if
you sort by last names.*

Once your database is set up, you can sort (organize) the information in a number of ways. If you don't have enough records to organize in your file yet, take a moment to add a few more. Then experiment with sorting.

1. From the Layout menu, choose "Browse" or "List."

2. From the Organize menu, choose "Sort Records...."
   You'll get the "Sort Records" dialog box, as shown below.

3. The "Field List" on the left contains every field in your database. Select the field you want to alphabetize by (such as "Last Name"), then click the "Move" button.

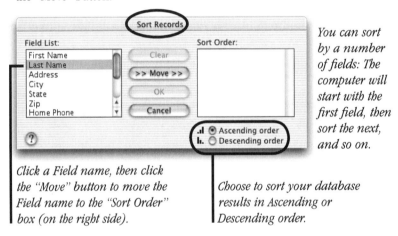

*You can sort
by a number
of fields: The
computer will
start with the
first field, then
sort the next,
and so on.*

*Click a Field name, then click
the "Move" button to move the
Field name to the "Sort Order"
box (on the right side).*

*Choose to sort your database
results in Ascending or
Descending order.*

Maybe you have a lot of people with the same last name, like your entire family. If you move "First Name" over to the "Sort Order" box *under* "Last Name," then the iMac will first alphabetize all the last names, and then alphabetize all the first names within that group. So "Gerald Williams" will be in the list before "Patricia Williams."

4. When you have arranged your sort orders, click OK to go back to your list, which is now organized per your request.

So think of it—you can sort by city, then by last name, then by first name. Your database will then display all of your information organized by city, with people's names alphabetized within each city. The possibilities are amazing. Enter a whole bunch of records and experiment. Enter your entire music CD collection, then organize them by genre, artist, and recording date from oldest recording to newest.

Find certain records

Often you will want to select, or find, just certain records. For instance, maybe you want to find the clients who live in a certain city or who owe you money. (Of course, if you want to find the clients who owe you money, you must have set up the database with a field for that information in the first place.)

1. From the Layout menu, choose "Find."

2. You see what looks like a blank record (shown below). Type the data you want to find in the field you want to find. For instance, if you want to find all the people with the last name of Williams, type "Williams" into the "Last Name" field.

   If you want to find all the people named Williams who live in the city of Santa Rosa, type "Williams" in the "Last Name" field, and type "Santa Rosa" in the "City" field.

   (If you want to find all the people who owe you more than $150 and you previously set up a formula field to figure that out, use the "Match" feature, under the Organize menu.)

   You can fill in as many fields as you need to narrow the search down to just what you want to find.

3. On the far left, click "All" if you want to find records within your entire database, or click "Visible" if you did a previous search or match and want to find files *within* that selection.

4. After you do a search, you probably want all of your records back. From the Organize menu, choose "Show All Records."

This is how you "find" a selection of records in your database.

Print your database

Of course you can print any of the information in your database. Often you will want to limit the records you print by first finding or matching certain criteria. When you print, only the visible records (the ones you found or matched) will print.

1. If you want to limit the records, find or match the ones to print, as explained on the previous page.

2. From the Layout menu, choose "Browse" if you want to print the data as the record displays it, or "List" if you want to print a list.

3. If you're printing a list, the fields might stretch across several pages. To check before you print, go to the Window menu and choose "Page View."

   You will get a preview of how your database will look on the printed page. You might need to enlarge the window as large as possible (drag the Resize corner in the bottom-right of the window). *Or* click the little mountain icon (in the bottom-left corner of the window) to reduce the picture on the screen.

   Directly in this preview window you can make the columns narrower and rearrange them so things fit on the page better (as you did on page 141).

4. From the File menu, choose "Print...." You might have to experiment with various arrangements in the preview window to get the printed results you want.

Make a Simple Spreadsheet

A *spreadsheet* is a very interesting and useful program. It lets you work with numbers and formulas and then play with the possibilities. It can automate just about any sort of scenario you want to create with numbers, such as the various options in a mortgage payment, the variety of discounts and taxable options in an invoice, the ups and downs of your income, and so much more. A spreadsheet is a very versatile program to have on your computer. And it does a lot more than crunch numbers—you can easily make forms, signs, calendars, tables of data, to-do lists, and more.

In this chapter, I'll show you the basics of working in a spreadsheet. Once you get the hang of just a couple of key features, you'll have fun creating all kinds of stuff.

Get ready to create a spreadsheet

Now, you might be in one of four different situations, depending on whether you've been following along or not. Choose the situation you're in and follow the directions:

This is the "Spreadsheet" button.

A. **You just finished the database exercise and that file is still on your screen.**

1. Save this file once again: press Command S.

2. Click the red Close button in the upper-left corner, or use the keyboard shortcut Command W (W for Window).

3. Click the "Spreadsheet" button in the Button Bar.

B. **You finished the database exercise, saved and closed it, and didn't quit AppleWorks. You still see the Button Bar.**

❂ You are exactly where you need to be! Click the "Spreadsheet" button in the Button Bar.

C. **You finished the database exercise, saved and closed it, and did not quit AppleWorks. BUT you don't see the AppleWorks Button Bar.**

1. Find the AppleWorks icon in the Dock. Single-click it.

2. After you click the AppleWorks icon, the "Starting Points" window and the Button Bar will appear at the top of the screen. Click the "Spreadsheet" button.

D. **You skipped the database exercise, or you turned off your computer and came back later, and AppleWorks is not open on your iMac.**

1. Open AppleWorks just like you did the first time: Single-click its icon in the Dock.

   (Or, go to the Applications folder, then open the AppleWorks folder. The AppleWorks *application* is inside the AppleWorks *folder!* Double-click the AppleWorks *application* icon.)

2. Click the "Spreadsheet" icon in the "Starting Points" window.

3. Go to the next page (of this book).

Create a spreadsheet document

Let's make a simple spreadsheet to become familiar with how a spreadsheet functions. It's a little different from other programs you've worked with.

Columns, rows, and cells

What you see on your screen, as shown below, is basically a huge sheet of grid paper.

Across the top are the alphabetic **column headings.**

Down the left side are the numeric **row headings.**

Each tiny block on the page is a **cell.**

Each cell has an **address,** which is the intersection of the column and row. In the example below, the selected cell's address is B2 because it is in column B and row 2.

Column headings.

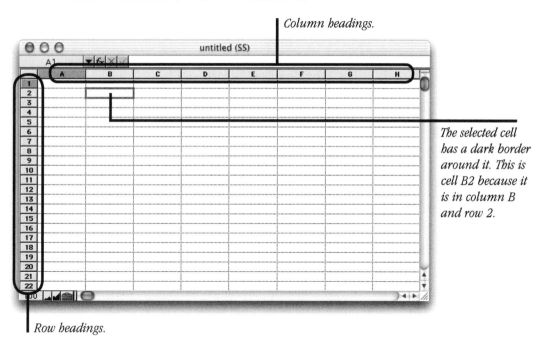

The selected cell has a dark border around it. This is cell B2 because it is in column B and row 2.

Row headings.

When a spreadsheet is open and active, the Button Bar changes to show buttons specific to spreadsheets. Hover the pointer over a button and that button's "Help tag" will appear, as shown above.

Entering data into the cells

At first, the oddest thing about a spreadsheet is that when you select a cell and try to type something into it, nothing seems to happen—the text does not appear in the cell. The text you type actually appears in the **entry bar,** *above* the spreadsheet itself, as shown in the example below. Try it: **Click in cell B2,** then type *Frogs R Us Web Design.* The text will appear in the entry bar. *(Make sure you click in cell B2 or the rest of this exercise won't work!)*

This is the entry bar.

This is cell B2.

It doesn't look like the text will fit into that tiny cell, and it won't. But in a spreadsheet, as opposed to a database, the text will just go right through the cell into the next one, as long as the next one is empty.

To make the text appear in the cell, you have to **enter** it: hit the Enter key (on the far-right, bottom end of your keyboard). Then it will look like this:

You still see the text in the entry bar because that cell (B2) is still selected.

Click in any other cell and that thick selection border will move to that cell.

Now experiment with this feature of a spreadsheet: Click on the word "Design," which looks like it is in cell C2. Does the text appear in the entry bar? No, because cell C2 is actually empty. Even though the text spills over to C2, it is *entered* into cell B2, and if you want to change the data, you have to *select* cell B2.

Tip: There are a number of ways to enter the data into a cell, depending on which key you press to enter the data:

Return key: Enters data and automatically selects the next cell *downward.*

Tab key: Enters data and automatically selects the next cell *to the right.*

Enter key or click the **check mark** in the entry bar: Enters data and keeps the *same selected cell* selected.

Format the spreadsheet text

Go ahead and format that text. Just like in the word processor and the database, you have to select the text first, then choose your formatting, right? In a spreadsheet, you select the text by selecting the *cell* in which it is entered.

1. So click once on **B2.**

2. Now go to the Format menu and choose a font, size, and color.
   For this example, choose the font Impact and the size 24.
   Oops, it doesn't fit, does it?

That's okay, let's just open up that row.

3. Position the spreadsheet cursor (⊹) **in the row heading** (*not* on the spreadsheet page) directly on the line dividing two numbered rows, as shown below. The cursor will change to a two-headed arrow. While it's the two-headed arrow, press-and-drag the line *downward* until the text fits in nicely. You might want to leave a little extra space at the top so the title is not too close to the top edge of the cell.

Position the cursor directly on this dividing line, then drag downward.

If you like, also drag the **right side of column heading A** to the left or right, depending on how far away from the left edge you want the title.

4. Save the spreadsheet! From the "File" menu, choose "Save As...."
   Name the file "Frogs R Us." Save the file in the "Documents" folder.

Add a graphic to the spreadsheet

1. From the File menu, choose "Show Clippings." You'll get a floating "palette" with a variety of images, called clippings, as shown below.

   Click on a tab at the bottom of the palette to see the different categories of graphics. Scroll up and down to see the images. Drag the title bar to move the palette around.

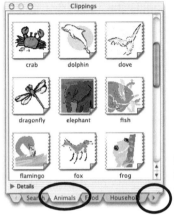

   Click on a tab to display the images in that category.

   Click the arrow tab to display more categories.

2. For this exercise, click the "Animals" tab. Scroll down the images and find the frog.

   Press on that frog and *drag* him to your spreadsheet; let go and he will drop right on the page. You'll see "handles" on each corner of the graphic; the handles indicate the graphic is selected.

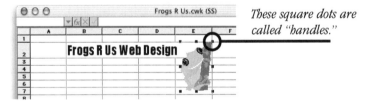

   These square dots are called "handles."

3. **Resize the frog:** Hold down the Shift key, then drag a corner handle to make it smaller.

4. **Flip the frog** if you want to: While the frog is still selected (click once on him if it's not), go to the Arrange menu and choose "Flip Horizontally."

5. **Move the frog:** Press in the *middle* of the graphic and drag it into the position shown above.

6. You can put the Clippings palette away now (click the red Close box).

Add names and numbers to the spreadsheet

Now that you've got a fun start, put some numbers in. Let's pretend this is a list of web design clients who owe you money, and you want to see the total of how much money they owe. You need a list of names and amounts.

1. Click in cell **C4.**

2. The entry bar is ready, waiting for you to type. Type the name of someone who owes you money—*but don't hit the Enter key yet!*

3. Instead of using the Enter key, use the **Return key** this time.
   This will enter the data *and* select the next cell *below* C4.
   (If you already hit the Enter key, don't worry. Select cell C5 now.)

4. Enter another name, then hit Return. Add three more names this way.
   It should look something like this:

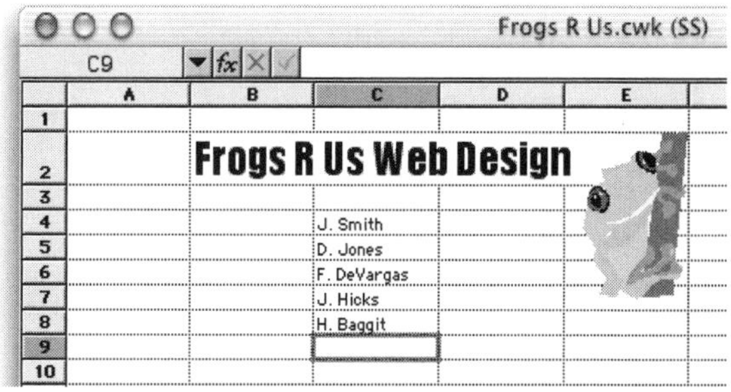

5. Next **align those names to the right** so they will be next to the numbers you are going to enter. To do that, select all the cells with names in them: press-and-drag from the first name to the last name. The selection will look like the example below. You just selected a "range" of cells.

6. From the Format menu, slide down to Alignment and choose "Right."

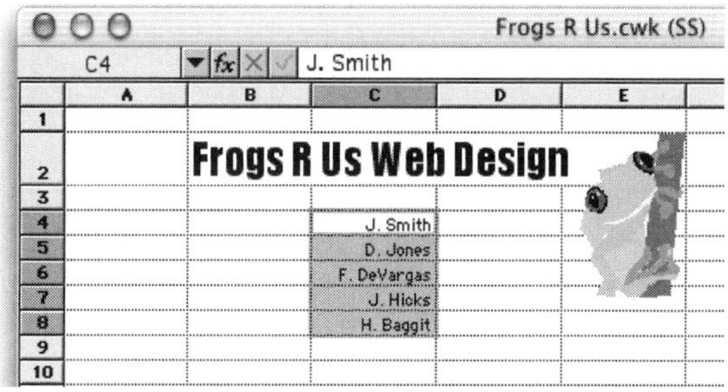

Notice that when you select a range of cells, only the first cell has a selection border around it, while the rest are highlighted. That's okay—that's what it does.

151

Now **enter** the numbers and **format** them.

1. Click in cell **D4.**

2. Type the amount this person owes you, *but don't use a dollar sign or commas.* Type just the number (decimal points are okay).

3. Hit the **Return key.** Enter the next amount. Continue down the column. The numbers should look something like you see below.

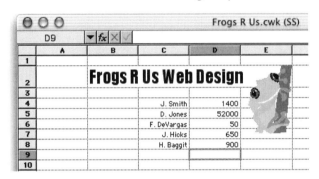

4. You need to *format* the numbers into dollars. First you must select them. This time, try selecting this way:

   Click in the first cell in the number list; *hold the Shift key down;* click in the last cell of that list (then let go of the Shift key). When you hold the Shift key down, everything between the two clicks is selected.

*Tip: You can also
double-click on any cell
(or range of selected
cells) as a shortcut
to open the "Format
Number, Date, and
Time" window.*

5. From the Format menu, choose "Number…" to open the "Format Number, Date, and Time" window, as shown on the opposite page. You're going to choose to format the numbers as "Currency," which will automatically apply the dollar sign. And you're going to choose how many numbers you want to appear after the decimal point, which is called "Decimal Precision." For instance, if you enter "2" in the Decimal Precision edit box, that means any number in the cell will always display two places after the decimal point. (If you enter more numbers after the decimal point, the computer will round them off to two.)

   If you want the currency to display in whole dollars (no cents), change the 2 to 0 (zero, not the letter O!). It's up to you. If you choose zero, any cents that may be in the cells will be rounded off.

a. Click in the "Number" radio button.

b. Press on the Number pop-up menu and choose "Currency."

c. Check the box to "Show Separators for Thousands," which will add commas in the proper places.

d. Enter "0" (zero) in "Decimal Precision."

e. Click OK.

6. After you click OK, take a look at those numbers!

$1,400
$52,000
$50
$650
$900

View the spreadsheet without the grid and headings

Let's take a quick look at how this looks without all the stuff around it.

1. From the Options menu, choose "Display...."

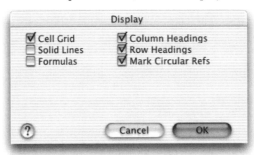

2. Uncheck "Cell Grid," "Column Headings," and "Row Headings." Click OK.

Your spreadsheet will look something like this:

3. Turn the cell grid and both headings back on so we can finish the project: Go back to the "Display" dialog box (choose it from the Options menu) and click those three boxes.

Add a function

Mathematical formulas and functions (functions are complex formulas) are integral parts of a spreadsheet. They enable you to speculate with the numbers. AppleWorks provides you with a huge number of pre-made functions that you just add the details to. We're going to use a very simple function, called Sum, to total how much these people owe you. (If you want to know more about functions, read the AppleWorks Help file; choose it from the Help menu in AppleWorks.)

You *could* use a simple formula, such as =D4+D5+D6+D7+D8 for your project, but it's faster and easier to use the function that is already set up.

1. First, **format the cell** in preparation for the number you're going to put into it:

    Double-click on the empty cell **D10** to get the number format dialog box.

    Choose "Currency," "Show Separators," and the same "Decimal Precision" you set in the other cells.

    Click OK.

2. Now put the Sum function in the *selected* cell **D10:**

    From the Edit menu, choose "Insert Function...."

    Type "su" to select the Sum function quickly, or just scroll down the list, admiring all the things you could do if you knew what the heck they were. Single-click on "SUM(number 1,number 2...)" to select that function.

3. Click "Insert." *Now **don't touch anything!***

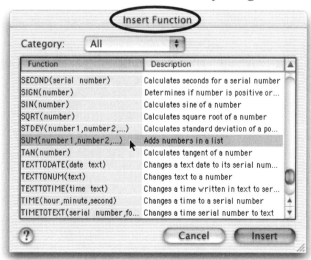

Tip: To enter your own formula, just type an equal sign in the cell. Then click in the cells whose data you want to add to the formula. **Be sure to hit the Enter or Return key as soon as you finish the formula!**

Note: With functions and formulas you can do all kinds of things with numbers.

You could have one cell add the numbers, subtract the percentage you owe your agent, and add the tax. Or you could create a "lookup table" where the cell would look up a chart and add a percentage based on the individual amounts owed, or add penalties daily.

The reason I yelled "Don't touch anything" on the previous page is because once you put a function in a cell or type an = sign to start a formula, *everything you click on becomes part of the formula.* It can make you crazy. So follow these directions carefully. If weird things happen, like strange stuff starts appearing in your entry bar, click the X in the entry bar and start over, selecting cell D10.

If things are going smoothly, you should see the function you selected in the entry bar. You need to substitute the "arguments" in parentheses (the first number, the second number, etc., that are to be added together) with the actual cell addresses that you want to add together.

4. So press-and-drag to select everything between the parentheses, like so:

Select this because you're going to replace it with the cell addresses.

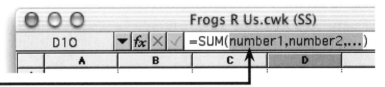

5. While it's selected, *press* (don't click!) in cell D4 and *drag* to D8, which will enter those cell addresses into the formula. The numbers in those cells will be summed. *Before you touch anything else, hit the Enter key* (or click the checkmark in the entry bar). Your entry bar should look like this:

And cell D10 should have the sum total of the money you are owed.

range: A range of cells is any selection of more than one. It is written with two dots between the first and last cell, as you see in your entry bar.

All the cells in a range don't have to be in the same row or column. For instance, you might select a range of cells like C4..D10.

6. **Change the amount someone owes you,** enter it, and the sum total changes instantly. Try it. If you had made a bar chart or pie chart, the chart would change instantly when you change data.

Move the data

Perhaps you decided you put all this information in the wrong place. That's easy to fix. Let's move the names and numbers one column to the left.

1. Select the cells you want to move: names, numbers, and total.
2. Hold down the Command and Option keys, and click in cell **B4.** Voilà—all the cell data moved over.

Now, click once in cell **C10,** the cell with the formula, and you'll notice that the cell range changed from the original settings of D4..D8 to C4..C8! That's a good thing because there's nothing left in D4..D8.

That formula you originally entered is what's called a **relative** reference, meaning it didn't *really* refer to D4..D8 specifically; it meant, "Sum the cells that are 2, 3, 4, 5, and 6 rows above *me.*" So when the formula moved, you didn't need it to add the cells above *D10* anymore—you need it to add the cells above *C10.* So a relative reference automatically changes the cells the formula refers to, according to the cell that contains the formula. You can also make **absolute** cells that do not change: see the Help file, under the Help menu in AppleWorks, for details.

Apply a border

The borders feature is what makes creating forms so very easy. You can apply a border to an individual cell or a range of cells; on any one side or on all sides. For instance, you could select cells in a column, such as B4 through B8 and apply a left border to make a vertical line.

For right now, put a border line under the logo.

1. Select all the cells through which the title extends (in my example, that would be B2 through E2), like so:

2. From the Format menu, choose "Borders...."
3. Click "Bottom." Click OK.

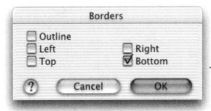

The border won't show up clearly while the grid is visible, but take a look at the finished example on the following page.

Change the color of cells

Do one more thing to this spreadsheet: color a cell or two. Colored cells can help the organization and clarity of a large spreadsheet.

1. Select the cell with the formula (so the total will stand out).

2. If you don't see a tool palette on the left of the screen, click the little "Tool Palette" button at the bottom-left of the window, next to the scroll bar.

Single-click this button to display the Tool Palette, shown to the left.

3. Single-click the "Color Palette" button and choose a color (below).

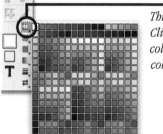

*This is the **Color Palette** button. Click on it and the collection of colors will appear. Click on any color to apply it to the selected cell.*

Or, from the Windows menu, choose "Show Accents." Click on a color in the "Accents" palette to apply it to the selected cell (below).

Click here, then click a color from the palette.

And this is your finished spreadsheet!

Make a Simple Painting

Paint programs are too much fun. Don't worry if you think you can't draw or paint—this is a fun exercise to walk through, even if you never plan to use this part of the application. Paint a monster because then no one can say it doesn't look like a monster, whereas if you try to paint a rose, you might not be very happy with your results (unless of course you really are a painter, like John).

So don't be intimidated; jump right in and follow the directions. Whether you ever plan to paint things or not, you will learn a lot more about your computer, and you will feel more comfortable and powerful.

If you like painting like this, explore more on your own. I can't tell you *everything* about this program in this short chapter, but AppleWorks has a great Help section: While the program is open, go to the Help menu and choose "AppleWorks Help." Click on the topics you want to learn more about, or type in the name of a topic you are looking for.

Get ready to paint

Now, you might be in one of four different situations, depending on whether you've been following along or not. Choose the situation you're in and follow the directions:

A. You just finished the spreadsheet exercise and the spreadsheet is still on your screen.

1. Save your spreadsheet (if you want): press Command S.

2. Click the red Close button in the upper-left corner, or use the keyboard shortcut Command W (W for Window).

3. Go to the next page in this book.

B. You finished the spreadsheet exercise, saved and closed it, and didn't quit AppleWorks. You still see the Button Bar.

✪ You are exactly where you need to be! Go to the next page.

C. You finished the spreadsheet exercise, saved and closed it, and didn't quit AppleWorks. BUT you don't see the Button Bar.

1. Find the AppleWorks icon in the Dock. Single-click it.

2. After you click the AppleWorks icon, the "Starting Points" palette and the Button Bar will appear at the top of the screen. Go to the next page of this book.

D. You skipped the spreadsheet exercise, or you turned off your computer and came back later, and AppleWorks is not open on your iMac.

1. Open AppleWorks just like you did the first time: Single-click its icon in the Dock.

(Or go to the Applications folder, then open the AppleWorks folder. The AppleWorks *application* is inside the AppleWorks *folder!* Double-click the AppleWorks *application* icon.)

2. Click the "Painting" icon in the "Starting Points" palette.

3. Go to the next page (of this book), but skip the first step because you just started a new document.

Open a new paint document

- To open a new, blank paint document, use the Button Bar: click on the "Painting" button with the little palette.

The paint Tool Palette.

AppleWorks 6 Painting button is in both the Button Bar and the "Starting Points" palette.

Check out the painting tools

Along the left side of the screen you now have special painting tools. Try this:

1. **Click once** on the paintbrush tool (circled, on the right).
2. Now position your pointer on the blank document page.
3. Press-and-drag the mouse around to draw any sort of shape.
4. If you want to undo the last thing you did, press Command Z for Undo.

Before you make an ugly monster, play with some of these paint tools. They're easy, and they teach you a lot about how other programs work. Follow along on the next several pages to experiment.

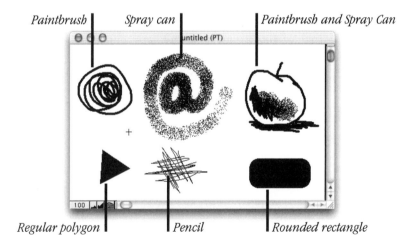

Paintbrush | Spray can | Paintbrush and Spray Can

Regular polygon | Pencil | Rounded rectangle

Erase anything or everything you just scribbled

- To erase part of your image, **single-click** on the eraser tool. Move the mouse over to the document, and press-and-drag over the area you want to erase.
- To erase everything on the page, **double-click** on the eraser tool.

The eraser tool in the Tool Palette.

The paintbrush tool in the Tool Palette.

Dip your paintbrush in a bright color

From the Window menu, choose "Show Accents" to get the palette shown below; click each of the tabs to see the wide variety of textures, patterns, colors, and gradients you can paint with. (The fifth tab is for use with the line tool.) Click a color or texture to paint with it.

To move the Accents Palette, drag its title bar. To close it, click the Close button in the upper-left corner.

Close button

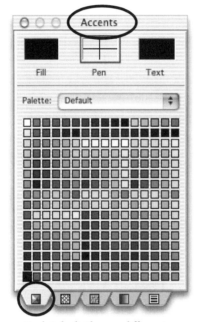

Each tab displays a different pane that contains its own collection of colors, patterns, or textures.

Click on a tab to see another palette. Be sure to check the "Palette" pop-up menu, as shown, to see what else is available in each pane.

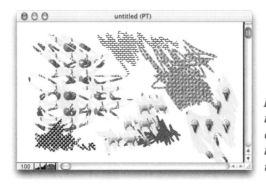

Experiment! Click various tabs in the Accents Palette; choose a color, pattern, or texture; then scribble away with the paintbrush.

Get a bigger paintbrush

1. **Double-click** on the paintbrush tool.

2. **Single-click** on any of those different "brush shapes," as shown below, then click OK.

3. Paint with that new brush: press-and-drag on the page.

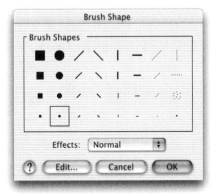

Click any of these brush shapes to choose it. Click "Edit..." to change the shape of the selected brush.

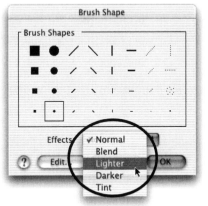

Choose an "Effect" here, then draw on top of something else. The effect will remain in the paintbrush until you change it back!

The trick to painting with your chosen fill and border colors

Experiment with using these colors and patterns! ***The trick is you must choose the color and/or pattern BEFORE you paint something.*** So choose a fancy fill texture and then paint on the page. Then experiment with painting over other items, changing the brush pattern and effect, spray painting, etc.

You can also **choose more than one color and pattern.** Select one of those black-and-white fill patterns, like this: ▨ , then choose a color that you want that pattern to appear in. (You can't change the color of the fancy textures or gradients.)

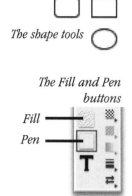

The shape tools

The Fill and Pen buttons

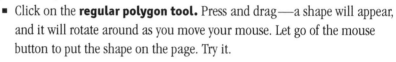

Fill ———

Pen ———

Paint using the shape tools

1. You're not limited to using the paintbrush. Choose one of the shape tools near the top of the Tool Palette, as shown to the left.

2. Click on the "Fill" button (shown to the left), then choose a pattern, color, texture, or gradient for the **inside** of the shape.

3. Click on the Pen button, then choose a pattern, color, texture, or gradient for the **border** of the shape.

   Also choose a **thickness** for the border: click on this symbol ▦ and choose a thickness.

4. With the shape tool, *press* on the page and drag diagonally to create a shape. Amazing.

Try these special tools

The regular polygon tool.

- Click on the **regular polygon tool.** Press and drag—a shape will appear, and it will rotate around as you move your mouse. Let go of the mouse button to put the shape on the page. Try it.

  Double-click the polygon tool to get a dialog box in which you can choose the number of sides you want in the shape.

The irregular polygon tool.

- Click on the **irregular polygon tool** shown to the left (I call this the spiderweb tool). On the page, ***don't press-and-drag***—instead, click once, then move the mouse and click somewhere else, then click somewhere else, etc. Cross over the existing lines, if you like. When you have created a shape, *single-click* directly on top of the first point you made, or *double-click* anywhere and the shape will close itself up. It will fill with the pattern or texture you had last chosen.

Remember, to stop the spiderweb tool, click directly on top of the first point you made, or double-click anywhere.

Use the spray can tool

I'll bet you know what to do: choose the **spray can tool.** Choose a color and/or pattern, then press-and-drag on the page.

In the Tool Palette, double-click the spray can tool to open the "Edit Spray Can" window and change the spray.

The spray can (airbrush) tool.

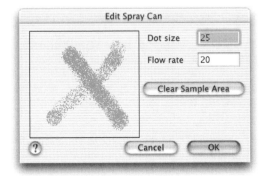

Pour paint into a shape with the paint bucket

1. Before you can pour paint, you need a shape to pour it into. So first:

    a. Double-click on the **paintbrush tool.** Choose any brush and the "Normal" effect, and click OK.

    b. Then choose a **solid color** from the color palette, and a **solid pattern** from the pattern palette.

    c. Paint a shape, like a monster head. It is extremely important that the shape be entirely closed (no holes anywhere) because *if there is the tiniest hole, the paint from the bucket will spill out of the hole and spread all over the entire page.*

2. Now choose the paint bucket tool:

3. Choose any color, pattern, or texture.

4. Position the bucket inside the shape that you want to fill with paint. The paint pours out of the very *tip* of the spilling point so make sure the tip is positioned to pour inside the shape.

5. Then just click and the paint will pour into the shape. If you don't like the color, *immediately* press Command Z to undo (or choose Undo from the Edit menu); choose another color or texture, and click again.

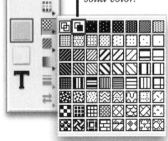

This little icon in the Pattern palette removes any pattern and makes the fill a solid color.

The paint pours out of the very tip.

Transform a shape

Here's an important technique to experiment with. Take a look at the Transform menu (it's in the menu bar across the top of the screen, not in the Button Bar or any palette). All the commands under Transform are probably gray, correct? That's because you must first *select* a shape that you want to transform (remember, select first, then do it to it). You have two selection tools, as shown to the left: a rectangular tool and a lasso tool.

The selection tools.

The rectangular tool selects a rectangular shape and picks up any background that it encloses. The lasso tool snaps to the exact shape of the object. To see the difference, draw a heart on the page with the brush. Then:

The rectangle selection tool selects the entire rectangular shape.

The lasso selects just the object.

1. Choose the **rectangular selection tool.** Begin outside of the heart, in the upper-left area, and drag diagonally down to the right.

   Then press the pointer in the center of that selected shape and drag. See, it drags the entire rectangle.

2. Now choose the **lasso tool.** Press-and-drag to draw loosely around the heart. When you let go, the lasso snaps to the heart shape. (You don't even have to draw entirely around the shape—when you let go, the lasso will find the other end of itself and snap to it.)

   To drag that selected shape, make sure you see the pointer—when the lasso tool is positioned on a draggable area of the image, it will turn into the pointer. The tool flips back and forth between lasso and pointer, so make sure you have the pointer before you try to move the object!

3. So that's how you select something. Now draw a shape, any shape.

4. Select that shape with either selection tool.

5. From the Transform menu, experiment with the choices. Choose something like "Perspective." Your selected object will display "handles," as shown below. Position the *tip* of the pointer tool in any one of those handles, then press-and-drag. Experiment with other options! (You must *re*select the object before you can transform again.)

Tip: *Try the "Pick Up" command. First paint a shape. Then select it with the lasso tool. Drag it onto some other shape that has a fancy pattern. While the shape is still selected and sitting on that other pattern, choose "Pick Up" from the Transform menu. Then drag the shape out to a clean part of the page. It will have picked up the pattern. You gotta try it to get it.*

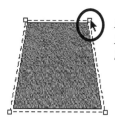

Each corner has a handle. Press-and-drag a handle to reshape the object.

Type some words and color them

You can also type words onto the page, and you can color those words. But keep in mind that you are painting, not word processing; that is, you won't be able to go back and edit the words or easily change their colors like you can in a word processor. And the text won't print as cleanly as text from a word processor. But it is great fun to do anyway. Follow the directions carefully.

The text tool.

1. Choose the **text tool.**

2. With the text tool, click on the left side of the painting page so you have room for the text to type out to the right. *As soon as you click, you'll see the menu bar change!* Now, while the insertion point is flashing on the page, you have menu items for text.

3. Before you type anything, go to the Text menu and choose the font, size, and color (you'll have to go to the menu three times, one for each choice). Unfortunately, you can't choose any of the patterns, textures, or gradients to type with. But you can choose any solid color.

4. Now type onto the page. Hit the Return key before the type bumps into the right side of the page. If you decide you want a different typeface, size, or color, press-and-drag over the text, then select your new choices. *But don't click outside of the little text box!* The very second you click anywhere outside of that text, the words become paint on the page and you cannot do any sort of editing—if you want to change anything after that point, you'll have to erase it and do it over again. It'll make you a little crazy for a while until you get the hang of it.

5. Once the type is set how you like it, click anywhere outside of the text box. Then you can select it (as described on the previous page) and move it wherever you like, transform it, delete it, etc.

*This is an example of paint text. You can, while typing, choose another typeface, size, and color and whatever you type **next** will be in the new formatting.*

I FOUND BETTER THINGS
IN THE DARK
THAN I EVER FOUND
IN THE LIGHT.

Ross Carter

So now paint an ugly monster

Use shapes or the paintbrush to create your monster. Use the paintbucket to fill in colors or textures. Paint the forest and the castle. Type a poem about your monster. You can't hurt anything, so experiment with all the tools and options—you'll learn a lot. Just remember to choose the tool, then the color/pattern/fill for the inside and the border *before* you paint.

See, isn't this a stupid-looking monster? So what!
Don't be afraid to paint something dorky—celebrate the dorkiness!

Make a Simple Drawing

A draw program can be less intimidating than a paint program because you mostly work with lines, boxes, and ovals ("lbo's," affectionately called "elbows"). The things you learn in this exercise will apply to many other programs that have draw tools as part of their features.

It's really a good idea to pair this draw exercise with the preceding paint exercise so you see the difference between a paint program and a draw program. You will not only learn which one to choose for a particular project, but you will feel more comfortable and knowledgeable when you understand the strengths and weaknesses of the two different sorts of applications.

Even if you think you can't draw a thing, go through the exercise and draw a little house. You'll be surprised. Even if your house turns out really silly (it can't be sillier than Robin's drawing), you will have learned a lot.

Remember, if you want to learn more, go to the Help menu in AppleWorks and choose "AppleWorks Help."

Let's draw!

Now, you might be in one of four different situations, depending on whether you've been following along or not. Choose the situation you're in and follow the directions:

This is the Drawing icon.

A. You just finished the paint exercise and the painting is still on your screen.

1. Save this document (if you want): press Command S.

2. Click the Close button in the upper-left corner, or use the keyboard shortcut Command W (W for Window).

3. Go to the next page in this book.

B. You finished the paint exercise, saved and closed it, and didn't quit AppleWorks. You still see the Button Bar.

✪ You are exactly where you need to be! Go to the next page in this book.

C. You finished the paint exercise, saved and closed it, and didn't quit AppleWorks. BUT you don't see the Button Bar.

1. Single-click on the AppleWorks icon in the Dock.

2. After you click the AppleWorks icon, the "Starting Points" palette and the Button Bar will appear at the top of the screen. Go to the next page of this book.

D. You skipped the painting exercise, or you turned off your computer and came back later, and AppleWorks is not open.

1. Open AppleWorks just like you did the first time: Single-click its icon in the Dock.

(Or, go to the Applications folder, then open the AppleWorks folder. The AppleWorks *application* is inside the AppleWorks *folder!* Double-click the AppleWorks *application* icon.)

2. Click the "Drawing" icon in the "Starting Points" palette.

3. Go to the next page, but skip the first step, the one that says, "Open a draw document," because you just opened one.

Open a new draw document

- To open a new, blank draw document, use the Button Bar: click on the button with the document and triangle icon.

 This is the Drawing button that appears in the Button Bar and also in the "Starting Points" palette.

Tip: *If you see a grid pattern in the background, you can choose to turn it off from the Options menu. Choose "Hide Graphics Grid" to make it go away.*

Check out the drawing tools

Along the left side of the screen you have the same Tool Palette, but the Paint tools are grayed out—if you did the painting exercise, you'll notice the paintbrush, spray can, pencil, paint bucket, eraser, and a couple of other tools are not available in the Draw module. So experiment with the Draw tools:

The Draw Tool Palette.

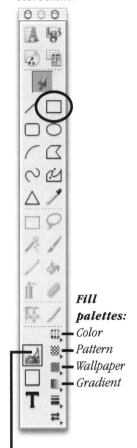

Draw and resize a shape

1. Click once on the **rectangle shape tool** (circled, to the right).

2. Now move the mouse over so you are positioned on the page.

3. Press-and-drag the mouse to draw a rectangle. The shape will **fill** with whatever color, pattern, or texture is selected in the Tool Palette.

4. Did you notice when you draw a rectangle you automatically get "handles" on each corner? (If the handles are gone, click once on any part of the object.) If you press the *tip* of the pointer in any one of those handles, you can drag the rectangle into a different rectangular shape. Try it.

*This is the original shape. Notice the handles. When an object is **selected**, you see its handles.*

Press-and-drag on any handle to resize the object.

You can resize any object at any time. It is never permanent.

Fill palettes:
Color
Pattern
Wallpaper
Gradient

Click this Fill button before you choose from the palettes.

Get rid of an object

- You've probably noticed you don't have an eraser in this Draw module. That's because each item in this program is seen as a complete object. You must remove an entire object—you cannot remove part of one. **To delete:** Select the item (click once on it with the pointer tool), and when you see the handles on the corners, hit the Delete key.

Change the fill and border thicknesses and patterns

1. One difference between a Paint program and a Draw program is that in Paint you must choose the fill and the border ("Pen") *before* you create the shape; in Draw you can change it whenever you feel like it.

Just like in the Paint module, in Draw you have palettes from which to choose the patterns and colors of the *inside* of a shape (the Fill), as well as the border thickness, color, and pattern of the *outside* (the Pen). You can use the buttons in the Tool Palette, or use larger palettes available from the Accents palette.

These are at the bottom of the Tool Palette:

Fill button (inside shapes)

Pen button (for lines and borders)

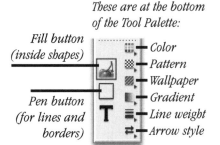

Color
Pattern
Wallpaper
Gradient
Line weight
Arrow style

From the Window menu, choose "Show Accents." The Accents palette looks the same in Paint and Draw.

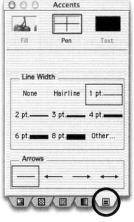

The tab on the far right is for lines and borders.

2. At any time—later today, next week, or next year—**click the object to select it,** then change the pattern or color of the inside, the thickness and color of the outside line, the size, or the position of the object. Try these actions (select the object first):

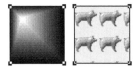

Change the pattern inside the shape (Fill).

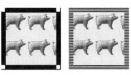

Change the thickness and pattern of the border (Pen).

From the Arrange menu, choose "Free Rotate." Then press on any handle, and drag to rotate the object.

Use the line tool

1. Choose the **line tool** by clicking once on it.

2. Press-and-drag on the page to draw a line.

3. After the line is drawn, make sure it is selected (you should see handles on both ends; if not, click once on the line with the *tip* of the pointer), then change the thickness, the color, and add some arrows to one or both ends.

From the Window menu, choose "Show Accents," then from the Accents palette (shown below, right) select the line attributes (Pen).

Or use the buttons at the bottom of the Tool Palette: Click any of the small buttons to reveal the pop-up palette.

This is the Line tool.

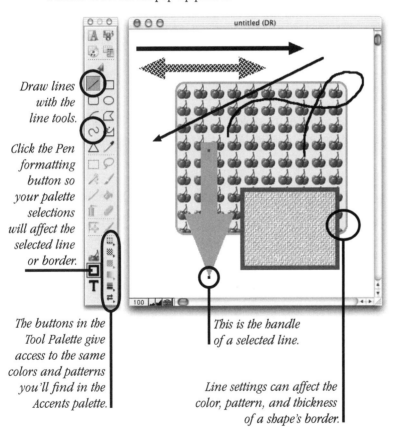

Draw lines with the line tools.

Click the Pen formatting button so your palette selections will affect the selected line or border.

The buttons in the Tool Palette give access to the same colors and patterns you'll find in the Accents palette.

This is the handle of a selected line.

Line settings can affect the color, pattern, and thickness of a shape's border.

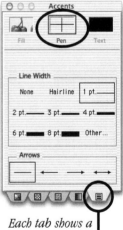

This pane of the Accents palette lets you change line widths, create arrows, and change the border width of a selected shape.

Each tab shows a different pane of the Accents window.

173

Use the freeform drawing tool

So far you have learned how to draw lines, boxes, and ovals (elbows, remember?). But you can also draw freeform shapes, then reshape them, and of course fill them with different colors or patterns, change the line thicknesses, and rotate and flip them to your heart's content.

You have two freeform tools: the freehand tool and something called the bezier tool. First try the freehand tool.

This is the freehand tool.

1. Choose the **freehand tool** from the Tool Palette.

2. Press-and-drag as usual, just like you did in the paint program or with any other draw tool.

3. Now this is the interesting thing about a freehand form in a Draw program: you can reshape it.

   If the shape doesn't have handles, select it by clicking once on it. Then from the Arrange menu, choose "Reshape."

4. Your cursor changes to a target (-⊕-), and the freeform shape gets little "points" on it (as shown below).

   Position the *center* of the target cursor on any of the points, press, and then drag. You have to play with it to get the hang of reshaping.

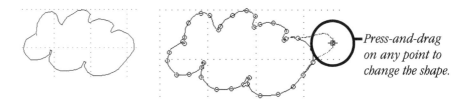

Press-and-drag on any point to change the shape.

Use the bezier tool

The bezier tool (pronounced *bay zyay*), which combines something called "bezier curves" with a polygon, is another freehand sort of tool.

This is the bezier tool.

1. Choose the **bezier tool** from the Tool Palette.

2. ***Do not press-and-drag!*** Instead, click once on the page, then move the mouse and click once somewhere else. Keep repeating the click-and-move action to create your shape.

3. When you have the basic shape you want, either double-click to finish the shape, or single-click directly on top of the first point.

4. While the shape is selected, from the Arrange menu, choose "Reshape." You get the same little points you saw with the freehand tool on the previous page.

   But if you click on one of those points with the target cursor, you get "control points" with long handles. Position the center of the target cursor on the end of one of those handles, and drag. Watch the shape change.

   This takes lots of experimenting before you begin to know what to expect when you drag. Try it!

Note: If you're wondering why curves drawn this way are called Bezier curves: a mathematician named Pierre Bezier invented this technique of drawing curves on a computer. John likes to call them "Pierre curves."

This is the original shape.

You can either drag the point itself . . .

. . . or drag either end of a point's handles.

The outlines display the original shape, plus the new shape, until you let go.

Now draw a silly little house

The tools are pretty easy to use, aren't they? Below are a few guidelines to help you use them. The trick to creating something fun in a drawing program (as in life) is to be creative with what you have.

- Keep checking to see which tool is selected. As soon as you draw something, AppleWorks switches back to the pointer tool.

- If you need to select an object and it's not getting handles when you click on it, check to make sure you have the pointer tool.

- No matter what patterns or colors are currently in the borders or the fills of any object, you can always change them.

- Make sure you have the right palette when you try to change a border (line) or a fill.

This is the text tool.

- Experiment with the text tool. Choose it, click on the page, and type. Edit the text just like you did in the word processor. The Text menu only appears after you have selected the text tool and clicked on the page!

- To select any object and send it behind the other objects or bring it in front: select the object, then use the Arrange menu.

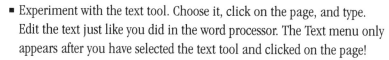

I used the "spiderweb" tool to create the sun's rays, the tree trunk, and the roof.

I drew one cat, then used the pointer tool to drag around all of the different objects that make the cat—this selected all the pieces. Then I held down the Option key and dragged to create a copy of the cat.

To create perfect circles and squares, hold the Shift key down while using the oval or rectangle shape tool.

Our house is a very very fine house.

After I drew this chimney, using the brick fill pattern and a brown color, I sent it behind the roof.

I used the freehand tool to create the cherry tree top and the chimney smoke.

Text in the draw program doesn't look any better **on the screen** *than it does in paint, but it* **prints** *beautifully. And you can edit (change) it as often as you like.*

Make a Simple (yet dazzling) Slide Show Presentation

AppleWorks includes a presentation module that makes it easy and fun to create professional-looking slide show presentations. Make slide shows for your family and friends, for school, or for work. Then present the slide shows on a computer, or print them onto transparencies so you can display them on an overhead projector. If you make your presentation on a computer, you can include movies, sounds, and visual transitions between slides. To aid you in your presentation, print a copy of the slide show and include notes to yourself. AppleWorks lets you set slide show playing options so you can design the presentation to suit your needs.

You can present your slide show on the computer, full screen, and use the arrow keys to go forward and back from slide to slide.

Get ready to create a presentation

Now, you might be in one of four different situations, depending on whether you've been following along or not. Choose the situation you're in and follow the directions:

This is the Presentation icon.

A. You just finished the drawing exercise and the drawing document is still on your screen.

1. Save this drawing (if you want): press Command S.

2. Click the red Close button in the upper-left corner, or use the keyboard shortcut Command W (W for Window).

3. Go to the next page in this book.

B. You finished the drawing exercise, saved and closed it, and didn't quit AppleWorks. You still see the Button Bar.

✪ You are exactly where you need to be! Go to the next page.

C. You finished the drawing exercise, saved and closed it, and didn't quit AppleWorks. BUT you don't see the Button Bar.

1. Find the AppleWorks icon in the Dock. Single-click it.

2. After you click the AppleWorks icon, the "Starting Points" palette and the Button Bar will appear at the top of the screen. Go to the next page of this book.

D. You skipped the previous exercise, or you turned off your computer and came back later, and AppleWorks is not open on your iMac.

1. Open AppleWorks just like you did the first time: Single-click its icon in the Dock.

   (Or go to the Applications folder, then open the AppleWorks folder. The AppleWorks *application* is inside the AppleWorks *folder!* Double-click the AppleWorks *application* icon.)

2. Click the "Presentation" icon in the "Starting Points" palette.

3. Go to the next page (of this book), but skip the first step because you just started a new document.

Open a new slide presentation document

To open a new, blank presentation document, use the Button Bar: single-click on the button that has a "slide" image on it.

Take a minute to look at the new document window and the Controls palette. If you don't see the Controls palette, click the "Show Controls" button in the Button Bar (shown circled, below). *Or* from the Window menu, choose "Show Presentation Controls."

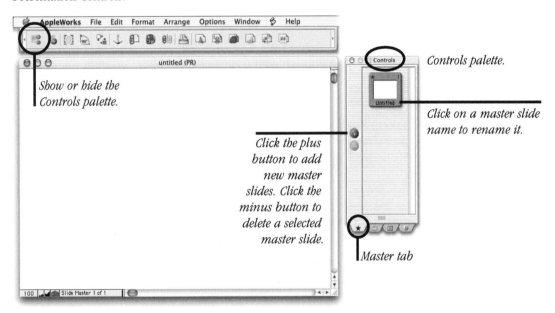

Show or hide the Controls palette.

Click the plus button to add new master slides. Click the minus button to delete a selected master slide.

Controls palette.

Click on a master slide name to rename it.

Master tab

Master slides and the Controls palette

A **master slide** is a *template,* or reusable slide, that includes design elements that will appear on other slides. It's a lot easier and faster to create a good-looking presentation if you don't have to build every slide from scratch. And when you use master slides, your presentation has a consistent, professional look.

You can use more than one master slide in a presentation. For instance, you might have a collection of photographs from your European tour, so you could create separate master slides for the sets of photos from each country.

The "Master tab" at the bottom of the **Controls palette** (shown above) displays a panel of small, thumbnail versions of the "master slides" you will create (as described on the following page). From here you can choose which master to use as a background for each slide.

Make a master slide

The master slide will be a consistent background on which you'll place the other, changeable elements of your presentation. You can use a solid color, a pattern, a design created in AppleWorks, a photo, or a combination of all those things. Use the tools and techniques you learned in Chapters 8 and 9 to create shapes filled with colors and patterns, then add some text to the page.

Leave large areas of the layout empty so your individual slides can use that space for text, photos, clip art, or movies.

Draw a round cornered rectangle, add a border, and fill with a solid color.

Add a text headline.

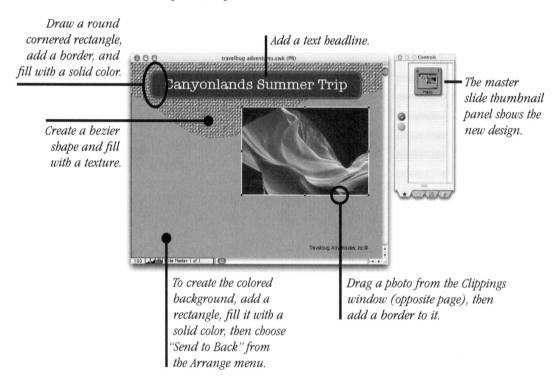

The master slide thumbnail panel shows the new design.

Create a bezier shape and fill with a texture.

To create the colored background, add a rectangle, fill it with a solid color, then choose "Send to Back" from the Arrange menu.

Drag a photo from the Clippings window (opposite page), then add a border to it.

Add a photo or clip art to the slide

Drag photos into the presentation window from any window on your Desktop. For instance, open your Pictures folder in which you have stored your photos. Make it a List View and resize it to tall and skinny over on the right side of your monitor. Then in AppleWorks, just drag a photo from your Pictures folder and drop it on the presentation window.

In the example presentation, I found the photo in the **Clippings palette,** provided by AppleWorks. The Clippings palette is a handy place to keep images, text, movies, and other items that you want to reuse in your documents. AppleWorks has provided lots of images already, but you can make your own collections (as separate panels) of art, logos, photos, or whatever. Almost anything that can be digitized can be dragged into the Clippings palette—photographs, movies, illustrations, scanned images, drawings and paintings you created in AppleWorks, etc.

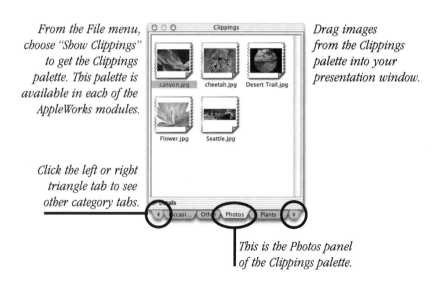

From the File menu, choose "Show Clippings" to get the Clippings palette. This palette is available in each of the AppleWorks modules.

Drag images from the Clippings palette into your presentation window.

Click the left or right triangle tab to see other category tabs.

This is the Photos panel of the Clippings palette.

Make the first slides of the presentation

Once you have a master slide, you can make a number of new slides using the master as a background.

1. Click the **Master tab** (the star) at the bottom of the Controls palette.

2. Single-click on the master slide thumbnail image you created.

3. Click the **Slide tab** (circled, below) at the bottom of the Controls palette.

4. Click the "plus" button to add a thumbnail of the master slide to the Slide panel. The new slide displays full-size in the document window, ready to be customized with your content.

5. Do something like add a new shape, fill it with a texture, then add text, as shown below.

*Plus button
(to add a slide)*

*Add a new rounded corner rectangle
shape, then add text on top of it.*

*The Slide tab displays the
Slide panel where you
create new slides and
where you can select any
slide to edit or delete.*

Make more slides from this master

To create another new slide using the same master, click the plus button again. A new thumbnail appears in the Slide panel, and the new slide displays in the document window, ready to be modified. Continue this procedure until you've created as many slides as you need.

The Controls palette features

The bottom of the Controls palette has several useful buttons.

> **To mark a slide to print (or not),** select the slide in the panel, then click one of the printer buttons.

> **To hide or show a slide in a slide show,** select the slide, then click the Hide or Show button.

> The **Transitions** button is explained on the next page.

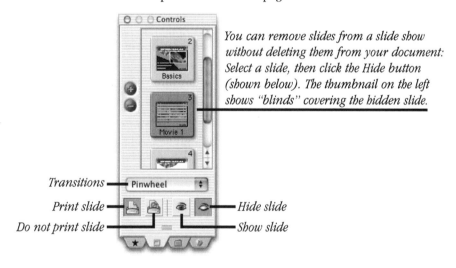

You can remove slides from a slide show without deleting them from your document: Select a slide, then click the Hide button (shown below). The thumbnail on the left shows "blinds" covering the hidden slide.

Transitions — Pinwheel

Print slide — — *Hide slide*

Do not print slide — — *Show slide*

Add transitions between slides

Add some visual interest to your slide show by creating "transitions" between slides. AppleWorks includes a pop-up menu full of different effects that you can apply with a click of the mouse. **To create a visual transition:**

1. Select a slide in the Slide panel to which you want to apply a transition. The effect will be applied between the selected slide and the following one.

2. Click the "Transition" pop-up menu in the Slide panel.

3. Choose one of the transitions in the list, as shown to the left.

When using master slides, some elements don't change from slide to slide, which makes some transitions look strange or minimizes their effect. In that case I usually prefer the "Fade" transition—it creates the visual illusion that most of the content of the original slide stays on the screen as the changing elements fade out and in. Of course, the entire slide is actually changing, but since some elements of the slide are identical, they *appear* to stay on the screen. When you switch to slides that use master backgrounds that are completely different, any of the transitions provide a great dramatic effect to emphasize the new background.

Preview your slide show

At any time you can play your slide show to evaluate it. It's a good idea to check transitions to see if they add interest—or not. You may also realize you have too many slides that are similar (thus boring), or too few slides to communicate your message.

1. Click the "Start Show" button in the Button Bar.

This is the "Start Show" button.

2. The slide show fills the entire screen as it plays.

Press the Right arrow on your keyboard to advance to the next slide. Press the Left arrow to return to the previous slide.

3. To stop the show and return to your Desktop, press the Escape key (esc) on the top-left corner of your keyboard, or press Command Period (.).

Single-click the Transitions pop-up menu in the Controls panel to choose an effect.

Add a movie to a slide

If you think a slide show presentation is fun, you haven't seen anything yet. You can even add QuickTime movies to a slide! Where do you get QuickTime movies? You can sometimes download them from other people's web sites (ask permission), and some digital cameras can make short QuickTime movies. Or if you're using iMovie on your iMac to edit home movies, you can export an iMovie as a QuickTime movie.

Tips: To start playing a movie, double-click it.

Stop play with a single click, even if the movie controls are not visible.

See below, left, to show the movie controls.

For this exercise, I have some QuickTime movies that I made with iMovie and that I placed in a Clippings panel. To add a QuickTime movie to a slide:

1. Select the thumbnail slide (in the Slide panel of the Controls palette) in which you want to add a movie, as on page 183.

2. Locate a QuickTime movie on your computer. Drag the movie's QuickTime icon from its location to the open presentation window.

3. Resize the movie if it's too large: Click on the movie to select it, then hold down the Command and Shift keys and drag one of the corner "handles."

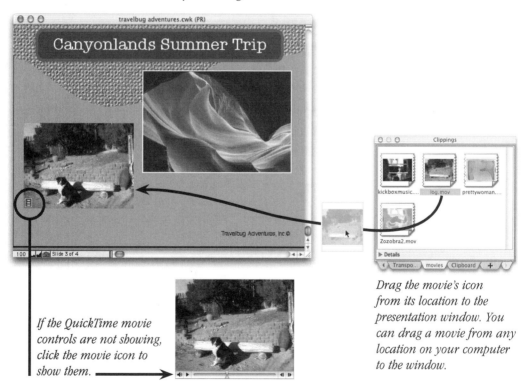

If the QuickTime movie controls are not showing, click the movie icon to show them.

Drag the movie's icon from its location to the presentation window. You can drag a movie from any location on your computer to the window.

185

More movie tidbits

You can put more than one movie on a slide. Drag the movies into any position and resize them to fit. Play each movie individually, or play them all at once. Your iMac is powerful enough to do everything.

Be careful when resizing movies in AppleWorks— smaller is okay, but if you resize a movie to a larger size, it looks bad (pixelated).

The Organize panel.

The Organize panel

Click the "Organize" tab to group, rearrange, rename, or delete slides in your presentation.

To add a folder, click the "plus" button.

To delete a folder (and all the slides in it), select it and click the "minus" button.

To rearrange the slides and folders into any order, or to move slides from one folder to another, press-and-drag them. The slides will show or print in the order they appear in this window.

The Slide Show panel

Use the Slide Show panel to customize settings for slides, movies, and sounds.

To make movie playback controls visible, as in the example shown above, click the "Show controls" checkbox in the "Movies and Sounds" section of this panel.

Play button.

The Slide Show panel.

Make slide notes

You can include notes with your slides to help you plan what to include in the slide content, or to help plan your verbal presentation. Print your slide notes to aid you in your presentation. **To make slide notes:**

1. Click the "Slide" tab at the bottom of the Controls palette.

2. Select a slide.

3. From the Window menu at the top of your screen, choose "Notes View." A checkmark will appear next to the item to indicate that Notes View is turned on.

4. Type your notes in the Notes "frame" that appears under the slide.

Tip: To return to a normal view of your presentation, go to the Window menu, then choose "Notes View" again to turn the notes off.

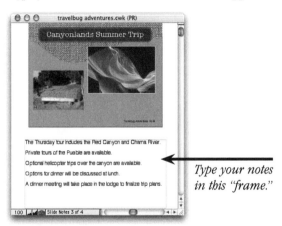

Type your notes in this "frame."

To print your notes:

1. From the File menu, choose "Print…."

2. In the Print window, choose "AppleWorks 6" from the pop-up menu.

3. Click the "Notes" button, then click "Print."

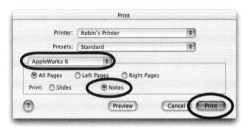

Notice you can also choose to print your slides from this dialog box.

Image format and size recommendations

AppleWorks will accept most common image file formats, such as TIFF, JPEG, PDF, and EPS. These are some format recommendations to help make your presentation more efficient.

All slides in an AppleWorks presentation document are a standard **size** of 640 pixels wide by 480 pixels tall (about the size of most 14-inch monitors). Photos that you insert should be that size or smaller, although you can resize a photo by dragging it to a smaller size in the presentation window.

Photos should have a maximum **resolution** of 72 ppi, but AppleWorks will accept higher resolutions. Higher resolution images won't look any better on the screen, plus they take up more disk space.

The **color mode** of an image should be set to RGB (red, green, blue) to look its best. If you use an image whose color mode is CMYK (cyan, magenta, yellow, black), the color looks over-saturated and dark. Digital cameras create RGB images, and scanners usually scan in RGB mode by default.

Photo specifications: 640 by 480 pixels, 72 ppi resolution, RGB color mode.

These are clip art images from the Clippings window.

Fax a Note to Someone 11

On your iMac you have the software called FAXstf X. With this software, you can create a letter in any application of your choice and fax it right from the screen. And you can also receive faxes into your computer (your iMac must be turned on), then print the fax on your own printer—or just read it on the screen and never print it at all. It's great and it's easy. In this chapter I'll walk you through sending a fax page, and I'll also show you how to set things up so your iMac will receive faxes.

This is the monster painting from the AppleWorks tutorial (Chapter 8). You can fax it to your friends and loved ones. They'll be so impressed.

FAXstf X

FAXstf™ X makes it possible to send and receive faxes straight from your iMac. FAXstf X works with the Address Book application to address faxes, and uses the Apple internal modem to send and receive faxes. If you have an AirPort wireless network, DSL, or cable modem connection, you must physically connect a **phone line** to the modem connection on the back of the iMac (and plug the other end into a phone jack) to use FAXsft X.

Install and set up FAXstf X

Before you can use FAXsft X, you need to install the application and perform a few basic setup steps.

To install FAXstf X

FAXstf X 10.0 Installer

1. To find the FAXstf X installer, click on the Applications button in any window Toolbar to open the Applications folder.

2. In the Applications folder, double-click the **Installers** folder to open it.

3. Double-click the "FAXstf X 10.0 Installer" icon and follow the simple installation directions.

FAXstf is actually two small applications, the **Fax Browser** and the **Modem Center.** These two applications, plus the Mac OS X **Print Center,** need to be set up before you send a fax.

First, set up the Print Center

Print Center

1. Open the Applications window, then open the "Utilities" folder and find the **Print Center** application.

   Double-click the Print Center icon to open the "Printer List" window, as shown below.

   (If the "Printer List" window does not automatically appear, go to the Printers menu and choose "View Printer List.")

2. You will get either the Printer List window or an alert message, both shown below. Click the "Add Printer…" or "Add…" button because you need to add the Apple modem printer to this list.

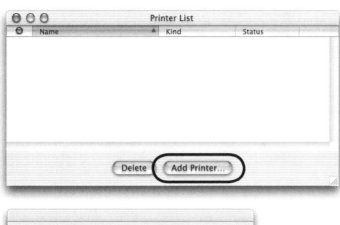

3. A "sheet" drops down in front of the list, and the sheet has a pop-up menu on it. From that menu, choose "FAXstf," as shown below.

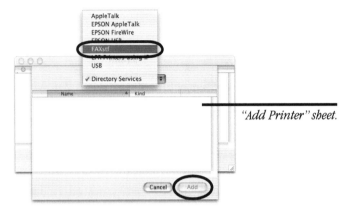

"Add Printer" sheet.

4. "Apple Internal Modem" will appear in the sheet below the menu; click on that name to select it, then click the "Add" button. The Apple Internal Modem will appear in the Printer List, as shown below.

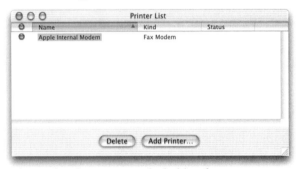

This is what the Printer List looks like after adding "Apple Internal Modem."

5. Now that "Apple Internal Modem" is added to the Printer List, FAXstf can fax from any application that is capable of printing.

6. You can **Quit** the Print Center now.

Second, set up the Fax Browser Preferences

The contact information you specify in the Fax Browser "Preferences" window appears on your fax cover sheet to identify you as the sender.

Fax Browser

1. Open (double-click) the Fax Browser application that's located in the FAXstf X folder.

2. From the Fax Browser menu, choose "Preferences…."
Click the "Identity" tab to show the Identity pane, as shown below.

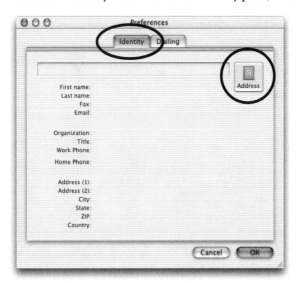

3. Single-click the "Address" button, circled above, to open the Address Book, shown below. If you don't already have one, you need to create a contact information card for yourself.

Each card in Address Book is called a **vCard,** or virtual card. **To create a card,** click the "New" button in the toolbar, then enter the information. You don't have to fill in every field, but you must enter a first name, last name, and fax number for the Fax Browser Preferences to accept it.

Click the "New" button to create a vCard for yourself.

While you're here, you might as well add cards for everyone you know.

—continued

4. Drag your personal vCard from the Address Book list and drop it in the text field at the top of the Identity panel.

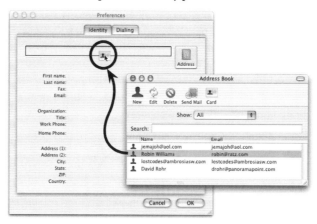

5. If you need a **prefix** before you call out from your phone line, such as a code for an outside line or a credit card number, click the **Dialing** tab.

Click the "Use prefix" checkbox and enter the number in the prefix field.

Sometimes you need a comma after a number or between a series of numbers to slow down the dialing operation—each comma makes the phone wait a few seconds before continuing. By default, a comma in FAXstf creates a two-second delay, but you can change that, if necessary; see the opposite page.

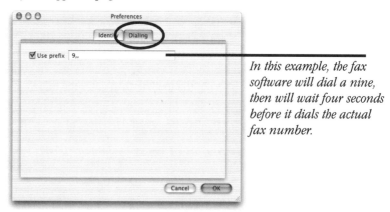

In this example, the fax software will dial a nine, then will wait four seconds before it dials the actual fax number.

6. Click OK.

Third, set up the Modem Center

1. Double-click the Modem Center application in the FAXstf X folder. Notice "Apple Internal Modem" appears as a result of setting up the Print Center.

    The current "Status" is "Idle," but when you send a fax, the changing states of the modem display in this window (dialing, connecting, sending, handshaking, etc.).

Modem Center

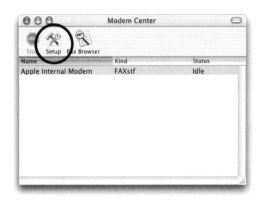

2. Click the "Setup" button, circled above, to show the setup sheet.

3. Click the **General tab,** if it's not selected, to show the General options.

    Name: Should already say "Apple Internal Modem."

    Station Message: Enter your fax number. This number is used to identify yourself to another fax device.

    Dialing: Select your type of phone service.

    Volume: Choose a volume for your modem speaker.

    On: Choose when you want the modem speaker turned on.

    Comma pauses: Specify a time delay that applies to commas in a number or prefix, as shown on the opposite page.

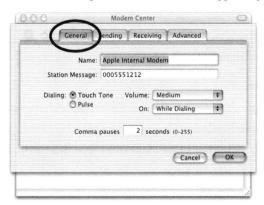

—continued

4. Click the **Sending** tab.

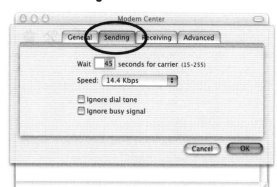

Wait: Specify the length of time to wait for a fax machine to answer.

Speed: Select a baud rate for the modem. Choose the highest option available, 14.4Kbps. This is the fastest speed that a fax can be sent.

Ignore dial tone: Forces FAXstf to dial a fax number even if it can't detect a dial tone, as when going through a hotel PBX switchboard.

Ignore busy signal: Forces FAXstf X to continue trying to connect when it detects a busy signal.

5. Click the **Receiving** tab.

Answer after: Set how many rings before FAXstf X answers an incoming fax call. If you don't want FAXstf X to automatically answer incoming calls, set this number to 0. (See page 200 for more info on this.)

Speed: Set the modem's baud rate for receiving faxes—choose the fastest option, 14.4Kbps. If you have trouble receiving faxes, try a slower baud rate.

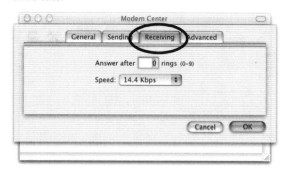

6. Ignore the **Advanced** tab. Click OK.

Send a fax

Now that you've set up FAXstf, you can finally send a fax. You can fax from any application on your iMac that ordinarily has a print option.

1. Open the document on your computer that you want to fax.

2. From the File menu, choose "Print...."

3. In the Print window, choose "Apple Internal Modem" from the Printer pop-up menu (as shown below).

4. From the lower pop-up menu, choose "Addresses" to show the Address pane of the Print window, as shown below.

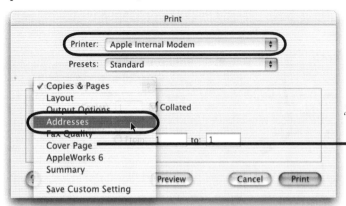

Notice from this pop-up menu you can also choose to add a "Cover Page" message, as well as adjust the quality of the fax.

5. In the Addresses pane, below, click the "Address" button on the right to open the Address Book, which is shown on the following page.

—continued

6. In the Address Book, find the vCard of a person to whom you want to send a fax. If there isn't one, click the "New" button and make one for that person. Make sure the vCard contains a fax number in the "Fax" field.

Drag the vCard and drop it in the Addresses pane of the Print window, as shown below. You can fax the document to more than one person at a time—just drag over a vCard for each recipient.

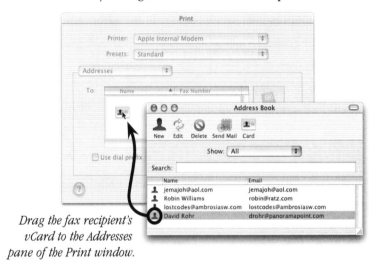

Drag the fax recipient's vCard to the Addresses pane of the Print window.

7. If you want to put a short message on the fax cover page, choose "Cover Page" from the lower pop-up menu (shown on the previous page).

In the Cover Page pane that appears, type a short message that will automatically print on a fax cover page.

8. Click the "Print" button in the lower-right corner of the Print window to send the fax.

FAXstf animated Dock icons

During a fax transmission, watch the FAXstf icon in the Dock. The inside of the circle will change and animate to illustrate the various stages of the fax operation.

 Idle
Pulsing green dot: You're ready to send or receive a fax.

 Dialing
Animated number keys: The modem is dialing a fax number.

 Ringing
Animated sound waves: The modem detects an incoming call.

 Connecting
Two buckles connect: The modem is connecting to another device.

 Sending
Data rising from a document icon: A fax is being sent.

 Receiving
Data falling into a document icon: A fax is being received.

 Handshaking
A page being torn away: The modem is "shaking hands," something that occurs during the transmission of pages.

 Hanging up
Two buckles moving apart: The connection is terminating.

 Error
Pulsing red dot: An error occurred during the fax transmission.

During a fax transmission, the Modem Center window automatically opens on the Desktop to display the modem status.

Receiving a fax

You cannot receive a fax unless you have instructed FAXstf X to automatically answer telephone calls, as described on page 196. I'll explain how to do this again because this is the one setting you might have to change regularly, depending on your phone line situation. How many rings you tell FAXstf to wait before it picks up depends on whether you have a dedicated fax line or whether your fax line is also the only phone line in the house.

If your iMac is connected to a **dedicated fax (phone) line,** set the value to 1 so FAXstf will answer as quickly as possible.

If you have an Internet connection that uses your modem, you cannot send or receive faxes while you are online, nor can you get online while you are sending or receiving a fax.

If your iMac is connected to a **phone line that is also used for phone calls,** set the value to 3, 4, or a higher number that gives you time to answer the phone, if you choose, *before* FAXstf automatically picks it up. Then when you are expecting a fax, let the phone ring until FAXstf picks it up.

If you have an **answering machine,** you'll have to set the number of rings to 0 (zero) while you're away from your desk so you can get messages. When you are back, change the rings to pick up.

To change the number of rings before FAXstf picks up to take a fax, or to **turn off FAXstf** altogether:

1. Open the Modem Center.
2. Click the "Setup" button in the toolbar.
3. Click the "Receiving" tab.

   Set the "Answer after" value to 0 rings to make sure FAXstf does *not* answer the phone (this effectively turns off FAXstf).

   Change the value to between 1 and 9 rings and FAXstf will answer any phone call that comes in (unless you leap for the phone and grab it first).

When a fax comes in, the Fax Browser automatically opens on your screen so you'll know what has arrived.

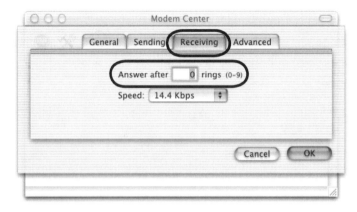

The Fax Browser window

Use the **Fax Browser** to view your fax documents. You can also choose a fax to print, delete faxes that you don't want to keep, and archive (save in another place) faxes that you need to keep. **To open the Fax Browser,** double-click the Fax Browser icon in the FAXstf folder.

Fax Browser

The Fax Browser window features a collapsible "Drawer"— click the **Trays** button in the toolbar (circled, below) to open and close the Drawer. This Drawer contains several "Trays" in which you can store and organize your faxes: Just drag any fax from the list area and drop it in a Tray.

Archive selected faxes by dragging them from the list area to the Archive Tray in the drawer.

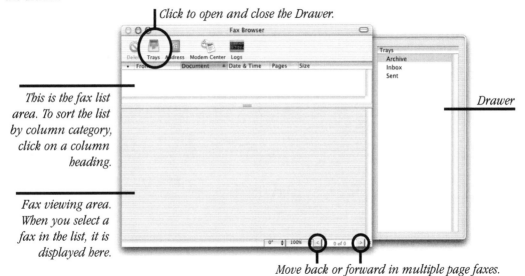

Click to open and close the Drawer.

This is the fax list area. To sort the list by column category, click on a column heading.

Drawer

Fax viewing area. When you select a fax in the list, it is displayed here.

Move back or forward in multiple page faxes.

The Fax Browser toolbar

Delete: Deletes the currently selected faxes in the fax list.

Trays: Opens and closes the collapsible Drawer that contains your fax Trays.

Address: Opens the Address Book application.

Modem Center: Opens the Modem Center where you can change your modem settings.

Logs: Opens the Activity Log file that contains a record of your fax activities.

Fax Browser

Viewing a fax

All faxes you receive are placed in the "Inbox" tray that appears in the Fax Browser Drawer, as shown below. Click on the "Inbox" tray to show a list of received faxes. A blue dot next to a fax in the list indicates that it has not been viewed.

Single-click on a fax in the list to display it in the viewing area of the Fax Browser window, as shown below. The controls at the bottom of the window let you rotate the selected fax, zoom in or out, and jump to specific pages of a multiple-page fax.

If you've used the Mail program, you'll find this browser window very similar.

Printing a fax

Select a fax in the Fax Browser list (single-click on it), then from the File menu choose "Print…." Make sure your printer (not the "Apple Internal Modem") is chosen in the Printer pop-up menu, as shown below.

Fax Browser

Select a fax in the Fax Browser list, then choose "Print…."

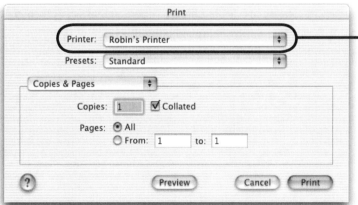

Make sure the printer chosen here is your actual printer, not "Apple Internal Modem"!

Modem Center

Modem Center Preferences

There are a few settings you can monkey with, if you like. To get the preferences, open the Modem Center, then go to the Modem Center menu (next to the Apple), and choose "Preferences...."

Windows

Click the "Windows" tab to choose if the Main Window and Active Modems will show when the Modem Center application launches. These settings don't really affect how you use FAXstf, and the Modem Center opens automatically when you send a fax. I prefer to leave the default settings alone.

Logging

Click the "Logging" tab to determine how often a New Activity Log is created. For most people, looking at a fax log file once is enough to satisfy their curiosity forever. Unless your life revolves around faxing, the "Never" option is probably sufficient.

Copy Files To and From Other Disks

Eventually, you'll realize that you need to put someone else's files on your computer. Or, you may need to give some of your files to someone else for a project they're working on. Even if you're not sharing files with someone, you'll need to make **backup copies** of important files for safe keeping. Sooner or later you'll start running out of storage room on your hard disk and have to find some other place to store lots of files that are just sitting there, taking up valuable space.

The following pages explain how to copy files to other disks. You'll notice I use two different spellings: **disk** and **disc.** It's not a typo, there's actually a difference.

Disc with a "c" refers to *optical* media, or a disc that's created by "burning" information onto it with a laser beam. This includes CDs and DVDs. To help make sense of it, remember that "discs" are round, like the letter "c."

Disk with a "k" refers to *magnetic* media, such as a Zip disk, your iMac's internal hard disk, or an external FireWire disk. (Yes, inside their cases these disks are also round, but the round disk is hidden by a square or rectangular enclosure. John would have named magnetic media "disq" ["sq" for "square enclosure"], but nobody asked him.

In this chapter "removable disk" often refers to both sorts of disks, so I use a "k." And who cares anyway.

What other disks?

Your iMac makes copying files onto external disks easy to deal with. You have one of these situations with your computer:

Your iMac has a CD-RW drive or a Combo Drive. You can copy files to a removable CD.

Your iMac has a SuperDrive. You can copy files to a removable CD or a DVD.

You bought an external drive that writes to removable hard disks (such as a Zip or Jaz drive). Connect the drive to your iMac and copy files to Zip or Jaz disks.

You bought an external hard drive (these usually do not have individual removable disks). If you bought a FireWire drive, you can copy files to the disk with blazing speed; other external hard disks are a little slower.

 Although these directions specifically explain copying from your "removable disk" to your "internal hard disk," you can use these same methods to copy from any disk to any other disk or volume (as long as there is room on the other disk).

Copying from a removable disk to the iMac

There are a couple of ways to copy files from your **removable disk** (such as a Zip disk, a CD, or a DVD) to your iMac's internal hard disk, depending on whether you want to copy *selected* files or the *entire* removable disk.

To COPY SELECTED FILES from a removable disk to your internal hard disk:

1. Insert the removable disk and wait for its icon to appear on the Desktop.

2. Double-click the removable disk icon to open its window.

3. Make sure you can see the folder, window, or column you want to drag the files *into*.

4. On the removable disk, selectively choose the files or folder you need to copy (see pages 64–65 about selecting more than one file at a time).

   Press-and-drag the selected files to your hard disk icon, or drag them directly into any folder on your iMac.

To COPY AN ENTIRE REMOVABLE DISK to your internal hard disk:

This method copies *every single item* from the removable disk to your internal hard disk. Make sure that's what you really want to do!

1. Insert the removable disk into its drive.

2. **What NOT to do:** If you drag the removable disk icon onto your hard disk icon, you'll notice a tiny curved arrow appears next to the pointer, as shown below. This indicates that dragging the item will create an *alias* (an icon that will go and *get* the real file) —it will *not* move the disk nor make a copy of the contents. That's not what you want.

*Dragging this removable disk into any window will create an **alias** to that removable disk.*

3. **What NOT to do:** Instead of dragging the disk icon, hold down the Control key and single-click on the removable disk icon. This will give you a "contextual menu," as shown below.

This is a contextual menu.

4. From the contextual menu, choose the "Copy" command.

—continued

5. Open the window you want to copy the entire removable disk contents into (the contents will copy into the *active* window).

6. From the Edit menu, choose "Paste item" (**or** Command-click in the open window or on any folder and use the contextual menu).

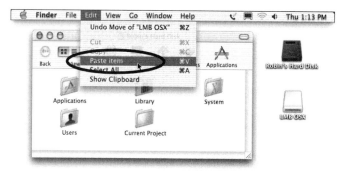

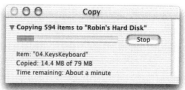

When you Paste, the contents of the removable disk you copied will be pasted into the active window or selected folder. You'll get the Copy message, as shown here.

7. When the copy/paste process is finished, you'll have an icon of the removable disk in the window. Don't get confused and think that this represents the actual removable disk! It doesn't—it is a *copy* of the entire contents on that disk. (The icon is actually a folder with a customized image.)

*This is the "folder" that holds a **copy** of the contents of the Zip disk.*

Copying files onto a CD

When you **copy files onto a CD,** it's called **burning a CD** because the computer uses a laser beam to burn digital information into the surface of a CD. You can't just burn any ol' CD, though—you need to understand the differences between CD-ROM, CD-R, and CD-RW.

CD-ROM (Compact Disc – Read Only Memory): You cannot erase information from or copy information to a CD-ROM, such as an old application installation disc that you don't need any more. If you've been saving that stack of AOL CDs to use for backups, forget it. They're CD-ROMS.

CD-R (Compact Disc – Recordable): CD-Rs are the most common type of disc for burning data and music files. Using Apple's CD-burning software, you can "write" once (a "single burn" session) to a CD-R.

Other CD burning software, such as Roxio's Toast, lets you burn "multiple" sessions of data files (but not if you're burning a music CD.)

CD-Rs hold between 650 and 700 megabytes of data and are very affordable, usually in the range of one dollar per disc or lower. The disc quality and dependability drop along with the price, however, so beware of buying really cheap CD-Rs.

You can't erase a CD-R.

CD-RW (Compact Disc – ReWritable): You can rewrite and erase CD-RWs many times, making these discs ideal for backing up files that change over time.

If you use Apple's CD-burning software, you can write to a CD-RW more than once, but only if you erase its current contents.

Other CD-burning software, such as Roxio Toast, allows you to selectively erase or rewrite files repeatedly on a single CD-RW, or you can choose to rewrite only files that have been changed since the last backup to the disc.

Depending on the quality of the CD-RW and the quantity you buy, the price per disc may be similar to CD-Rs, or up to two to three times more.

Do not use CD-RWs for creating music CDs—they only work in computers, not CD audio players. Use CD-Rs.

To burn a CD:

Please read the previous page before you burn your first CD.

1. Before you burn a CD (or DVD), make sure your Mac will not go to sleep during the process: Open the System Preferences, and choose Energy Saver. Set the top slider (System Sleep) to "Never," and uncheck the bottom two options (Display Sleep and Hard Disk Sleep). See page 71 if you need more explicit directions for Energy Saver.

2. Insert a blank CD.

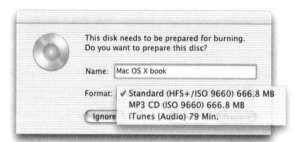

Is "compact disc" spelled with a "c" or a "k"? Well, as you can see in this alert box, even Apple can't keep it straight.

Mac OS X book

This is the CD icon before burning. The letters "CDR" indicate this is a CD-Recordable disc that has not been burned.

3. This disc needs to be prepared. Name the disc, and choose a format based on the information below.

Choose **Standard** format to copy data and multimedia files to a CD that can be read by a Mac or a PC. These data files can be recognized by a computer, but not by a CD player or MP3 player.

Choose **MP3 CD** to create a *data CD* in which music files are *stored* in MP3 format. MP3 compression enables you to store the maximum number of songs possible on a CD.

Music in this format can be played on computers using software such as iTunes, or loaded onto MP3 players such as Apple's iPod. You cannot play an MP3-formatted CD on a standard CD player.

Choose the **iTunes** format to create music CDs that you can *play* on standard CD players or on your computer. If you select this format when preparing to burn a CD, iTunes opens so you can select a Playlist (or selections from a Playlist) to burn. (To learn how to make iTunes Playlists, please see Chapter 18.)

4a. If you chose the **Standard** or **MP3 CD** format, drag the folders and files you want to copy and drop them on top of the CD icon on your Desktop. A "copy" window opens to show the progress. This does *not* burn the CD—the iMac just makes a list for itself of the files you *want* to burn; go to Step 5.

4b. If you chose the **iTunes** format to create a music CD, select a Playlist (or songs in a Playlist) from the iTunes window that opens, then click the "Burn CD" button in the top-right corner of the iTunes window. Skip to Step 6.

5. It sounds strange, but now drag the CD icon to the Trash. As soon as the CD icon moves, the Trash icon changes to the "Burn CD" icon.

6. As your files are prepared, burned, and verified, the "Burn Disc" window shows the progress.

This is the "Burn CD" icon.

7. The letters "CDR" are gone from the icon, indicating that this disc has been burned. Eject the disc—select it and press Command E.

This is the CD icon after it has been burned. Notice the letters CDR are gone.

Tip: *If you burn a lot of CDs and DVDs, add the Burn icon to your Finder window Toolbar.*

1. *Hold down the Shift key and single-click on the Hide/Show Toolbar button.*
2. *Drag the Burn icon up to the Toolbar.*
3. *Click "Done."*

Copying and burning files onto a DVD

If your iMac has a "SuperDrive," you can copy files to a DVD-R. The advantage of a DVD is that it holds 7 or 8 times as much information as a CD, and 47 times more than a 100-megabyte Zip disk. When you buy a DVD-R, the packaging usually claims the capacity of the disc is 4.7 gigabytes (that's 4,812 megabytes, in round numbers), but the actual capacity of useable space on the disc is closer to 4.2 gigabytes.

1. Use the Energy Saver preferences to make sure your hard disk does not go to sleep (see page 71).

2. Insert a blank DVD.

3. In the box that appears, enter a name, then click the "Prepare" button. A DVD disc icon appears on the Desktop.

Robin's iMac backup

This DVD icon will appear on your Desktop after you name the disc and click the "Prepare" button.

4. Drag the selected files to the DVD icon.
The "Copy" window appears to show the files being copied (not yet burned) to the disc.

5. Control-click on the DVD icon, then choose "Burn Disc" from the contextual menu that pops open, as shown to the left.

6. In the message box that appears, click the "Burn" button.

This contextual menu will appear when you Control-click on a DVD.

7. The "Burn Disc" status bar indicates the progress. When the procedure is finished, press the Media Eject key on the keyboard to eject the DVD.

Customize
Your iMac with
System
Preferences

The **System Preferences** allow you to change the settings of a number of features on your computer. This will become a familiar process to you as you work with your iMac. There are too many items in System Preferences to cover them all in this book, so I'll show a few of the ones that you're most likely to use initially. When you're ready, refer to *The Little Mac OS X Book* for a description of every item in System Preferences.

System Preferences

The **System Preferences** program holds all of the individual preferences.

To open System Preferences:

This is the System Preferences icon that is in the Dock.

- The icon shown to the left should be in your Dock. Single-click on it.

- **Or** you can always go to the Apple menu and choose "System Preferences…."

Then single-click any icon to open its preference pane. The new pane will replace this one you see.

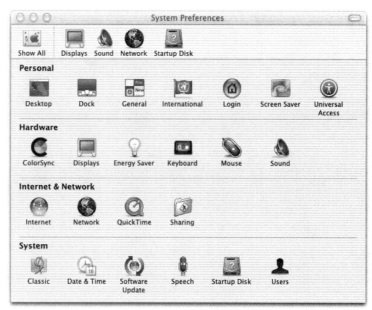

To come back to this main pane, *single-click the "Show All" button in the upper-left of the window, or press Command L.*

The following preferences are explained elsewhere in this book:

Classic is on pages 408–409, Chapter 23.

Dock preferences are on page 44.

Energy Saver is on page 71, Chapter 3.

Internet preferences are on page 317.

Mouse preferences are on pages 46–47, Chapter 2.

Network preferences are in Chapter 15.

Desktop

Open the Desktop preferences as explained on the opposite page.

Use the **Desktop** preferences to change the color of your background on the monitor. Instead of a color, you can choose a photograph or an abstract image. You can also use any photo or graphic image of your choice. Just put that photo or image in your Pictures folder, then choose "Pictures Folder" from the Collection menu (circled, below) to add the photo.

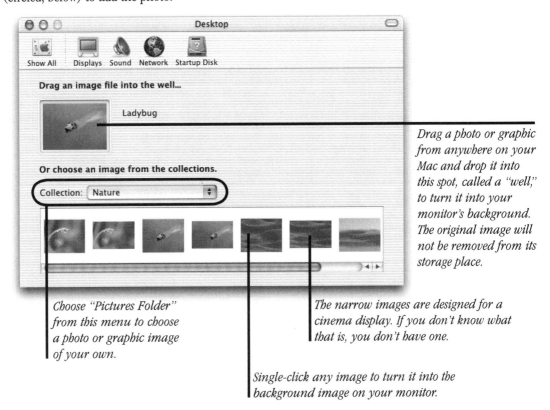

Drag a photo or graphic from anywhere on your Mac and drop it into this spot, called a "well," to turn it into your monitor's background. The original image will not be removed from its storage place.

Choose "Pictures Folder" from this menu to choose a photo or graphic image of your own.

The narrow images are designed for a cinema display. If you don't know what that is, you don't have one.

Single-click any image to turn it into the background image on your monitor.

Tip: *If you have a digital camera and iPhoto, see page 299 for an even easier method of quickly changing your Desktop.*

General

General

Open the General preferences as explained on page 214.

The **General** preferences pane offers a variety of options, most of which are self-explanatory. Experiment—you can't hurt your iMac with these preferences.

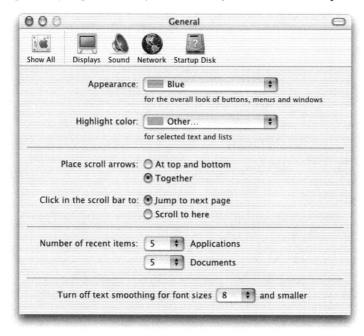

Most of the items above are self-explanatory, except:

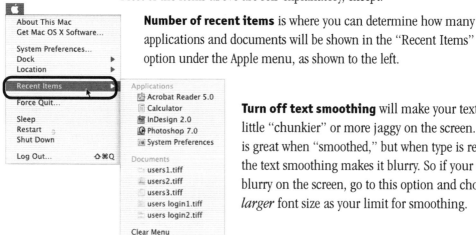

Number of recent items is where you can determine how many applications and documents will be shown in the "Recent Items" option under the Apple menu, as shown to the left.

Turn off text smoothing will make your text look a little "chunkier" or more jaggy on the screen. Large text is great when "smoothed," but when type is really small, the text smoothing makes it blurry. So if your type looks blurry on the screen, go to this option and choose a *larger* font size as your limit for smoothing.

Screen Saver

Open the Screen Saver preferences as explained on page 214.

Screen Saver

The **Screen Saver** preferences let you set up a series of images that will automatically appear on your screen. The basic function of a screen saver is to prolong the life of your monitor and to prevent static images from being "burned" into the screen. But on your iMac, an image is not going to get burned into your screen even if you left it on for a month. To prolong the life of your flat screen display, you should probably use the Energy Saver monitor option (see page 71).

Although the screen saver is not necessary to protect the *monitor,* you can use it to protect the *data* on your computer by **requiring a password:** After the screen saver automatically activates, a person would have to enter a password before the screen saver would go away (see the following page).

Tip: If you have a digital camera (and if iPhoto is installed), see page 299 for an even easier method of quickly changing your screen saver.

And even though it's not necessary, this screen saver is really quite lovely and makes for a nice look in an office with all the monitors dissolving into various photos of beaches and forests and the universe. If you are a web designer, make screen shots of your web sites and use them as the screen saver to impress your clients. If you're an illustrator or photographer, use your own images as the screen saver.

To turn off the Screen Saver so you can work again, click anywhere, tap a key, or wiggle the mouse.

Choose the "Slide Show" option and the iMac will use the photos in your Pictures folder as the Screen Saver.

Or choose "Slide Show," then click the "Configure" button to choose any other folder of images that you have on your iMac.

—continued

Screen Saver Activation

You can determine **when** you want the screen saver to automatically appear, and whether or not to require a **password.** The password that will wake the screen saver is the password for the current user.

If you are the only user, you were asked to provide a password and a hint when you first set up your Mac. If you've *forgotten* your password, type in the wrong one three times and your hint will appear.

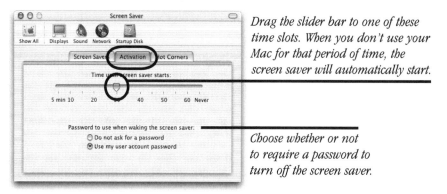

Drag the slider bar to one of these time slots. When you don't use your Mac for that period of time, the screen saver will automatically start.

Choose whether or not to require a password to turn off the screen saver.

Screen Saver Hot Corners

The **Hot Corners** pane lets you select a corner that will **turn on** your screen saver when you shove the mouse into it. For instance, in the example below there is a checkmark in the upper-right corner of the screen image. If you push your mouse into that corner (*without* pressing the mouse button down), the screen saver instantly activates without waiting for the prescribed period of time (as chosen above). If you set a hot corner with a minus sign, you can shove your mouse into that corner and the screen saver **will not activate** as long as the mouse stays in that corner, even if the time's up.

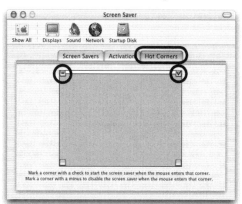

To check the corner boxes:

If a checkbox corner is empty, click once to put a check in it.

Click once again to change the check to a minus.

Click once again to clear the checkbox.

Sound

Open the Sound preferences as explained on page 214.

Sound

The **Sound** preferences let you choose an alert sound (the sound you hear when the Mac wants to yell at you about something), how loud that alert is, and how loud the general sounds on your Macintosh are, like music and video. You can also choose to put a sound volume icon in the menu bar so you don't have to open this preferences pane to change the volume.

Notice you have **two volume settings!** One is for the alert sounds, and the other is the main volume control on your computer.

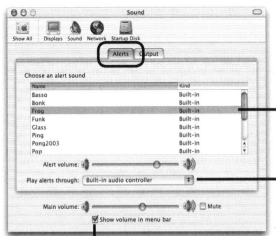

As you click each of these, you'll hear its sound. The last one you choose is the one that will be your new alert sound.

If you have installed extra speakers for your Mac, you can choose to have the alert sounds played through your speakers.

Click this box to put a Sound icon and menu in the menu bar.
It will appear on the far-right of the menu bar.
Uncheck this box to remove the icon from the menu bar.

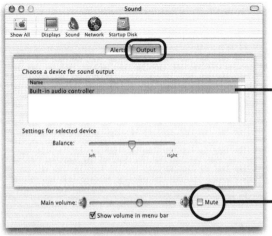

If you have installed extra speakers for your Mac, you can choose to have all of your sounds, such as from video, music CDs, etc., come out of your fancy speakers instead of the Mac's built-in audio controller.

*This will mute **all** sounds on your Mac, including alert sounds.*

When you press the Mute key on your keyboard (in the numeric keypad, above the /), it checks this button.

Software Update

Open the Software Update preferences as explained on page 214.

The **Software Update** preferences let you determine when your computer will go to the Internet and check to see if any of your **Apple software** has downloadable versions of free updates. If you have a fast and permanent connection, such as ISDN, DSL, T1, cable, etc., then it is safe to tell your Mac to automatically check for updates.

If you have to dial-up to connect to the Internet, check the "Manually" option, then when you have time to let the computer go do its updating, log on through your dial-up and click the "Update Now" button.

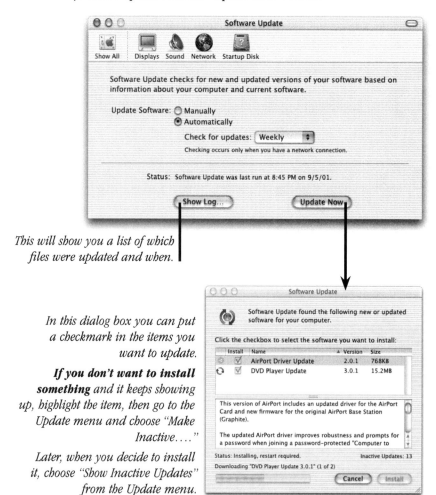

This will show you a list of which files were updated and when.

In this dialog box you can put a checkmark in the items you want to update.

If you don't want to install something *and it keeps showing up, highlight the item, then go to the Update menu and choose "Make Inactive...."*

Later, when you decide to install it, choose "Show Inactive Updates" from the Update menu.

You can also find downloadable software updates by using the option in the **Apple menu** called "Get Mac OS X Software...." This menu option will connect you to the Internet (if you're not already), open the Internet Explorer browser, and take you to a page that looks similar to the one below.

Click the name of the software to get a detailed description of it.

Click the "Download" link to download (copy) this software from Apple's server to your iMac.

Beta *software is not really ready yet, but you can try it out for free to see what it's like. It usually has bugs in it and can create problems.*

Demo *software will work for a limited time for free, or with limited features.*

Shareware *is free to download, but if you decide you like it, you should send in the small fee required.*

Freeware *you can download and use for free, with blessings to the developer.*

Users

You might think you are the only user of your iMac, but how about when the grand-kids come over? Or houseguests stay for a week and want to check their email? Or a partner sometimes asks to use your machine to type up a résumé? And of course if you have kids in the house, they want to use the iMac. It's irresistible.

In Mac OS X, you can create a number of "users" of one machine. All users get their own Home and Documents folders that no one else can access. All users can customize the Mac using any of the preferences, customize the Dock, the applications, and they even get their own Trash baskets that no one else can get into. The big advantage of this, to you, is that you can safely let anyone else use your computer, even little children or spouses, and they cannot accidentally destroy anything, read your email, or even change the time.

All users can use the applications in the Applications folder, although any customization they do will belong just to them; for instance, they can all use the same Internet Explorer browser, but all users will have their own set of bookmarks (favorites) and preferences.

When you set up your machine the first time it was turned on, the iMac created a user—you—and you are considered the "Administrator." Now you, as "Admin," can set up other users. I hope you remembered your password.

When someone else needs to use your machine, you will go to the Apple menu and "Log Out," and the other user can "log in." When he is finished, he logs out or shuts down, and you log back in to your own machine.

To create another user:

1. Open the Users preferences as explained on page 214.

2. Click the button "New User...."

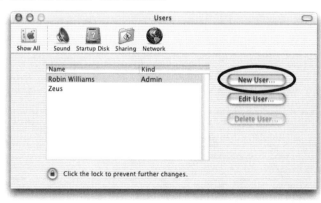

If you're in the position of having to set up iMacs to share files and users, it would be a good idea to get The Little Mac OS X Book. *That book includes every gory detail about setting up users, logging in, sharing files between users on one Mac, sharing files between a number of Macs, setting privileges for files, folders, and disks, and more (as well as sharing files with the rest of the world).*

There is a Shared folder (in the Users folder) in which you can put files for all users to read. And each user has a Public folder where she can put files to share with you, and a private Drop Box where you can put files for her.

3. In the "Identity" pane, as shown below, type the name of the user, or type a generic name that everyone else except you will have, such as "Guest."

4. A shortened version of that name will appear in the "Short Name" edit box, but you can change it to whatever you like, as long as it's no longer than eight letters, all lowercase, and no spaces or funny characters.

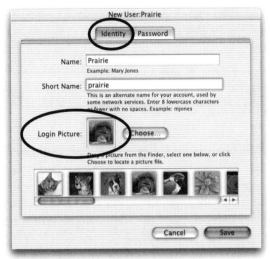

You can click one of these images, and at the log-in window, this picture will identify the other user.

Or drag any picture on your computer into the "Login Picture" space.

5. Click the "Password" tab. Enter a password (twice) and a hint to yourself in case you forget the password. You don't *need* a password. In fact, if the other user is a small child, skip the password; at the log-in screen, all the child will need to do is single-click her picture.

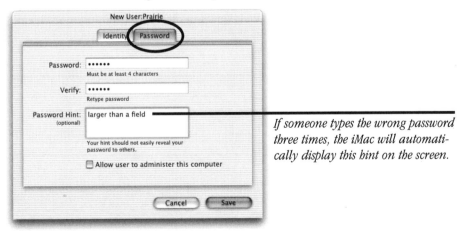

If someone types the wrong password three times, the iMac will automatically display this hint on the screen.

6. Click "Save." Go to the next page and set up the Login screen.

Login

Open the Login preferences as explained on page 214.

The Login preferences are handy even if you are the only user (see the previous two pages about other users). You can make certain applications start up automatically when you turn on your iMac, have a song play, or have documents open and ready for you to work on. You can also make some adjustments to the log-in window, which is especially useful after you have more than one user.

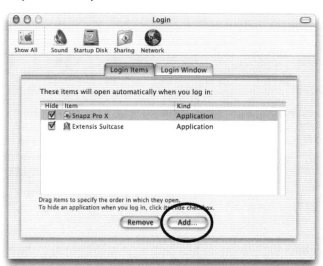

Each user can set up their own Login Items—click the "Add…" button and find the file or application.

If you are setting up a small child's login, you might want their favorite software application to open automatically.

To change the Login Items for a user, *you must log in as that user.*

Note: *Only the Administrator (you) can change this pane.*

Only one user can be chosen to "Automatically log in." This should be you, although if automatic log-in is on, other users can log in without needing your password.

If you "Display Login Window as" ***entry fields,*** *everyone must type in their names and passwords.*

If you choose to display a ***list of users,*** *the picture chosen in User Identity (previous page) will be visible. The user clicks on the picture and types a password (if she has one).*

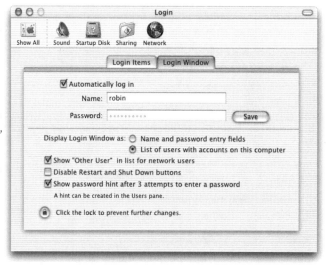

The Internet and the World Wide Web

The "i" in "iMac" stands for Internet. If you are sitting in front of an iMac, you are sitting in front of the easiest and most cost-effective solution to connecting to the Internet. You might have gotten a "cheaper" solution, such as a WebTV box that hooks up to your television, but then you wouldn't be able to do anything else with that machine *except* use the Internet—you wouldn't be able to do your personal accounting, burn CDs, or edit movies.

This section discusses what the Internet actually is, what the World Wide Web is, and the sorts of things you can do there. If you didn't set up your iMac to connect to the Internet in Chapter 1, then follow the directions in Chapter 15 to get connected; otherwise skip that chapter. In Chapter 16, learn how to *surf*.

log on: *When you use your computer to connect to a communication system such as a phone line to get to the Internet, or a network (system of connected computers) in a large office, the process is called **logging on,** and then you are **online.** Usually to log on you have to enter a password.*

*When you are done, you **log off,** and then you are **offline.***

The process of logging on and off is similar to calling up a friend and saying hello (logging on), chatting for a while (being online), then saying goodbye (logging off).

surf: *Wander around the World Wide Web.*

Note: *In the Apple menu, you have an option to "Log Out," but that refers to using the iMac itself, especially in reference to multiple users on one Mac (as explained on page 222).*

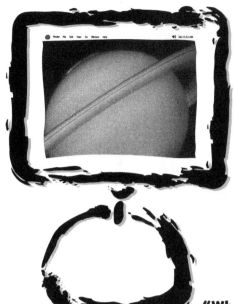

"What planet did you say this came from?"

Impressed scientist

What is the Internet?

This Internet thing has been around for over thirty years. In the late 1960s, the United States government's Advanced Research Projects Agency (ARPA) wanted to encourage scientists in academic, military, and research institutions to work together to catch up to the Soviet's advances in science. The scientists demanded computers, which were enormously expensive at the time, and ARPA realized they would need fewer computers if the machines were connected by means of a network.

So this connectivity has grown to include literally millions of computers all around the world, all connected, all capable of sending messages to other computers, sometimes through telephone lines, sometimes through other sorts of specialized lines, and sometimes with no lines (wireless). And it's this worldwide connection that's now called the Internet.

Think of the Internet as being similar to the electrical wiring in your house. In your house, the wires go into every room, out to the garage, the back porch, the laundry room, and other places. And that wiring allows you to plug in a variety of devices, such as a refrigerator, washing machine, coffee pot, microwave oven, computer, and lamps. The wiring itself doesn't do anything—it is just the system that allows everything else to work.

The Internet works (hypothetically) like your electrical wiring. It potentially connects every home and office on earth, and allows all sorts of things to "plug into it." In this chapter we'll talk about some common uses, such as email, newsgroups, and mailing lists, and the new technology that has changed the world, the **World Wide Web.** The web is not the Internet, just like a lamp in your home is not the electrical system. The web *uses* the Internet to display pages on your computer, just like a lamp uses the electrical system to brighten a room.

Email

Email stands for "electronic mail," which is a message similar to a letter that is delivered to your mailbox. The difference, of course, is that it is created electronically (in a computer) and is delivered over the Internet straight to another computer. You "open" the electronic mail and read the contents, and you can send an email response instantly. When you receive an email, the phone doesn't ring; your computer doesn't have to be turned on; you can choose to open the email or delete it unopened; you can read it anytime of the day or night; and you can answer it anytime of the day or night.

No matter where the recipient of your message lives or how long the message, it doesn't cost anything extra (anything more than the cost of your monthly Internet service). You can send hundreds of messages a month. It's much quicker and cheaper than using the post office, it's much more fun, and you don't have to get dressed.

Electronic mail can be simply text, or it can include pictures, web pages, or files such as spreadsheets or word processing documents.

When you sign up for Internet access (if you haven't already), you will usually be offered an email account; if not, ask for one. You can tell them what you want your email name to be. If you get an email account with a large "provider," such as EarthLink, you might have to get creative with your name because there are so many millions of names taken already.

See Chapter 20 for details on how to get your email and how to send others email.

Your address will look something like this:

john@something.com or **john@ratz.com**

An email address always has the @ symbol, pronounced "at," and the period is always called a "dot." (There is never a space in an email address.) (Well, except in some America Online addresses, before the @ symbol.) So the address above is pronounced:

John at Something dot Com   or   *John at Ratz dot Com*

If you chose the EarthLink option when you first set up your iMac (Chapter 1) to connect to the Internet, your email address will look something like this:

yourname@earthlink.net

Examples of email

Below are a couple of examples of email. If you use some software other than America Online or Mail (the application that comes with Mac OS X), your email window may look different from those below, but it will be similar. On the examples below, circle these common items:

To field: Where you type the email address of the recipient.

Subject field: Where you type a subject so the receiver knows what this email is about.

Message area: Where you type your message.

Attach button: Click to find and attach an extra file to send to someone, such as a photograph, newsletter, business report, sound, etc.

Send button: Click to send the message.

*A **field** is a box in which you type information. In the example of the email form, you can see fields for To, Cc, and Subject.*

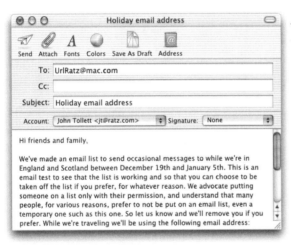

An email message created in Mail, the email application that came with your iMac.

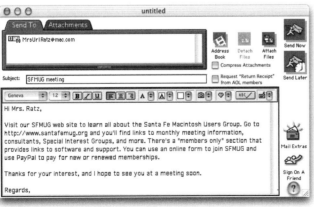

An email message created in America Online.

Newsgroups

One of the popular features of the Internet is **newsgroups,** which are groups of people around the world who have common interests, such as rugby, pet cheetahs, leukemia, pregnancy, hair salons, gay children, Robert Burns, Judaism, various eras of history, collections of all sorts, etc. There are about 30,000 different newsgroups. People in each group "post" their news or questions or comments on the Internet, which is kind of like pinning messages on a bulletin board in the community laundry room, and everyone in the group can read them and post their own answers, comments, or questions at any time. It's a wonderful resource.

Some newsgroups are intended for discussion, and some for announcements and queries. Some groups are moderated, where someone reads the postings and perhaps censures messages before posting them.

protocol: Set of rules, sometimes spelled out, sometimes expected to be understood.

Newsgroup members often bond together into a tight clique, depending on the newsgroup and its particular members. Thus the one thing you never want to do is bounce into a newsgroup and holler, "Hey! What's goin' on here?" The *protocol* is to "lurk" for a while, just hang around and listen to people, catch the tone, find out what's already been talked about, discover the different personalities, etc. When you do join in, stay on the topic.

*flame: An irate message or posting, often to new users who didn't read the FAQ. If someone sends you a nasty message, you have been **flamed.** When people start posting nasty messages back and forth to each other, that is a **flame war.***

Also, you must **always** read the "FAQ" (pronounced "fak") which is the list of Frequently Asked Questions. If you dare jump into a newsgroup and ask a dumb question that was covered in the FAQ, you are guaranteed to get pounced upon by some annoyed member.

NEVER TYPE IN ALL CAPS. Online, all caps is the equivalent of shouting, and people won't hesitate to point it out to you.

Find a newsgroup

To find a newsgroup that is centered around your particular interest, go to the web site **www.google.com** and look for the link called "Groups" (don't worry, I'll tell you how to "go" there in a few minutes, on page 252). The current site is shown below, but it changes all the time. (In addition to newsgroup searches, Google is my favorite site for doing any kind of search, as described on pages 258–259.)

To find people talking about your interest:

1. Click the "Groups" link on Google's home page.

2. In the text field on the Google Groups page (circled, below), type in what you want to talk with other people about.

3. Click the "Google Search" button.

4. You will get a list of results; click to read any of them. When you read a "posting," you will find a link to add yourself to that newsgroup.

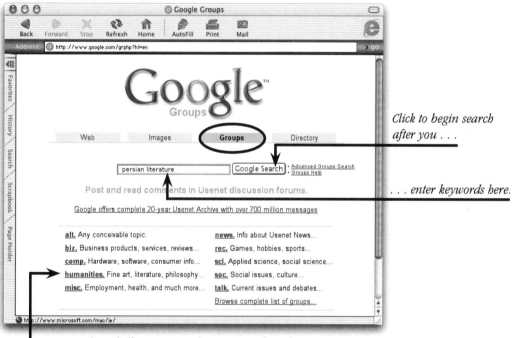

Click to begin search after you . . .

. . . enter keywords here.

You can also "drill" your way down to specific subject matter: first click one of the main topics on the bottom half of the page, then choose more specific options on subsequent pages.

Mailing lists

Using the Internet you can also join any of 90,000 mailing lists, or listservs, which are similar to newsgroups except instead of posting messages on a bulletin board, you get email delivered to your computer. Once you join a mailing list, any email message sent by anyone on the list automatically goes to everyone else on the whole list. In an active list, this can mean *lots* of mail.

Find a mailing list

To access a vast list of mailing lists, go to this address when you get connected to the Internet (don't worry, I'll tell you how to go to an address on page 252): **www.liszt.com**.

Click on any topic to get more information, and then if you like you can "subscribe," which is the process of joining the list so you get the mail. You'll usually find a button called "Join this list."

Or type in a topic in the search field (circled, to the left), click the "Search" button, and see how many mailing lists there are on your favorite topic.

The most important thing to remember!

If you join a mailing list from the web site shown above, most lists will have the nice feature of including a button in each email that you can click when you want to unsubscribe from the list.

But generally, one of your first pieces of email from a mailing list will be *instructions on how to get off the list.* **Keep these instructions!** There is only one way to get off that list and stop all the email, and if you don't have the specific directions you will end up accidentally emailing *everybody* on the list telling them you want to get off, and they will all email you back nasty messages, and you will still be on the list.

An email list is not run by a human; it is run by what's called a "robot," which is actually software, of course. But unless you send the precisely worded message to the right robot, you can't get off the list. So keep those directions in a safe place.

What is the World Wide Web?

You will definitely be using email, and you might want to join a newsgroup or a mailing list, but the place you'll find most incredibly useful, informative, and downright fun is the **World Wide Web.** The Internet itself has been around for thirty years, but it wasn't incredibly popular because you had to be a nerd to know what was there and how to access it. There were no pictures, no sounds —just ugly yellow or green text on a black background and you had to type in weird codes to get what you wanted. Then the Macintosh was invented and changed the way people used computers and changed our expectations of what a computer should do. We grew to expect graphics, sound, and attractive stuff on our monitors.

So several years ago new technology was developed that allows us to send not just text email messages and news postings, but full **pages** through the Internet that include color, sound, graphics, animation, interactivity, and video. And the individual pages have "links" that connect them to each other.

The World Wide Web is actually many millions and millions of individual pages; the more simple web pages are very much like the word processing pages you might be used to making. The information and graphics on these pages are sent around the world using the connection called the Internet.

*A **web site** is a collection of web pages. This is an example of an "entry page" to a web site. It leads to the "home page," or table of contents to a site. (Not all web sites have an entry page; often the first page will be the home page, or table of contents.) You will click a "link" to go to the next page.*

This is a typical "home page," or table of contents page of the web site. On this page you will find "links" that take you to other pages in the site.

These are other pages in the site. Each of these pages may lead to other pages, using links. The other pages do not have to be in the same site— you might go to a page in Japan or Istanbul or next door.

What's a browser?

Of course, to see web pages, first you have to be connected to the Internet. And you also need special software, called a **browser.**

A browser is just like any other software that has a special purpose. If you want to type a letter, you use the software called a word processor, right? If you want to crunch numbers, you use the software called a spreadsheet. If you want to see World Wide Web pages, you use the software called a browser.

The browser that is already installed on your iMac is **Internet Explorer.**

> **Note:** Internet Explorer is not the only browser in the world. Someday you might like to try others, especially if you prefer not to support Microsoft (when not writing this book, I keep a Microsoft-free environment). The other most common browser is Netscape Navigator. If you want to use the Netscape browser you can download it from the Netscape web site. Go to **www.netscape.com** and click the "Download" button at the top of the page. If you have never downloaded software before, you might want to have someone walk you through it.
>
> Another browser I like is OmniWeb from Omni Group; you can download it from **www.omnigroup.com**.

The same web page will often look slightly different in each of the browsers, and will look slightly different again if you use America Online.

Since Internet Explorer is already installed on your iMac, I'll use it for the examples in this book.

 This is the icon that represents the Microsoft Internet Explorer browser.

My name is Browser. I'm a netHound.

Let's look at a web page

Once your iMac is connected to the Internet (in the next chapter, if you haven't done it already), the rest is easy. Below is a typical web page, displayed on the screen using a browser.

I'll go into detail in exactly how to surf the web in Chapter 16, but for right now just take a quick look at a typical web page. One of the most important features on a web page is **links.** You click on a link with your mouse, and the browser "jumps" to another web page with different information. You know an item (either text or a graphic) is a link when you position your mouse over the item and the pointer turns into a little pointing hand, like this: 👆 . You can usually tell a *text* link even without the pointing hand because the text is usually <u>underlined</u> (but not always).

Another important feature of a web page is its **address.** Every web page has an individual address, just like a house address. The address is also called the **URL** (pronounced "you are ell"). If someone says, "Hey, what's your URL?" they mean, "What's the address to your web site?"

URL: an acronym for Uniform Resource Locator, the technical name for a World Wide Web address.

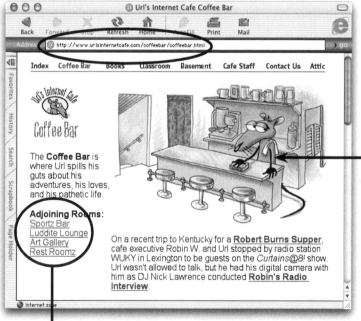

Url: This "Url" (pronounced "Earl") is a sleazy rat with his own web site. He's known world-wide, and he's resourceful, but there's nothing uniform about him.

When text is underlined, that means it's a "link."
Click on links to "jump" to other web pages.

And what's a modem, anyway?

It's kind of interesting to understand why you have to use a modem to get online. You see, the computer is **digital,** meaning it can only do things in whole chunks. It can count from 0 to 1; it can understand "on" and "off." It can understand stuff that is counted in whole numbers, like ice cubes.

The connection lines, however, are **analog.** Analog is flowing, infinite, and can be broken down into smaller and smaller pieces. Water is an analog thing.

So to get information from the digital computer to go through the analog lines, the modem takes the digital information (ice cubes) and turns it into analog information (water) to send it through the lines. On the other end, another modem takes the analog information (water) and turns it back into the exact same digital information (ice cubes) for the other computer.

How fast a modem can do this is called its "baud rate." The bigger the baud rate number, the more information (ice cubes) it can process. The chart below shows what these numbers mean.

Speed	Say it	Write it	How fast is it
2400	twenty-four hundred	2400 (2.4)	s l o - o - o - o - w
9600	ninety-six hundred	9600 (9.6)	not much better
14,400	fourteen-four	14.4	minimum for the Internet
28,800	twenty-eight eight	28.8	the Internet is do-able at 28.8
33,600	thirty-three six	33.6	pretty good
56,000	fifty-six k	56K	pretty fast*

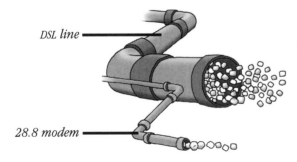

DSL line

28.8 modem

The faster the modem, the more information it can process at one time.

*You have a 56K telephone modem built into your iMac. However, the baud rate is still dependent on how "clean" your local phone lines are. Rarely will you actually get data at 56K!

*You might use something like **cable** or **DSL** to connect to the Internet. Those are very high-speed lines that go through special external modems, not your iMac's internal telephone modem.*

Connect to the Internet

15

You probably set up your iMac to connect to the Internet when you first turned it on and followed the step-by-step instructions in the Set Up Assistant. But just in case you didn't, this chapter tells you how to get an Internet Service Provider (ISP), what settings to make, and how to connect. Even if you've already set up your iMac with an Internet connection, you may change ISPs or change settings at some point.

Mini-glossary

This chapter uses some terms that may be unfamiliar if you're new to the Internet. Take a moment to scan these brief explanations.

America Online (AOL): America Online is an "online service." It is a self-contained entity that offers content and services of its own, but also provides access to the World Wide Web (Chapter 1).

broadband: Technically, "broadband" refers to telecommunications in which a wide band of frequencies are available to transmit information. Simply, it's an Internet connection that can send a lot of information in a short period of time, such as DSL or a cable modem.

cable modem: A cable modem is a device that connects your computer to the Internet through a service provided by your local cable TV company. It's similar to (but more complex than) a telephone modem. It connects to your computer with an Ethernet cable instead of a telephone cable.

dial-up: Dial-up refers to an Internet connection that requires your modem to "dial up" your ISP on a phone line. This is the slowest type of connection.

DSL: Digital Subscriber Line is a type of very fast Internet connection referred to as "broadband." A DSL connection is convenient because your connection to the Internet is always on. It is fast enough to enable continuous transmission of complex and large files (video, audio, and 3-D) over the Internet. To get DSL service you must be located within a certain distance of a telephone company's "central office" where "switching" equipment makes DSL connections possible.

EarthLink: EarthLink is a *national* ISP that can provide you with Internet access, email accounts, web site storage, and global connectivity services (Chapter 1). They offer dial-up as well as a variety of broadband services.

IMAP: IMAP (Internet Message Access Protocol) is a type of email account in which you can access your email from anywhere because it's stored on the ISP's server (page 346).

Internet: The Internet is a network of millions of computers around the world that can communicate with each other through phone lines, wireless technology, and other sorts of specialized lines (Chapter 14).

ISDN: ISDN (Integrated Services Digital Network) is a type of fast Internet connection (broadband), although not as fast as DSL.

ISP: An ISP (Internet Service Provider) is a company that you pay to provide access to the Internet. Your computer connects to the ISP's computer, which is connected to the Internet (Chapter 1).

iTools account: iTools is a suite of very cool tools and services that Apple offers free to Mac users who use Mac OS 9 or Mac OS X (Chapter 19).

log on, log off: When you connect to the Internet or a network, it's called "logging on." When you disconnect from the Internet or a network, it's called "logging off."

modem: A device that transmits information between your computer and the phone lines. The iMac has an internal modem built in.

network: When computers are connected with cables (or sometimes wirelessly) so that you can send files back and forth between computers, you have a network. The Internet is a network that connects all the computers in the world.

POP: POP (Post Office Protocol) is a type of email account in which your messages are downloaded to your computer when you check your mail (page 346).

server: A server is a special computer that "serves" content (web sites, audio, video) up to the Internet.

URL: URL (Uniform Resource Locator) is the technical name for a web address, such as http://www.ratz.com.

World Wide Web: The World Wide Web consists of the millions of web pages that contain text, graphics, and other kinds of content. (Chapters 14 and 16).

1. Connect your telephone modem

If you chose not to set up your Internet connection when you first started your iMac, you can do that now. Unless you've made special arrangements with an ISP for a broadband connection (such as DSL or cable modem), you will connect to the Internet using a telephone modem connection.

- Plug one end of the telephone cable that came with your iMac into a phone connection in the wall. If your phone has a "data port" connection you can plug into that (but make sure your phone is connected to the wall connection).

- Plug the other end of the phone cable into the modem port.

This is the modem port on the back of the iMac.

If you plan to use only America Online, double-click the AOL icon in the Installers folder that's located in the Applications folder. The AOL installer will take you step-by-step through setting up a new account or accessing an existing one—and you can skip the rest of this chapter.

If you are in a school or large business with a network (all the computers are connected and can send messages to each other, even without the Internet), you should talk to your network administrator first because you will need to know several technical details to go through the process.

If you are at home or a small business and you either have an *existing telephone modem (dial-up) service* with a **local ISP** that you want to get set up on your new iMac, or you want to start a *new account* with a local ISP, follow the steps and fill in the information in the Network preferences window on pages 244–248.

[If you chose EarthLink as your ISP]

If you want to use EarthLink (a national ISP that has worked with Apple to make it easy to set up an account on your iMac; see page 10), follow the steps below, **then skip the rest of this chapter.**

EarthLink

1. In the Applications folder, double-click the "EarthLink Connect" icon.

2. Follow the step-by-step instructions that appear on your screen. The second window you see lets you choose to set up a "New" or "Existing" account. Click "Setup New" to create a new account and connect to the Internet.

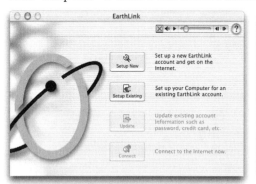

The instructions include EarthLink information about fees and services. The first thirty days are free and the set-up fee is waived. Your membership includes eight email addresses, a Personal Start Page, a subscription to BLink magazine, and ten megabytes of free web site storage. It's a good way to get connected right away while you decide if you want to keep the EarthLink account. After you've completed the on-screen forms for billing and credit card information, you see the window on the right with the necessary information filled in.

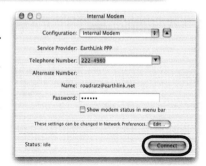

3. Click the "Connect" button.

   The Status panel of the Internal Modem window shows the status of your connection (bottom, right).

4. When the Status panel indicates that it is connected, click the "Internet Explorer" icon in the Dock to start browsing the World Wide Web. (Learn about Internet Explorer in Chapter 16.)

For more information about Internet connect and how to go directly to it, see page 250–251.

2. Open the Network preferences

If you skipped the Internet setup when you first turned on your Mac, it's okay because you can just **enter the information yourself.** You'll use the Network and Internet preferences, as explained below and on the following pages. You will also need to use these preferences when you decide to switch ISP providers, when you upgrade to a broadband connection from a dial-up, when you connect your Macs over Ethernet to share files, when things go wrong, etc.

1. To open the Network preferences:

a. From the Apple menu, choose "Preferences...," *or* click on the System Preferences icon in the Dock.

b. Single-click the "Network" icon. There is probably a Network icon in the toolbar across the top of the System Preferences pane, and there is one in the third row of preferences. They're exactly the same thing.

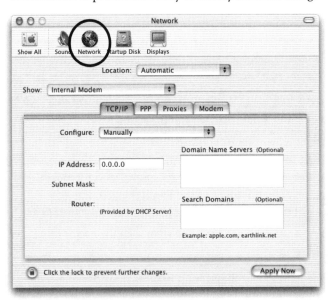

Many of these settings you don't have to worry about, so don't let all this scare you.

2a. Do you need to make a Location?

Read this only if you use more than one type of connection (dial-up, DSL, AirPort, etc.).

If you have a simple situation with your home or office computer in that you have one Internet Service Provider and you won't be switching between your dial-up connection and an AirPort connection and your office network, then **skip the following information** about making a Location. You will be just fine with the "Automatic" Location that Apple will create for you.

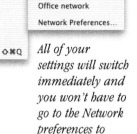

If you think you're going to add other connections, like an AirPort connection when you take your laptop to your treehouse or a network connection in your office, it's a good idea to make a new **Location.** A Location is simply a collection of your specifications (a "configuration") for that particular connection. If you have several Locations, you can just switch Locations from the Apple menu and all the rest of the changes are made for you.

Once you've made a Location, you can go to the Apple menu, choose the "Location" item, then choose the name of your Location.

All of your settings will switch immediately and you won't have to go to the Network preferences to change everything.

To make a new Location:

1. In the Network preferences, click on the "Location" pop-up menu and choose "New Location…." Type in a name and click OK.

2. From the "Show" pop-up menu, choose your method of connection. For instance, if this is a dial-up account through your telephone modem, choose "Internal Modem."

   (If you don't see your connection method in that menu, which is unlikely, choose "Active Network Ports" from the Show menu and make sure all of the ports available to your Mac are checked on. To get back to the main Network pane, from the "Show" menu, choose the port through which you want to connect, such as "Internal Modem.")

3. Follow the steps on the next pages to set up the configuration for this Location.

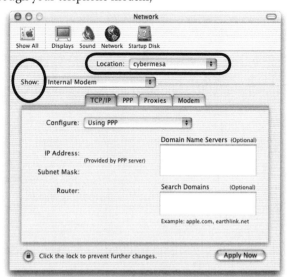

3. Enter the TCP/IP information

TCP/IP is what sends your messages out and makes sure the messages you receive are put together properly.

Below you see the TCP/IP pane for a **telephone modem connection.** Your service provider will most likely give you an "IP Address" to enter in that edit box, shown below, left.

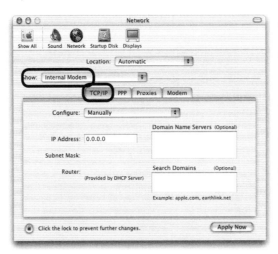

No one expects you to know whether to use a manual configuration, as shown above, or the option of "Using PPP," as shown below. Get this information, plus an IP address if necessary, from your Internet Service Provider.

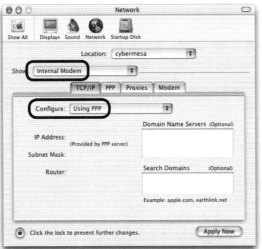

Ask your ISP if you should enter the numbers for DNS (Domain Name Servers). They will be in the same format as the IP address; that is, something like 192.254.10.93.

You'll probably use this "Using PPP" configuration.

4. Enter the PPP information

If you are setting up the configuration for a **telephone modem,** click the **PPP** tab. Enter the name of your service provider, the phone number they told you to dial, and an alternate (if they give you one) in case the first one is busy.

The account name and password, in this case, is your account name and password with your service provider. **Often it is different from your email name and password!** You can change your email password whenever you like, but your account password for your ISP is given to you by your provider and cannot be changed unless you call them up and arrange it.

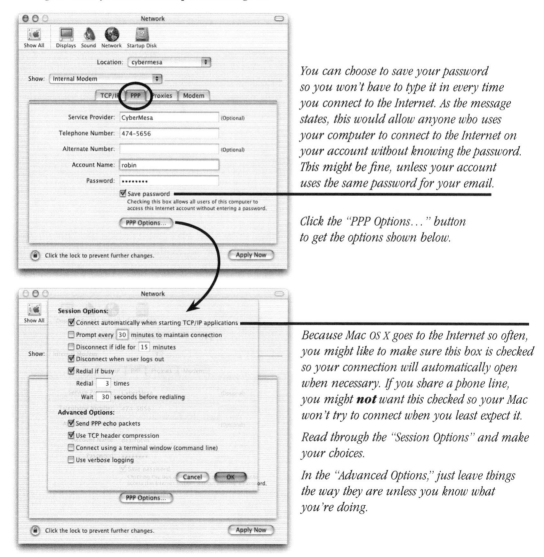

You can choose to save your password so you won't have to type it in every time you connect to the Internet. As the message states, this would allow anyone who uses your computer to connect to the Internet on your account without knowing the password. This might be fine, unless your account uses the same password for your email.

Click the "PPP Options…" button to get the options shown below.

*Because Mac OS X goes to the Internet so often, you might like to make sure this box is checked so your connection will automatically open when necessary. If you share a phone line, you might **not** want this checked so your Mac won't try to connect when you least expect it.*

Read through the "Session Options" and make your choices.

In the "Advanced Options," just leave things the way they are unless you know what you're doing.

5. Choose your Modem preferences

In the **Modem** pane, the Mac has already chosen your internal modem for you.

Sound: Annoying as the sound of the modem is, it's a comforting feeling when you hear it connecting. I usually leave it on because then I can instantly tell whether things are working properly or not.

Dialing: If you have a very old telephone that uses a pulse instead of a tone, choose "Pulse." If you actually dial a round wheel to make phone calls, you've got a pulse phone. If you can play little songs with the musical tones when you punch the buttons to make a call, choose "Tone."

Wait for dial tone before dialing: If you're outside of North America, you might want to uncheck this box because most foreign phone systems use a dial tone that your built-in modem won't recognize.

This is the modem status in the menu bar.

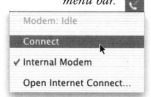

Show modem status in menu bar: Check this box to put a little phone icon on the right side of the menu bar. Choose this modem status menu to connect, change your port, or open Internet Connect (which is shown and explained on page 250–251).

Once these settings are entered, go to the next chapter and **log on** to the Internet (page 250). You'll use Internet Connect.

Proxies pane

If you are a home or small office Mac user, you won't need to bother with the **Proxies** pane. If you work in a large corporation or university, ask the network administrator if you should change any of the Proxies settings. Proxies are designed to work around a *firewall,* which is a system designed to prevent unauthorized access to or from a private network, such as a corporate *intranet* (a private, in-house network). A firewall might be implemented with software or hardware, or a combination of both.

Broadband connections: The TCP/IP pane

If you have a **broadband connection,** you need to choose "Built-in Ethernet" from the "Show" pop-up menu, circled on the next page, because your Mac connects to the special broadband modem with an Ethernet cable.

To get a broadband connection, someone will have to come to your house and set up a special modem that connects to a broadband service, such as DSL, or a cable connection from your local cable TV company. Broadband service costs extra, but the advantages of broadband outweigh the cost. With a broadband connection you never have to dial up, log on, or log off—you're connected to the Internet any time your computer is on. Just leave your browser open all day so you can click the browser icon in the Dock to instantly surf for information, check the news or get your email. A full-time connection allows you to have your email program automatically check for mail at specified intervals. You can click web links that may be in a word processor or PDF file and you'll go straight to the Internet. You can be working on a research paper, pop over to the Internet, get information, then switch back to your research paper. You gain a huge increase in speed of downloading (and uploading) pages and files from the Internet. Plus, there are some Internet technologies that don't work well enough with slow connection speeds to be useful.

The **TCP/IP** pane, shown on the next page, contains the settings necessary for you to connect through a broadband service. The settings will vary, depending on your broadband ISP.

In the **TCP/IP** pane, the necessary information has probably been filled in by the technician who brought you the modem and set up your connection. If not, you can get the information from your provider (the IP address, the Subnet mask, and the Router number) and fill them in yourself: From the "Configure" pop-up menu, choose "Manually" and fill in the blanks.

If your connection doesn't work, call your provider and go through these settings over the phone to make sure all information is correct and in the right places.

DHCP stands for Dynamic Host Configuration Protocol, which is used for assigning dynamic IP addresses.

PPPoE is Point-to-Point Protocol over Ethernet, generally used in apartment houses or office buildings sharing one DSL so online sessions can be individually monitored for billing purposes. If you use PPPoE, ask your provider what to enter in that pane.

AppleTalk is networking software that allows your Mac to connect with other kinds of networks. You'll use it when you start file sharing.

Let's Go to the Web!

This chapter walks you through your (possibly) first adventure on the World Wide Web. I have to assume you worked through the previous chapter or set up your Internet connection yourself already.

Step 1: Log on to the Internet and open a browser

How you actually *get* to the Internet (log on) to read email or surf the web depends on what kind of "connection" you have. It's one of the following three options.

If you have a broadband, or "always on" connection

A "broadband" connection provides permanent, high-speed access, sometimes called "always on." You would know if you had a broadband connection because someone had to come to your house and set it up, and you most likely have a special modem that sits outside your iMac. It might be cable, DSL, a T1 line, satellite, or an office or school network.

Internet Explorer

The Internet Explorer icon is in the Dock.

To log on: You're already there, you're already connected to the Internet, all the time. To surf the web, all you need to do is **open your browser:** single-click the Internet Explorer icon in the Dock. To get your email, just open your email program.

To log off: You don't need to. Your connection is always on, for the same price (usually). (Some providers, like QWest, have a cheesy setup where you're supposed to log on and log off, but that defeats the purpose of a broadband connection and you might want to look for another provider.)

If you have a dial-up account

You might have signed up with a local ISP (Internet Service Provider, as explained in Chapter 1), or maybe you're using EarthLink, a national ISP. Your iMac has a telephone cable from the computer's internal modem to a phone jack, and it *dials* a phone number to connect to your ISP. You have a **dial-up account.** (EarthLink is not *always* a dial-up; they also provide several broadband options.)

In either Chapter 1 or Chapter 15 you should have *set up* your iMac to connect to the Internet, where you entered the correct phone number and other settings. If you haven't done that at all, you must go through the steps in Chapter 15 before you try to log on.

Internet Connect

To log on: Open the application "Internet Connect" (go to the Applications folder, then double-click the "Internet Connect" icon). You'll see the dialog box shown on the opposite page. The phone number should already be in the dialog box; if it isn't, enter it.

Type in your password, then click "Connect." You'll hear the modem "squeal," which is annoying but good because that means it's working. When the "Status" comment says "Connected," you can **open your browser or your email program** and you're on the Internet.

To log off: You don't need to quit either your browser or your email program—you can just leave them open so they are available next time you log on. You *do* need to go to the Internet Connect window and click "Disconnect." If you don't, your phone line will stay tied up. After a while, your ISP will disconnect you from their end anyway.

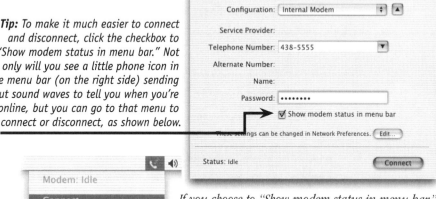

Tip: To make it much easier to connect and disconnect, click the checkbox to "Show modem status in menu bar." Not only will you see a little phone icon in the menu bar (on the right side) sending out sound waves to tell you when you're online, but you can go to that menu to connect or disconnect, as shown below.

If you choose to "Show modem status in menu bar," you can connect (log on) and disconnect (log off) the Internet without having to open the Internet Connect dialog box.

If you're using America Online

If you're already using America Online or if you want to **sign up** for an AOL account, you need to install the AOL software (if you haven't already). To install it, go to the "Installers" folder (which is inside the "Applications" folder), double-click the "Install AOL for Mac OS X" icon, then follow the directions. (See Chapter 1 for more information about America Online and how it relates to ISPs.)

America Online

To use AOL, install the software, as described to the left.

Log on: If you have a **broadband** connection as described on the previous page, all you have to do is open the AOL application and "Sign On."

If you have a **dial-up** connection, as described on the previous page, open the AOL application. It will dial its own special number and connect when you "Sign On."

Go to the web: America Online is not the web. Click the Internet button in the AOL toolbar, then choose "Go to the Web," or type a web address in the bar across the top.

Log off: You can "Sign Off" America Online without actually quitting the application, but if you have a dial-up connection you are still connected—use the log-off directions at the top of this page (you can leave AOL open).

Step 2: Enter a web address

Enter any web address you may have. If you don't know any specific web addresses, try this one:

www.UrlsInternetCafe.com

Type the address in the "location box" at the top of the window, as circled below. **Then hit the Return or Enter key.** The browser will find that page and display it. If you enter **www.UrlsInternetCafe.com,** this is the page that appears:

*Type a web address in here.
You don't have to type "http://." If you leave
that part off, the computer will fill it in for you.*

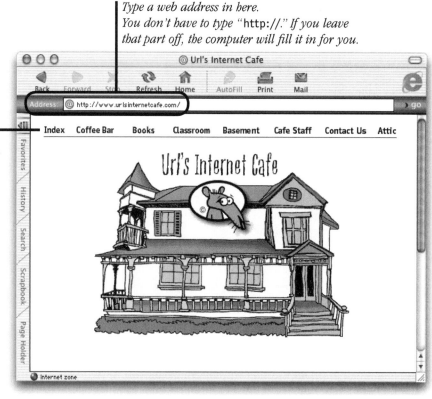

*This is called a
"navigation bar"
because it has links
that help you navigate
around a web site.
A good site has a
clear navigation bar
that always tells you
where you are within
the entire site and
lets you get to every
other section of the
site from every page
you happen to be on.
Check it out—
browse around Url's
web site and watch
the navigation bar
change as you go
from room to room.*

*See the following pages for more information
about how to get around a web page.*

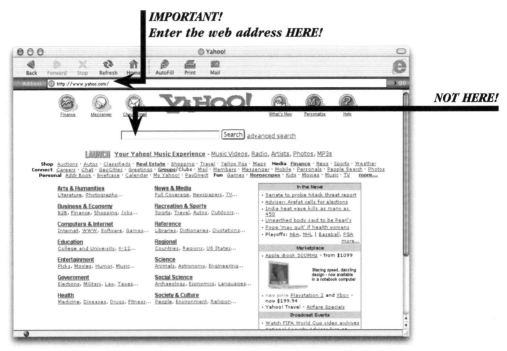

IMPORTANT!
Enter the web address HERE!

NOT HERE!

If, instead of the web page you expected, you get a page of links to lots of other web sites, you entered the address in the wrong place. Make sure you enter it in the box across the top of the window, labeled "Address," **not** in the "Search" box—as labeled "NOT HERE," above.

Tip: In a web address, it doesn't matter if you type capital letters or lowercase **in the first part,** as in www.UrlsInternetCafe.com. But after the first slash (/, which will appear automatically after the .com), **you must type exactly** any capital or lowercase letters or you may not be able to get to the page.

www.UrlsInternetCafe.com
www.urlsinternetcafe.com
WWw.URLSinternetCAFE.com ⎤ ── *Before the first /, it doesn't matter what you type in capital letters and what you don't— any combination will find the page.*

BUT:
www.UrlsInternetCafe.com/**c**lassroom
www.UrlsInternetCafe.com/**C**lassroom ⎤ ── *The actual web address to this page uses a lowercase "c" after the slash. If you type a capital "C," you will not get to the page!*

Poke around this web page

This web page is a window just like every window you've used on the iMac! You already know how to use the scroll bars, close the window, resize it, minimize it, move it around the screen, etc.

Everything you see **underlined** is a **link.** Single-click on any link to jump to another page: to get to the web page shown below, go to **www.UrlsInternetCafe.com** (you might already be viewing that page), then click the "Classroom" link at the top of the web page.

On most web pages, most **graphics** are also **links.** And on some pages, text is a link, but there is no underline. Just move your mouse around a page, and when it turns into the pointing hand, that indicates a link. Oh, there are so many places to go before you sleep.

When a page is "loading," this logo spins around.
When the logo stops, the page is fully loaded.

__Single-click__ the Back button to go back to the page you were just at.

__Press__ (hold the mouse button down) on the Back button and you will get a menu listing all the pages you have been to; drag down and select one.

Click __Forward__ to go forward __after__ you have backtracked.

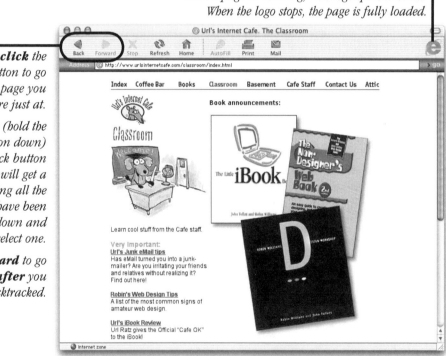

Step 3: Find a corporate web site

Just about every major corporation has a web site. You can often find them easily by typing in what seems to be a logical address. For instance, Toyota can probably be found at **www.toyota.com.** The NFL website is probably at **www.nfl.com.** Apple is probably at **www.apple.com.** Try it.

In fact, if the address ends with "**.com**," most of the time you don't even have to type **www.** or **.com** — just type the middle part. For instance, if you want to go to **www.adobe.com,** just type "**adobe**" and hit Return. Try it — try typing **cnn, nytimes, esprit, nfl, disney, mgm,** or any other favorite.

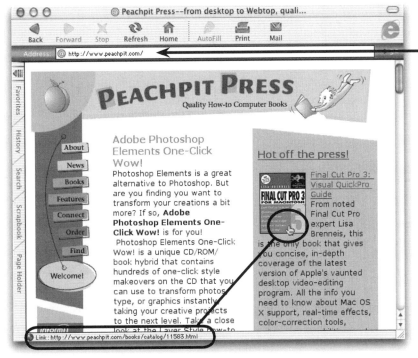

Type the corporate name in here (make sure you delete everything else first). Then hit Return or Enter. The browser will fill in "www" and ".com."

Occasionally this technique doesn't work; if not, type the "www" and the ".com."

*The trick above **only works** with **.com** addresses. That is, if the address ends with .edu, .gov, or any of the other domain "extensions," you have to type in that extension.*

Most graphics on web pages are also links. *If your pointer turns into a browser hand when you slide over a graphic (like the one above, on the book), that graphic is a link. Check the status bar at the bottom of the window to see the address of where the selected graphic link will take you.*

Do you see Peachpit's navigation bar, down the side? Of course it looks different from Url's. Navigation bars come in lots of different forms, but every decent web site will have a "nav bar."

Step 4: Set a few defaults

Before you go much further, I suggest you make a couple of changes to your browser default so all of your web pages look better. It's easy. I suggest you change the typeface default so some of the text on your web pages will be easier to read (as shown below). And you can also set the "Home" button to go to the page of your choice whenever you click on it (as shown on the opposite page).

To change the typeface defaults

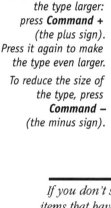

*Tip: On most web pages you can make the type larger: press **Command +** (the plus sign). Press it again to make the type even larger.*

*To reduce the size of the type, press **Command –** (the minus sign).*

1. From the "Explorer" application menu, choose "Preferences...."
2. On the left side of the dialog box, click on "Language/Fonts."
3. Change the "Proportional" font to New York. Its size is probably already "12." That's good.
4. Change the "Monospace" font to Monaco.
5. Change the "Sans serif" font to Verdana. (In fact, if you like the clarity of Verdana, which really looks great on the screen, you can set the "Proportional" font to Verdana as well.)

Go to the opposite page and change a couple of other settings.

If you don't see the items that have blue dots, click the small triangle next to "Web Browser" to disclose all the subcategories.

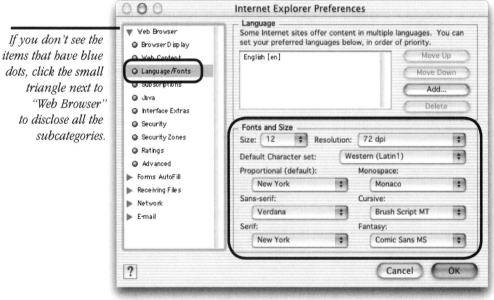

When you open any browser, it opens to the **Home** page that is chosen in the Preferences (shown below). Also, when you click the little "Home" icon in the toolbar at the top of the browser, you will go back to this chosen page. (This has nothing to do with the home page in any web site!) For instance, you might want your browser to open to your own web site every morning, or perhaps to your company site. Robin's browser opens to Google (a search tool) because she usually wants to looks for something whenever she goes online; John's browser opens to a customized Netscape page where he gets news updates fed to him, the weather for his favorite places in the world, links to his favorite Macintosh sites, etc. (You can set up a customized page for yourself as well, at **www.netscape.com.** If you use EarthLink, customize your EarthLink page.)

- To change your browser's home page to one of your choice, click "Browser Display" in the left panel of the Preferences.

  In the "Home Page" section, type the web address, including **http://**, that you want your browser to automatically open to. When you click the "Home" button, it will go to this page.

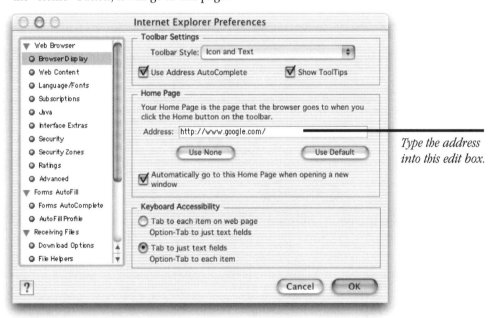

Type the address into this edit box.

- In this same panel, you can customize your toolbar across the top of your browser. In the "Toolbar Settings" section, at the top of this Preferences window, click on the "Toolbar Style" pop-up menu and choose "Text Only" or "Icon Only." This will give you more room on the web page.

Step 5: Search for something on the web

There are several billion individual web pages on the Internet. If you don't already know the exact address of the page you want, you need to use a **search tool** (often called a search engine) to find it. Learning how to *really* search the Internet is a valuable skill that takes some time to learn, but everyone needs to know at least a little about how to search.

You don't have to buy the search tools, nor do you have to install them. They are just there on the web. They are "just" web pages.

You can also use the Sherlock feature on your iMac, right at your Desktop, to search for a variety of information on the Internet. Click the Sherlock icon in the Dock; see Chapter 24.

The most important thing to realize about search tools is that when you type in something you want to find, such as a particular dog breed, the search tool does not go instantly all over the World Wide Web at that moment and try to find something for you. No, it looks into its own *database,* or collection, of information to find something. Each search tool chooses what to put into its database, based on varying criteria. Thus you can do the same search with three different search tools and you will get three different lists of results (responses) to your request.

Try a quick search. **Google** is my favorite search tool on the web. Type this into the Location box in your browser: **google**. Hit Return. You'll see a page like this:

Type "google" in here.

Type your search query in here.

Tip: *Click the "Images" tab and you will get pictures of whatever it is you're searching for, like "bull snake." Try it!*

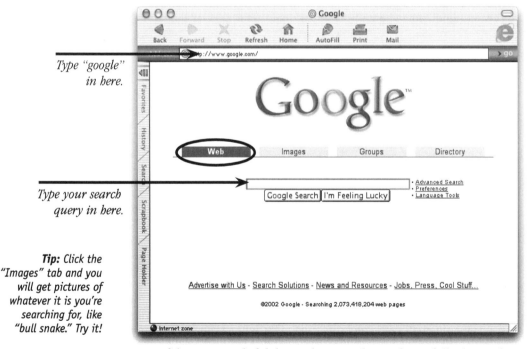

One of the most wonderful things about Google is its beautifully designed page. It's a welcome relief from every other search page.

How to use Google

Google's main page is a "word search" engine that uses automatic software called "spiders" or "robots." If you are looking for a word or phrase that might not have an entire web site devoted to it, Google is a good place to search.

In the *search query box* (shown on the opposite page), type the word or phrase you want to find, then click the "Google Search" button. If you type a phrase or first and last name, put quotation marks before and after the phrase or name, like so:

"Santa Fe Railroad"   "George Washington"   "French sheepdogs"

If you *don't* put quotation marks around something like "Santa Fe Railroad," Google will find every page with the word "Santa" on it, *plus* every page with the word "Fe," *plus* every page with the word "railroad." The quotation marks limit the results so you are more likely to find something useful.

All search engines have tips for narrowing the search. Look for the "Tips" or "Help" button and follow the guidelines. One technique you can use in most search engines goes by the scary name of "Boolean operators." All that means is you can use AND, OR, and NOT (some search tools use + instead of AND and − instead of NOT). Most search tools ignore commas, hyphens, capitalizations, and common words like **it, the,** or **of.**

For instance, let's say I'm looking for people who breed Briards.

This is my Briard, Reilly. He's very large. He adores me.

If I enter **briard breeder** I will get every page with the word "briard" on it, plus every page with the word "breeder" on it.

If I enter **"briard breeder"** with quotation marks I will only get pages that have the words "briard" and "breeder" directly next to each other.

But if I enter **briard AND breeder** I will get pages that have both the word "briard" and the word "breeder," even if they are not next to each other.

And if I enter **briard NOT breeder** I will get pages that have the word "briard" but *not* the word "breeder."

What would the following search find you?

briard AND breeder "sacramento california"

See the results of a search for **briard AND breeder** on the following page.

Below you see the results of a search for **briard AND breeder**.

Single-click on any of these results to go to a web page.

*If that web page doesn't satisfy you, use the **Back** button to come back to this results page and try another link.*

How to use a directory to search for information

Many search tools provide what is called a "directory." On the Google page, click the "Directory" tab, as circled below. You see on the Google page a number of categories. These categories have been put together by **humans** who have decided which web sites belong in the directory and under which category. If you are looking for whole web sites about a particular topic, a directory is a good tool to use.

One way to use a directory is to "drill down" through the categories, as shown below; as you click on links, the topics narrow down to exactly what you want.

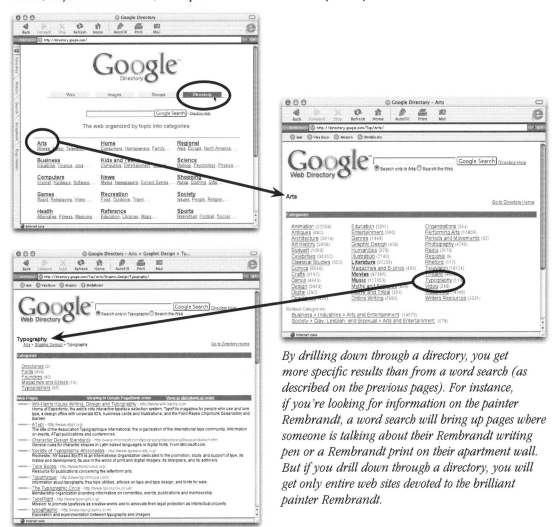

By drilling down through a directory, you get more specific results than from a word search (as described on the previous pages). For instance, if you're looking for information on the painter Rembrandt, a word search will bring up pages where someone is talking about their Rembrandt writing pen or a Rembrandt print on their apartment wall. But if you drill down through a directory, you will get only entire web sites devoted to the brilliant painter Rembrandt.

Here you see more specific subsections about typography, as well as a number of web sites devoted to type.

Other search tools to use

These are the addresses for some of the most popular search tools. The description that follows each address does not mean that is the only thing the tool does—it just indicates one of its strengths. Go to each one and play around. You'll find one or two you like best.

If you seriously need to learn to search, get the book Search Engines for the World Wide Web: Visual QuickStart Guide, *by Alfred and Emily Glossbrenner. Published by Peachpit Press.*

Google	**www.google.com** (see the previous pages)
About.Com	**www.about.com** (fabulous resource—hundreds of human guides search the web for you and compile selected results here; try this!)
Yahoo	**www.yahoo.com** (best used as directory to "drill" down to find whole web sites)
AltaVista	**www.altavista.com** (word search; can search for images, video, news; has a directory as well)
HotBot	**hotbot.lycos.com** (can find sites with specific technology, such as sites that use JavaScript, ActiveX, or Shockwave; can find images, video, MP3s; very popular general search engine as well)
Ask Jeeves	**www.ask.com** (type in a question, such as "What's the difference between apple juice and apple cider?")
Electric Library	**www.elibrary.com** (30 days free access, then a fee; search magazines, maps, pictures, over 2,000 books, more than 150 newspapers and newswires, radio, and TV transcripts)
Northern Light	**www.northernlight.com** (over 7,000 sources, including newswires, newspapers, business and trade magazines, academic and scientific journals, analyst reports, and much more. Just incredible.)
Search.Com	**www.search.com** (search for people, software, travel, and of course much, much more)
software	**www.shareware.com** (shareware and freeware)
	www.download.com (commercial software)
	www. versiontracker.com (links to software updates)

shareware: Software that someone has created and that you can download (copy) right off the web. If you decide to keep it, you send the author a small fee, as explained in the Read Me file that will be with the shareware.

freeware: Software that someone has created that you can copy and use for absolutely free.

Step 6: Send email from a web page

Most web sites have email links (circled, below). You click the link, an email form pops up, you type the subject and your message, and click the "Send" button. The form is automatically return-addressed from you. Try it. (Just don't be upset if you don't get a response when you send someone you don't know unsolicited email.)

If you can't find any other web site with an email address, feel free to go to **UrlsInternetCafe.com,** click "Contact Us" in the navigation bar, and send Url an email. Send *someone* an email message!

Note: *When you click an email link on a web page, it will open the Mail program. If you use a different email program, you can tell your iMac to open these mail links in the program you prefer: Open the System Preferences and click the Internet icon; click the "Email" tab and make your "Default Email Reader" choice.*

This is an email link. Even if it didn't say so, you can always tell because email addresses always include the @ symbol. Also check the status bar—notice it doesn't display a web address, but the code "mailto." That is another clue that if you click this link, you'll get an email form.

The "To" field is already filled in for you. Just type your message in the message area and click "Send." The email will be marked "From" your email address.

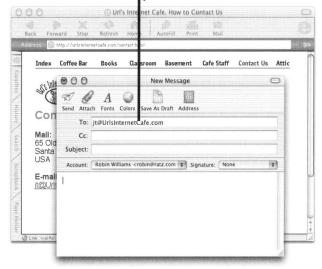

Step 7a: Log off the Internet (for AOL, see below)

If you have a **broadband** connection (as explained in the beginning of this chapter), you do not have to log off. Ever. You can leave your browser and your email applications open all day long and just pop over to do what you need to do at anytime. It's great. If you're using America Online, you do need to "Sign Off"; if you don't, AOL will sign out for you after a certain amount of time.

If you have a telephone **dial-up** connection, you do need to *log off,* or hang up. Quitting the browser *does not* close the connection; if you don't close it, it's the same as having your phone off the hook. (You can leave your browser open, ready and available for the next time you log on.)

To disconnect your dial-up connection (log off):

- If the Internet Connect window is open (shown below, labeled "Internal Modem" at the moment because it's connected to a dial-up; if you're connected to an AirPort, this window is labeled "AirPort"), click the "Disconnect" button.

- If the "Internal Modem" window is not open: Click once on the "Internet Connect" icon in the Dock to open it, then click the "Disconnect" button.
- If you clicked the button earlier to "Show modem status in menu bar" (as explained on page 251), you can just go to the menu and choose "Disconnect."

Step 7b: Log off from AOL

If AOL is acting as your ISP (you call a phone number AOL gave you), when you "Sign Off" in AOL, the connection is discontinued (you have logged off), but the AOL program is still open. When you "Quit" AOL, the program will quit *and* you will disconnect.

But if you log on through a different dial-up ISP to use AOL, *when you quit AOL you are still connected to the Internet,* so you must disconnect as shown above.

Your iMac Is Your Digital Hub

The iMac is designed to be the center (the hub) of your digital lifestyle. If you think you don't have a digital lifestyle, think again. You have an iMac, and that means you can be productive and work digitally with programs like AppleWorks, Mail, Address Book, and Quicken. Even better, you can have fun and be creative with art, photography, music, and video. Your iMac provides you with all the software you need to get started with a digital lifestyle that's exciting and inspiring.

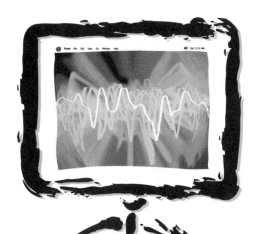

"I love iTunes. I've loved it from the moment I first saw it. I even remember precisely when that moment was."

Bob LeVitus, author

iPhoto: Organize and Share Your Digital Photos

iPhoto is an application made exclusively for Mac OS X. It makes managing your digital photo collections both easy and fun. You can effortlessly import photos straight from most digital cameras, as well as from other sources, such as a digital card reader, CD, Zip disk, or from a location on your iMac's hard disk. Use iPhoto to organize and edit your photos, then share them with friends, relatives, or business associates in a number of different ways.

Even if you don't own a digital camera, you can send your exposed film to companies that offers digital film services. These companies can process your film and put your photos on a CD or post them on the web for you to download. Visit **www.Ofoto.com** or **www.Shutterfly.com** to see what services are available.

For a list of compatible cameras, printers, and digital card readers, see the iPhoto web site **(www.apple.com/iphoto).** If your digital device is not listed as compatible, there is still a chance that it may work—try it before you buy a new one.

And if you want still more details on iPhoto, pick up Adam Engst's great book, *iPhoto for Mac OS X: Visual QuickStart Guide.*

First, install iPhoto

If iPhoto is not already installed on your iMac (look in the Applications folder for the "iPhoto" icon), you need to get the iPhoto CD that came with your iMac and install it.

1. Open the iMac CD tray (press the Media Eject key in the upper-right corner of the keyboard) and insert the iPhoto CD, label-side up. Press the Media Eject key again to close the tray.

iPhoto

2. Double-click the "iPhoto" CD icon that appears on your Desktop. This will open the CD window (shown below).

3. Double-click the "iPhoto" folder.

It's always a good idea to read the "Read Me" file.

4. The window now has a "package" named "iPhoto.mpkg." Double-click the package icon.

Follow the instructions in the next series of panels to guide you step-by-step through the rest of the installation.

Note: *The version of iPhoto we used in this chapter is 1.1.1. If you have an earlier version, you can download the update (if you want) from www.apple.com/iphoto.*

5. **Authorization:** You must enter the Administrator name and password that you created for your "user account" when you set up your iMac.

Single-click the small padlock to open the "Authenticate" panel.

6. **Authenticate:** Enter your Administrator name and password, then click OK.

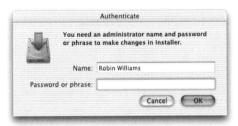

7. **Important information:** This is the licensing information. Read it (if you can get through it), then click "Continue." A "sheet" will drop down on top of the panel—click the "Agree" button to continue installation. (If you "Disagree" with the license agreement, the installation will quit.)

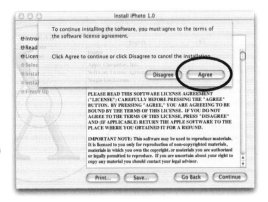

8. **Select a Destination:** Single-click on a disk icon to select a destination disk for the installation of iPhoto. Disks that you cannot install on, such as the iPhoto CD, shown in this example, are grayed out. Click "Continue."

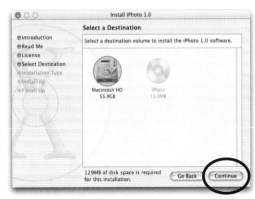

9. **Easy Install:** Click the "Install" button. A "progress bar" will indicate the progress of the "Installation" and the "Finish Up" procedures.

When the installation of iPhoto is finished, a Desktop message tells you that "Your software has been successfully installed." You can eject the CD (press the Media Eject key) and start using iPhoto.

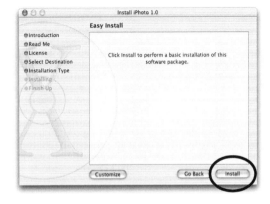

iPhoto

Open iPhoto

Go to the Applications folder (click on the Applications icon in the Toolbar of any open Finder window), then double-click the "iPhoto" icon. The iPhoto window (below) opens, although yours will be empty if this is the first time you've used it.

Click here to see your entire collection of photos.

Albums.

Album pane.

Resize button (drag).

Viewing area.

File Information.

Play Slide Show.

Add new Album.

File information: (click to show Info, click again to show Comments pane).

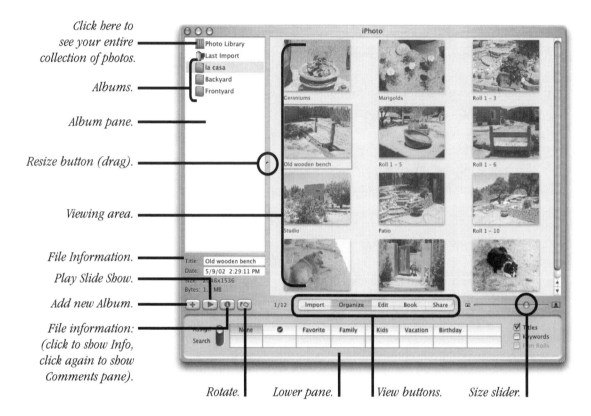

Rotate.   *Lower pane.*   *View buttons.*   *Size slider.*

The iPhoto main window

Before you can use iPhoto's various features, you first have to **import** the photos into the Photo Library, as explained on the following pages and shown in the example above. When you import photos, iPhoto considers each import a "Film Roll." That's why iPhoto automatically names each photo with a "Roll" number and an "image" number. A photo named "Roll 1 – 6" indicates that in "Film Roll" number one, this photo is the sixth image. You can **rename** any photo with a name that makes more sense, as shown in the example above: Just click on the photo *name* to highlight it, then type in the new name.

The **Library** stores all the photos you ever import. Create separate **Albums** (pages 276–277) to store customized selections from the Library.

Import your photos to iPhoto

When a digital camera or a memory card reader is connected to the computer (with a USB cable) and recognized by iPhoto, the "Import" view button is automatically selected. The next few pages explain how to import your photos directly from a camera, a digital card reader, a CD, or a location on your hard disk.

Import photos from a digital camera

You can transfer photos directly into iPhoto if your camera has a USB port and if it is compatible with iPhoto (see page 267 regarding checking for compatibility).

1. Turn your camera off.

2. Connect the camera's AC power adapter to the camera, then plug the adapter into a power outlet.

3. Use the USB cable that came with the camera to connect the camera to your iMac's USB port. **Turn on your camera.** These things happen:

   An icon representing the digital card in your camera (shown to the right) appears on the Desktop, indicating it has been *mounted*.

   The iMac automatically recognizes the camera and opens iPhoto.

   iPhoto opens with the Import pane showing at the bottom of the main window (shown below).

   A camera icon and the name of the attached camera appears on the left side of the Import pane.

VIKINGFLASH

When you connect a digital camera to your iMac, an icon appears on your Desktop named for the brand of memory card that's in the camera.

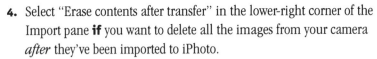

4. Select "Erase contents after transfer" in the lower-right corner of the Import pane **if** you want to delete all the images from your camera *after* they've been imported to iPhoto.

5. Click the "Import" button on the right side of the Import pane.

6. After the photos have been imported, drag the digital card icon on the Desktop to the Trash to *unmount it.* **If you do not unmount the card before disconnecting the camera, you'll get an error message warning that you could possibly damage any images left on the memory card.**

7. Turn the camera off and disconnect it from your computer.

The imported photos are placed in the Photo Library, as shown on the opposite page.

Import photos from a digital card reader

You can import your photos from a **digital memory card reader,** even if your digital camera is not directly supported by iPhoto.

1. Make sure the card reader is connected to your iMac using the proper cable.

2. Take the digital memory card (CompactFlash, SmartMedia, or Memory Stick, etc.) out of your camera and insert it into the card reader.

   The card's icon appears on your Desktop, as shown to the left, indicating it has *mounted.*

3. iPhoto automatically recognizes the digital card and opens; if iPhoto is already open, it switches to "Import" view. The card reader, instead of a camera, is identified on the left side of the "Import" panel, shown below.

4. If you want to erase the contents of your digital card after importing the photos, select "Erase contents after transfer" in the "Import" pane.

5. Click the "Import" button in the bottom-right. The lower pane of the iPhoto window shows the import in progress, plus a thumbnail (small version) of the current image being copied to iPhoto.

This icon appears on your Desktop, named for the card that's in the reader.

The most common types of memory cards are CompactFlash™ SmartMedia™ and Memory Stick™. Some card readers can read only one type of memory card, while others can read two or more types of cards.

6. *Unmount* the digital card when all is done: drag its icon from the Desktop to the Trash.
   Or Control-click on the digital card icon and choose "Eject" from the contextual menu that pops up.

The imported photos are placed in the Photo Library. (They are also temporarily available through the "Last Import" icon in the Album pane, explained on page 274, until the next import session when another batch of photos becomes the "last" import.)

Import photos from a CD or from a location on your hard disk

1. Press the Media Eject key on the upper-right corner of your keyboard to open the CD tray.

2. Place the CD that contains photos you want to import into the tray, and press the Media Eject key to close the CD tray.

3. Open iPhoto if it is not already open.

4. From the File menu, select "Import..." to open the "Import Photos" window, shown below. Find the CD you inserted, or choose a location somewhere on your hard disk where photos are stored.

5. Select an entire folder of photos, an individual photo, or multiple photos, then click the "Open" button.

The selected photos are placed in iPhoto's Photo Library. They also appear in the "Last Import Roll" shown in the Album pane, as shown on page 270.

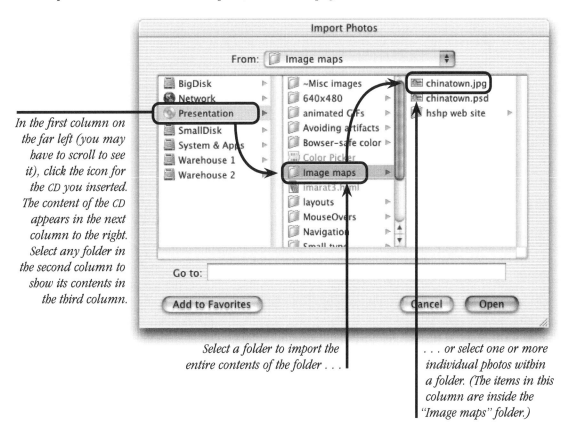

In the first column on the far left (you may have to scroll to see it), click the icon for the CD you inserted. The content of the CD appears in the next column to the right. Select any folder in the second column to show its contents in the third column.

Select a folder to import the entire contents of the folder . . .

. . . or select one or more individual photos within a folder. (The items in this column are inside the "Image maps" folder.)

Viewing your photos

Once you've imported photos to iPhoto, there are several ways to view them within the main viewing area.

- Single-click the **Photo Library** icon (upper-left) to view all photos that have been imported into iPhoto during your various Import sessions.

- Single-click the **Last Import** icon in the Album pane (the white pane on the left) to show only the photos from the most recent Import session.

- Single-click an **Album** icon in the Album pane (the white pane on the left) to show only photos that have been placed in that specific Album (how to create an Album is explained on page 276).

- From the Edit menu, choose "Arrange Photos."
  By Film Roll arranges photos into the groups in which they were originally imported.
  By Date arranges photos by the date they were taken in the camera, **if** you set the date in your camera *before* you took pictures.

The View buttons

Each **View button** beneath the viewing area gives you different options and tools to work with, as displayed in the lower pane. Each of these views is explained in detail on the following pages.

Import view: Supplies information and options for importing photos.

Organize view: Provides tools for organizing and searching.

Edit view: Displays a larger version of the selected photo in the upper viewing area, and the lower pane switches to editing tools.

Book view: Provides tools for creating a hard-bound book.

Share view: Displays various tools that let you share your photos with friends, relatives, and co-workers in a variety of ways.

File information and comments

iPhoto gives you file information about photos, such as date created, size in pixels (dimensions) and size in kilobytes (how much space it takes up on your hard disk). Titles and comments you type in will be used in albums, books, or web pages created by iPhoto.

1. Single-click on a photo to select it.

2. Click the "Information" button once to show the File Information.

3. Click the "Information" button again to show the Comments pane. Type any comments you want in the text field.

4. Click the "Information button" once more to hide both the File Information and Comments pane.

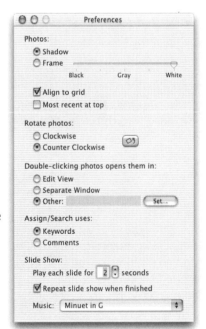

Title.

File Information.

Comments pane.

Information button.

iPhoto Preferences

You can set some basic characteristics that affect how you view your photos. Go to the iPhoto menu and choose "Preferences...."

- **Shadow:** Show photos in the viewing area with a drop shadow effect against a white background.

- **Frame:** Adjust the slider to set the background between black and white.

- **Align to grid:** Keep all photos neatly aligned within an underlying invisible grid.

- **Most recent at top:** Affect the order in which photos are displayed in the viewing area.

- **Rotate photos:** Choose which direction photos will rotate in when you use the Rotate tool.

- **Double-clicking photos opens them in:** Choose "Separate Window" if you want to have access to a customizable Edit toolbar. You can also choose to have them automatically open in something like Photoshop.

- **Assign/Search uses:** What you choose here changes the Assign/Search area in the Organize pane (pages 280–281).

- **Slide Show:** Set the Slide Show behaviors, including the music soundtrack.

Create an Album and add photos to it

Create **Albums** to help organize your photos, make them easier to find, and sort them in any order you wish.

You can put the same photo in any number of Albums because iPhoto actually just "points" to the original photo stored in the Library, which means you don't end up with sixteen copies of the same photo taking up space on your hard disk.

1. **To create a new Album,** click the "Add" button in the lower-left corner of the iPhoto window, circled below.

2. In the "New Album" dialog box that appears, enter a name for the Album and click OK. Your new Album appears in the Album panel of iPhoto's main window.

3. **To add photos to the Album,** drag images from the viewing area and drop them on the Album icon.

*The Photo Library is currently selected, which displays photos from **all** Import sessions. Each "Roll" in the Viewing area represents a separate Import session from a digital camera.*

After you click the "Add" button (below) and name an Album, the new Album appears here.

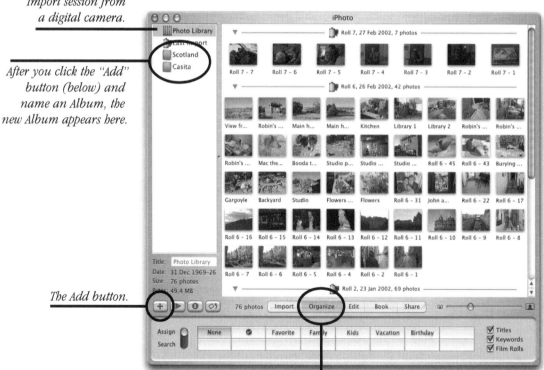

The Add button.

Use the "Organize" view to arrange, name, organize, or delete photos, as well as assign keywords and conduct searches for photos. See the following pages for details.

To rename an existing Album:

Double-click the Album name and type a new name.

To delete photos from an Album or from the Photo Library:

If you delete a photo from an Album, this will *not* delete it from the Photo Library (remember, the image in the Album "points" to the stored image in the Library).

But if you delete a photo from the Photo Library, it *will* disappear from every Album that contained it.

1. Select the Photo Library icon, **or** select an Album from which you want to delete one or more photos.

2. Click the "Organize" view button if it's not already selected.

3. Select one or more photos to delete.

4. Press the Delete key.

To duplicate an Album:

You can duplicate an entire Album. In the duplicate, you can rearrange the photos, delete some, add others, and it won't affect the original Album.

1. Single-click an Album in the Album pane to select it.

2. From the File menu, choose "Duplicate," **or** press Command D.

3. Double-click the new Album icon in the pane, then type a new name over the default name assigned by iPhoto.

The Organize view

After you've imported all the photos from the camera to iPhoto, you can begin organizing and arranging them. The Organize view gives you tools for organizing and makes searching for photos fast and easy.

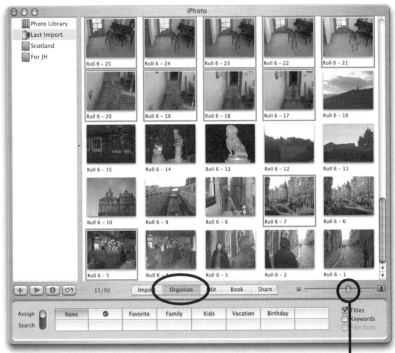

Double-click a thumbnail to display a large version of that photo in the Viewing area. This automatically switches iPhoto to the Edit view.

To return to the Organize view, click the Organize button.

In either Edit or Organize view, you can enlarge or reduce the photos or thumbnails: slide the Size button left or right.

Organize into Albums

At this point, for the sake of organization, you may choose to place selected images into an existing Album or create a new Album, as explained on the previous pages. (Briefly, to create a new Album click the "Add" button [the plus sign], name the new Album, then drag photos into it.)

Delete unwanted photos

If you delete a photo from an Album, this will *not* delete it from the Photo Library. **But** if you delete a photo from the Photo Library, it *will* disappear from every Album that contained it, as explained on the previous page.

To delete any images you don't want to keep: Single-click an image (or Command-click to select multiple images), then press the Delete key.

Arrange the order of the photos

In Slide Show, Book, and HomePage (web site) projects, your photos will appear in the same order that they appear in the Album's viewing pane. There are a couple of ways to arrange photos in an Album or in the Library.

- To change the order of photos in an Album (this doesn't work in the Library), drag one or more images to the location desired. As you drag, a black vertical bar indicates where the photos will be placed when you release the mouse button.

- In the Library, you can arrange the photos by the date they were taken (if you set your camera's date before you took the pictures) or by import session ("Film Roll"): From the Edit menu, choose "Arrange Photos," then from that submenu, choose "by Film Roll" or "by Date."

Add titles and comments

The titles and comments that you insert in the Information pane are used by the Book and HomePage features to add headlines and captions. When you export photos, they will have this title instead of something like DSCN0715.jpg.

1. Single-click a thumbnail photo to select it.

2. Click the "Info" button (the "**i**" beneath the Album pane) to show that photo's Info area.

3. Click in the "Title" text field, then press Command A to select any existing text, that might be in that field, such as "Roll 1-6."

4. Type a new title into the "Title" text field.

5. Click the "Info" button again to show the "Comments" field. Click inside that field, then type a caption for the photo.

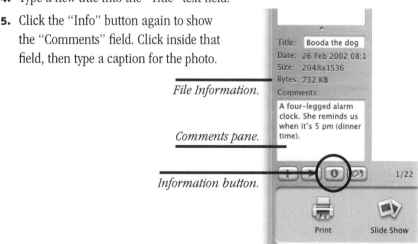

File Information.

Comments pane.

Information button.

Keywords and searching

The Organize view makes searching for photos fast and easy, especially if you previously assigned keywords to your photos. The toggle button on the left side of the Organize pane enables you to assign keywords *or* search for photos.

The checkmark (see below).

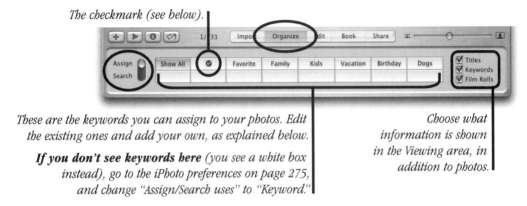

These are the keywords you can assign to your photos. Edit the existing ones and add your own, as explained below.

If you don't see keywords here *(you see a white box instead), go to the iPhoto preferences on page 275, and change "Assign/Search uses" to "Keyword."*

Choose what information is shown in the Viewing area, in addition to photos.

Assign keywords to photos

By assigning keywords to photos, you make it possible to search for photos based on those words. If you take the time now to assign keywords, you'll save a lot of time later when you're trying to find a certain photo.

1. In the "Organize" view, move the toggle button to "Assign."

2. Select a photo or an Album. To select multiple photos, drag across a group of them, *or* hold down the Command key and click on individual photos.

3. Single-click one of the preset keywords in the Organize pane ("Family," for instance). That keyword is now attached to the selected photos.

To assign multiple keywords to a photo, select the photo again and choose another keyword.

Edit keywords

You can edit the keywords while you are in the Organize view. From the Edit menu at the top of your screen, choose "Edit Keywords." This makes the keyword buttons in the lower pane become editable fields so you can replace existing keywords with new ones or add keywords to empty boxes. Just click in a box and type.

The checkmark

The checkmark is sort of a temporary keyword, useful for marking photos for which you haven't decided on a keyword or category. You can search for all photos with a checkmark.

Search for photos

1. In the Organize view, move the toggle button to "Search."
2. Click on the Album you want to search, or click "Photo Library" to search your entire collection.
2. Single-click one of the keyword buttons. The photos that match the selected keyword are shown in the viewing area.

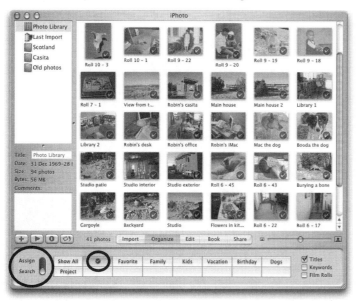

This search result shows all photos that had the checkmark assigned to them. Notice each found photo has a checkmark in its lower-right corner.

If in the Preferences (as shown on page 275) you choose to Search by "Comments," the Search bar turns into this white box. Type in a word that you might have used in either Titles or Comments; as you type, only those photos that match your text appear in the viewing area. Click on an Album icon to display the photos again.

The Edit view

In the Edit view you can perform basic image-editing operations which include adjusting brightness and contrast, cropping, rotating, red-eye reduction, and converting an image from color to black-and-white. The following pages explain how to use each of the tools available.

Edit tools

View a photo for editing

Select a photo, then click the "Edit" view button (beneath the viewing area). Two things happen:

- The selected photo fills the entire viewing area.
- The lower pane displays iPhoto's editing tools.

To choose the previous or next photo in the collection without leaving Edit view, click the "Previous" or "Next" buttons in the bottom-right.

Undo editing changes

As you make the changes described on the following pages, you can use the Undo command (Command Z, or "Undo" from the Edit menu) to undo your steps, one at a time.

Once you quit iPhoto, you cannot use Command Z to undo any changes you made last time you used iPhoto. **But you can** go to the File menu and choose "Revert to Original" and the original photo will magically reappear.

Create a duplicate photo before you do anything drastic

When you drag a photo from the Library into an Album, iPhoto doesn't make a separate *copy* of that photo—it puts a "link" from the Album to the original photo that's still stored in the Library. This prevents your hard disk from getting full of multiple copies of the same photo.

So when you edit a photo, you not only affect its appearance in the Photo Library *but in all other Albums in which that photo appears.* To avoid changing the photo's appearance in every instance, create a *duplicate* of the photo and edit the duplicate.

1. Select a photo in the Photo Library or in an Album. If you duplicate a photo in an Album, it will appear in *both* the Album and the Library; any changes you make will apply to *both duplicates* (since they're actually the same photo).

2. From the File menu, choose "Duplicate," **or** press Command D.

3. Rename the duplicate photo: select it, then enter a new name in the Title field of the Information section (click the "Info" button beneath the Album pane to show the Title field, as shown below).

4. Edit the duplicate photo.

Warning:
It's possible to duplicate an entire Album (select the Album name, then press Command D), but any editing changes you make to photos in the duplicate Album will apply to the original photos!

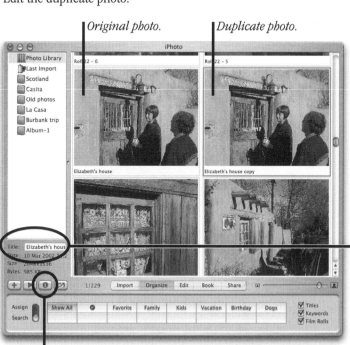

Original photo. *Duplicate photo.*

While the duplicate is selected, type in a new title.

Info button.

Cropping this photo brings more attention to Booda's warm eyes.

Crop an image

The Crop tool lets you select the most important part of a picture and delete the rest of it. Thoughtful cropping makes your photos stronger and more visually interesting.

1. Select a photo.

2. Click the "Edit" view button.

3. Select an option (explained below) from the Constrain pop-up menu, which is on the left side of the Edit pane.

   The Constrain menu gives you common proportion ratios to apply to the Crop tool. Choose "None" if you want no restraints on your cropping. Choose one of the other options to limit your cropping area to a specific ratio. For instance, if you plan to use the photo in an iPhoto book, select the "4 x 3 (Book, DVD)" option.

4. Position the pointer at one corner of the desired cropping area, then press-and-drag diagonally to select a cropping area.

   To move the crop selection, *press* inside the rectangular cropping area and *drag*.

   To resize the crop selection, position the tip of the pointer in any corner of the cropping selection; when the pointer changes to a "pointing finger," press-and-drag the selection to the desired size.

5. Single-click the "Crop" button.

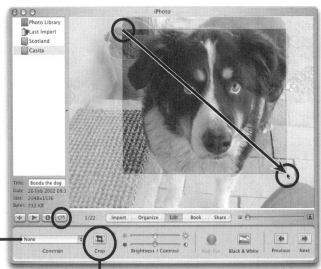

Limit the shape and proportion of the cropped area by selecting an option from the Constrain pop-up menu.

Drag the arrow pointer diagonally to draw a cropping area within the selected photo. The "faded out" area will be deleted when you click the "Crop" button.

Click the "Crop" button after you draw a selection.

Rotate an image

You can rotate a photo from any view mode except "Share." Just select a photo and click the "Rotate" tool to rotate the image 90 degrees, counterclockwise (if that's what you chose in Preferences, page 275). Additional clicks will continue to rotate the image in 90 degree increments.

This is the Rotate tool.

Option-click the Rotate tool to rotate the photo in a clockwise direction (or opposite of the direction chosen in Preferences).

Reduce red-eye

Use the Red-Eye tool to eliminate or reduce the red glare in a subject's eyes when taking flash photos. The results may vary with different photos.

1. Select a photo that needs red-eye reduction.

2. Click the "Edit" view button (if you're not already there).

3. In the Edit pane, choose "None" from the Constrain menu so you will be able to draw freely.

4. Press-and-drag a selection around the area of one eye. Select as small an area as possible. If necessary, zoom in on the photo before making your selection: drag the Size control toward the right.

5. Single-click the Red-Eye tool. iPhoto will remove all red from the selected area. Repeat for the other eye.

If you're not satisfied with the results, press Command Z (Undo) one step at a time, or from the File menu, choose "Revert to Original."

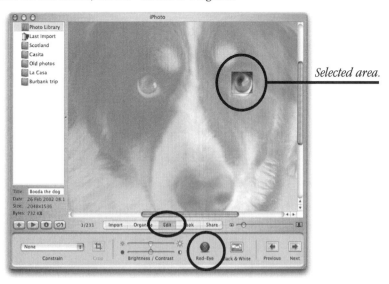

Selected area.

Convert a photo to black & white

To convert a photo to black and white, select it and click the Edit button. In the Edit pane click the "Black & White" button.

Remember, this will affect how this photo looks wherever it appears in iPhoto. If you don't want to affect other occurrences, make a duplicate of the photo, rename it, and convert the duplicate to black and white.

Adjust the brightness and/or contrast

When a photo is a little too dark or too light, you can adjust the brightness and contrast. It's an easy way to juice up a flat photo.

To adjust the brightness and/or contrast, select a photo while in Edit view. Drag the "Brightness/Contrast" sliders left and right until you like the results.

The settings for this photo have not been altered.

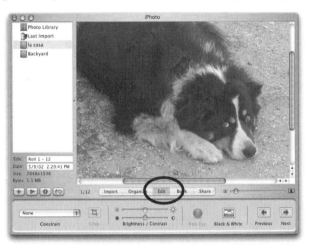

In this photo, I decreased the brightness (moved the Brightness slider to the left) and increased the contrast (moved the Contrast slider to the right).

Even photos that don't need brightness and contrast adjustments can be manipulated to create different and unusual effects.

Open photos directly into another image-editing application

iPhoto's editing tools are fairly limited. For additional image editing, you might want to open a photo in another program, such as Adobe Photoshop (for professionals) or Adobe Photoshop Elements (for home users).

1. From the iPhoto menu, choose "Preferences...."

2. In the Preferences window, find "Double-clicking photos opens them in." Click the "Other" button, as circled below.

3. Click the "Set..." button to get an "Open" dialog box. Find and select the application you want to use for more advanced image editing. Click "Open" (bottom-right corner).

Click the "Other" button, then click "Set..." so you can choose another application.

4. Close the Preferences window.

5. Double-click on a photo. iPhoto will open the photo in the image-editing application you selected.

Edit a photo in a separate window

You can choose to edit a photo in its own, separate window rather than in the iPhoto window. This lets you customize the window Toolbar to display the tools you use most.

To open a photo in a separate window, hold down the Option key and double-click a photo.

Tip: If you want photos to open into individual windows every time you double-click, choose that option in the Preferences; see page 275.

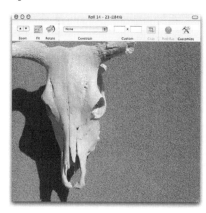

This separate window lets you edit the photo without losing the entire window view of thumbnails. You can open a number of separate windows—just Option-double-click on any number of thumbnails.

Click this icon to display the Customize Toolbar sheet.

Just like in your Finder window Toolbar, you can:

Drag toolbar items sideways to rearrange them.

Command-drag items off the toolbar.

Click the Hide/Show button in the upper-right to hide or show the toolbar.

Change how the buttons are displayed (use the Show menu).

The Book view

Through iPhoto, you can create a professionally printed hard-bound copy of a Book you design with your photos and captions. It might be a catalog, picture book, story book, portfolio, or any other sort of Book you dream up. After you create it, you can order it with the click of a button and your beautiful Book will be delivered to your door. A ten-page book costs $30, and it's about $3 for each additional page.

To create a Book with your own photographs:

1. First create a new Album (as explained on page 276), or select an existing Album that contains the photos you want to use in a Book. The order that photos appear in an Album determines the order in which they appear in the book that you create. The first page in the Album will be the cover of your Book.

2. With your Album open, click the "Book" button to show the layout in the large viewing area, a scrolling thumbnails pane, and the layout tools in the lower pane.

3. Choose one of the design themes from the "Theme" pop-up menu.

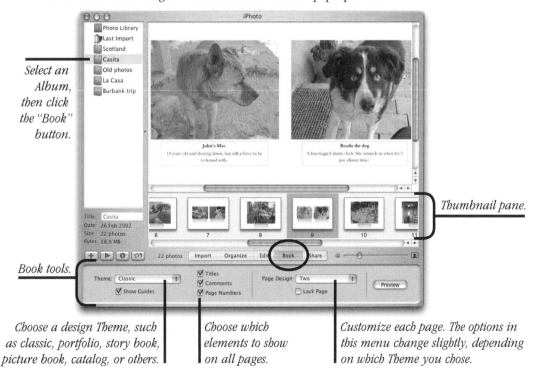

Select an Album, then click the "Book" button.

Thumbnail pane.

Book tools.

Choose a design Theme, such as classic, portfolio, story book, picture book, catalog, or others.

Choose which elements to show on all pages.

Customize each page. The options in this menu change slightly, depending on which Theme you chose.

4. Select a thumbnail page, then from the "Page Design" pop-up menu, choose a layout.

5. You can add titles and comments to each photo (see page 279).

   To edit the text on a Book page, select the text in the text box and type your changes.

   To add text directly to a Book page, click inside any text box and it will enlarge so you can see your text as you type.

   To choose a font, go to the Edit menu and choose "Font...."

   If you need to rearrange photos, add or delete photos, or edit individual photos, click the "Organize" button to go back to your Album. Your Book for this Album will stay as you left it; when you return to the Book, it will reflect the changes you made in the Album.

6. Choose to show or hide "Titles," "Comments," and/or "Page Numbers" on the Album pages by clicking (or *not* clicking) their checkboxes. These options affect the entire Book, not individual pages.

7. Click the "Preview" button to see how your finished Book will look.

Yellow triangle?

When you create a Book, some images may display a low-resolution warning (a yellow triangle containing an exclamation mark). iPhoto warns you if a photo has a resolution that is lower than that recommended for quality printing. Such photos will still print, but they may look pixelated and jaggy, or appear to be of lower quality. If you plan to shoot photos for a Book, set your camera to at least a medium-quality setting, or even high-quality.

If a caution sign appears on a photo in Book view,
it means the photo may print at a very low quality.

Congratulations! You've designed and built a great looking coffee-table Book. To order copies of this Book with a single click, see the opposite page.

To order your Book:

After you create a Book (as explained on the previous pages), you can order hard-bound copies of it using your Internet connection.

Order Book

1. With the Book open on your screen, click the "Share" button.

2. Click "Order Book" in the lower pane. Your iMac will connect to the Internet (if it isn't already) and open the "Order Book" window, shown below. A "Progress" window opens on the Desktop as the "Assembling Book…" process takes place.

3. If the button in the lower right says, "Enable 1-Click Ordering," click it. You will be asked to start an Apple account and provide your name, address and credit card information (don't worry—this is safer than giving your card to an unknown waiter who takes it to the back room), as well as your shipping preferences. If you already have an Apple account, you will be asked to turn on 1-Click Ordering. Click OK.

4. In the "Order Book" window, choose a color for the cover, the quantity of Books (they will all be copies of this one Book), and the shipping options.

5. Click "Buy Now With 1-Click."

6. You'll see a "Transferring book …" progress window that indicates the files for your Book are being transferred via the Internet to the publisher. Your Book will arrive on your doorstep in about a week.

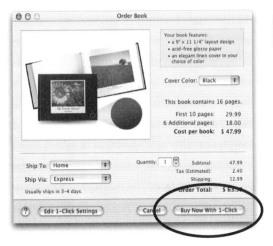

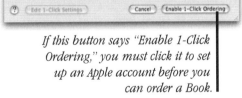

If this button says "Enable 1-Click Ordering," you must click it to set up an Apple account before you can order a Book.

Once you have this Apple account, you can order prints of your photos (see page 296) in iPhoto, and even order hardware and software from the Apple web site with one click.

The Share view

The Share pane contains tools that let you share your photos with others in a variety of ways. You can print your photos in various formats, create a Slide Show to play on your computer, export a QuickTime slide show for others, order professional prints over the Internet, order a professionally bound, hard-cover book, create a web site and publish it with blinding speed, burn your photos to a CD, and more.

Print

Print your photos to your desktop printer

1. Select a single photo, multiple photos, an Album, or the Photo Library.
2. Click the "Share" button (beneath the Viewing area).
3. Click the "Print" button in the Share pane.

4. In the Print window, click the "Style" pop-up menu and choose Contact Sheet, Full Page, Greeting Card, or Standard Prints. Each option will display different parameters; check it out.
5. Enter the number of copies to print.
6. Put photo-quality paper in your printer and click "Print."

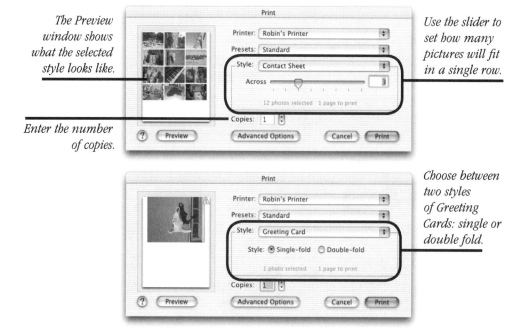

The Preview window shows what the selected style looks like.

Enter the number of copies.

Use the slider to set how many pictures will fit in a single row.

Choose between two styles of Greeting Cards: single or double fold.

Create a Slide Show to view on your iMac

With the Slide Show tool in the Share pane you can quickly create a slide show with a sound track that will play full-screen on your monitor.

Slide Show

1. Select an Album, the Photo Library, or a group of photos within either collection.

2. Click the "Share" button to display the Share pane, as shown below

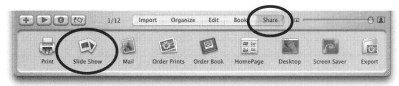

An advantage of creating a separate Album for a slide show (or for any project) is that you can arrange the photos in an Album in the order you want them to appear.

3. Click the "Slide Show" button. The "Slide Show Settings" window will open, as shown below.

4. Enter the number of seconds for each photo to play.

5. Choose if you want the Slide Show to repeat.

6. Select the music you want to use for a sound track: From the "Music" pop-up menu, select one of the few sound tracks that Apple has provided for you, **or** choose "Other..." so you can select any MP3 or WAV file you have on your computer.

7. Click OK to start the Slide Show.

Any sound files you choose through "Other..." will stay in this list.

Choose "Edit List..." to remove songs.

—continued

Slide Show quick-play

You don't have to go through the Settings window to play a Slide Show, or even be in the Share view: Just select an Album while in any view (or a group of photos in the main viewing area), then click the "Play" button. You might have to wait a few seconds while iPhoto prepares the show.

Play Slide Show.

Preferences settings

You can also set up the Slide Show settings in the Preferences window. All Slide Shows will play with the same preferences, whether you choose them in the Settings window as on the previous page, or here in the iPhoto Preferences.

To set the Preferences, go to the iPhoto menu and choose "Preferences...." Adjust the settings at the bottom of the window, then close the window.

This will pick up the settings you made on the previous page, and that window will pick up any settings you choose here.

Slide show keyboard commands

Use keyboard commands to control the playback of your iPhoto Slide Show:

- **Up arrow:** Speeds up the Slide Show.
- **Down arrow:** Slows down the Slide Show.
- **Spacebar:** Toggles the Slide Show between Play and Pause.
- **Left and right arrow keys:** Shows the previous slide or next slide.
- **Mouse:** Stops the Slide Show.

Send your photos through email

One way to share your photos is to send them to someone through email. iPhoto makes it incredibly easy to do just that.

1. Select one or more photos in the viewing area; you can choose photos from any Album or from the Library.

To select multiple photos, hold the Command key as you click on your photo selections.

Selected photos show blue borders.

Note: *People using the current versions of America Online (version 5.0 for Macs, version 7.0 for PCs) will not see the iPhotos you send this way. Dang. I hope they fix that.*

2. Click the "Share" view button.

3. Click "Mail" in the lower pane to open the "Mail Photo" window.

4. In the "Mail Photo" window, choose a photo size from the pop-up menu, and choose whether to include titles and comments that you may have added to photos (as explained on page 279). Click the "Compose" button.

5. Compose your email message in the "New Message" window that opens (as shown to the right). Your photos are already sized and placed in the message area.

6. Click the "Send" icon in the email window Toolbar. Your iMac will connect to the Internet (if it isn't already) and send the photos. Amazing.

Order traditional prints of your photos

You can order regular, real, hold-in-your-hand prints of any photo or collection of photos. Your first **ten** 4x6 prints are **free!**

1. Make sure you're connected to the Internet.

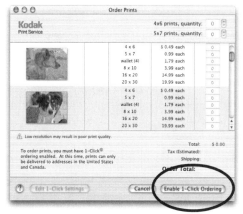

2. Select an Album or a group of photos within an Album or the Photo Library.

3. Click the "Share" view button (if it isn't already).

4. Click the "Order Prints" button in the lower pane.

5. If the button in the lower right says, "Enable 1-Click Ordering," click it. You will be asked to start an Apple account and provide your name, address, and credit card information, as well as your shipping preferences.

   If you already have an Apple account, you will be asked to turn on 1-Click Ordering. Click OK.

6. If necessary, click the "Order Prints" button again in the Share pane to reopen the Order Prints window.

7. Select the size and quantity you want of each photo in the "Order Prints" window:

   In the top-right corner you have options of 4x6 and 5x7 prints. Any quantities you enter in these two boxes will apply to every photo you selected; that is, if you enter "2" in the 4x6 box, you will get 2 prints of every picture.

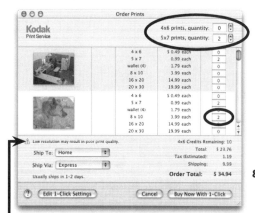

   In addition to **or** instead of the above, you can select individual photos and buy separate prints, like a 16x20 or a collection of four wallet-sized.

As you enter a number to order each photo, the amount is instantly calculated in the window. You can always type in "0" to change your mind.

8. Click the "Buy Now With 1-Click" button. Wow.

Notice there is a warning that one or more of the photos in the collection are low resolution (the photo will appear with a warning icon displayed in the corner). The larger the photo, the more important it is that you originally shot the photo in the highest resolution. You can get away with creating small prints from low-resolution photos.

Build a web site with your photos and put it on the web—free

If you signed up for a free Apple iTools account (see Chapter 19), iPhoto will automatically create and publish a web site of your selected photos and store it **free** on Apple's Internet servers. It's really incredible.

HomePage

1. Select an Album or a group of photos within an Album. The order in which photos appear in the Album determines the order in which they appear on the web page that iPhoto creates. To rearrange photos, drag-and-drop them into new positions.

2. Click the "Share" view button.

3. Click the "HomePage" button in the lower pane. Your iMac will connect to the Internet and open the "Publish HomePage" window, as shown below. Your selected images are displayed on a web page template that you can customize.

Tip: If you want to create a web page with your photos that you can upload to a site you already own, see page 301.

If your web page appears with only one photo on it, perhaps you accidentally had one photo selected in the Album. Click "Cancel" and go check.

Click one of the thumbnails to choose a photo frame style. Each style has a different typeface, but they all have the same layout.

4. Click one of the thumbnail images at the bottom of the window to choose a style for the frames that will border your photos. The same frame will border every photo on the page.

5. Select the existing captions on the page (press-and-drag over the text) and replace them with your own words. If you had given titles to photos (explained on pages 275 and 279), those titles would appear as captions.

Tip: To remove a HomePage Photo Album, log in to your iTools account, then click the "HomePage" button. You'll see a list of the Albums you have posted. Single-click on the name, then click the minus sign right below the list.

—continued

6. From the "Publish to" pop-up menu at the bottom of the window (shown on the previous page), select your iTools account name.

7. Click the "Publish" button. After the files have been transferred to Apple's iTools server, a notice will appear telling you the web address of your new web site; this notice has a button called "Visit Page Now." Click it to open your brand new HomePage Photo Album.

This is the iPhoto HomePage Photo Album as it appears on the web. As you add other Albums, each one will have its own link, as shown here.

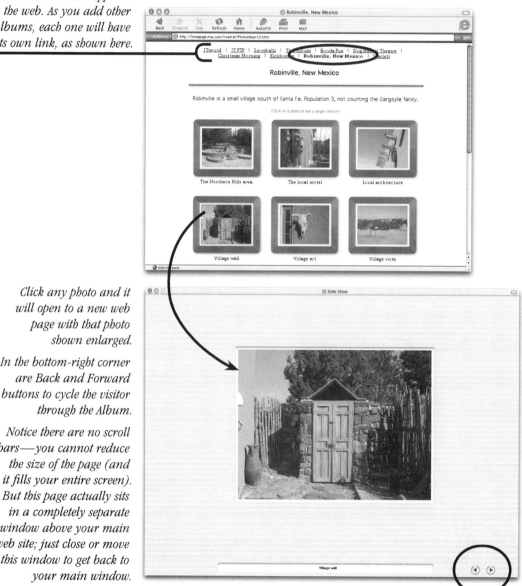

Click any photo and it will open to a new web page with that photo shown enlarged.

In the bottom-right corner are Back and Forward buttons to cycle the visitor through the Album.

Notice there are no scroll bars—you cannot reduce the size of the page (and it fills your entire screen). But this page actually sits in a completely separate window above your main web site; just close or move this window to get back to your main window.

Use a photo as your Desktop background

Select one of your photos to use as a Desktop image. It's a great way to personalize the appearance of your iMac. Any photo you choose will fill the Desktop space.

Desktop

1. Single-click **one** photo in any Album or from the Photo Library.

2. Click the "Share" view button.

3. Click the "Desktop" icon in the lower pane. The selected photo displays instantly on your Desktop.

This is a picture of Mac The Dog as an iMac Desktop image. Notice I selected a photo that won't interfere with the visibility of the Desktop icons in the upper-right corner of the screen.

Make a Screen Saver from your photos

Create your own Screen Saver that will activate after the amount of time you set (see pages 217–218 on how to set the Screen Saver preferences). The images will appear on the screen, move forward, recede, and fade into each other. Way cool.

Screen Saver

1. Click the "Share" view button, if it isn't already.

2. Click the "Screen Saver" icon in the lower pane.

3. In the "Screen Saver" dialog box, a menu contains the names of all your Albums. Choose the Album you want to use as a screen saver, or choose the option of "All Albums."

4. Click OK. Your Slide Show will play when your monitor sleeps, or when you move your pointer to the "Hot Corner" of the screen (as explained on page 218).

Export

Export copies of your photos in various formats

There are still more ways to share your photos with iPhoto. The following export functions are available when you click the "Export" button.

Export copies or convert photos to other file formats

You might want to export photos to a different project folder, or convert them to another file format. This does *not* remove the photos from the Photo Library. The converted or exported photos will be *copies* of the originals; any changes you make to those copies will not affect the originals.

To export and/or convert photos:

1. **Select a single photo,** an Album, or a group of photos within an Album or the Photo Library.
2. Click the "Share" view button, then click the "Export" button (above).
3. In the "Export Images" window that appears, click the "File Export" tab.

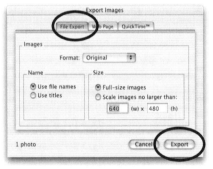

4. From the **Format** pop-up menu, select a file format in which to save photos: "Original" saves photos in whatever format they currently use. "JPG," TIF," and "PNG" are the other options. If you're not familiar with file formats, "JPG" is a safe choice that anyone can use. Most digital cameras create photos in this format.

5. **Name:** "Use file names" means the exported photos will have the default names your digital camera assigned (such as DSCN0715.jpg). "Use titles" will name the photos with the titles you gave them in iPhoto (page 279).

6. **Size:** "Full-size images" will export photos the same size as the original. Or you can enter specific dimensions (in pixels).

7. Click "Export." In the "Export Images" dialog box (left), iPhoto automatically chooses the "Pictures" folder. If you want to put your copied photos into another, separate folder, click the "New Folder" button, and name the new folder. The pictures will be saved into that folder, which you can find in the Pictures folder.

8. Click "Save."

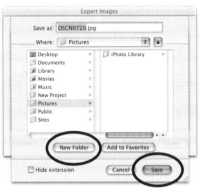

Export your photos as a web page

Export

The Web Page option of the "Export Images" window is very different from the HomePage feature as explained on page 324. This Web Page tool creates a slightly plainer web site and saves it on your computer—it does not post this site on Apple's server for you. You can upload this site yourself to a server of your choice, or you may want to burn the site to a CD to share with others.

1. Select an Album or a group of photos within an Album. The order the photos appear in an Album is the order they will appear in a Web Page.

2. Click the "Share" view button.

3. Click the "Export" button in the lower pane.

4. In the "Export Images" window that appears, click the "Web Page" tab.

5. Enter a title for the Web Page, and choose how many columns and rows of photographs to create on the start page (the first page).

6. Choose a background color: click the "Color" button, then click in the little box to the right of the button to get the color palette.

   If you want to use a background image instead of a color, click the "Image" button, then click "Set...." Find the image you want to use as a background; click OK.

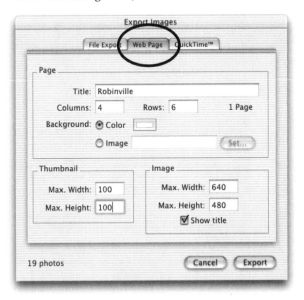

—continued

7. Set maximum widths and heights for thumbnail images (the small, clickable images on the first page) and for full-size images (the large ones that will appear each on their own page).

8. Click "Export."

9. iPhoto automatically chooses the Sites folder in which to store your Web Page. You really need to create a new folder so all of these files will be nicely contained, and so you can create another Web Page someday without overwriting this one.

   So click the "New Folder" button and name it. Then click OK. Your new Web Page and all of its related files will be stored in this folder.

To see your new Web Page (which is really a web *site,* not an individual web *page*), find the new folder you just made (it's in the Sites folder in your Home window, unless you put it somewhere else).

Double-click the file named **index.html.** It will open in your web browser (Internet Explorer), *but it's not online!* You're actually just opening files on your own hard disk. That is, if you wanted other people around the world to see this web page, you'll have to invite them to your house. This Web Page feature just builds the site for you—it's your responsibility to upload it to a server if you want it online.

Web Page creates a "start page" that contains thumbnail versions of your selected photos. Single-click any thumbnail to open a page that displays a full-sized version of that photo.

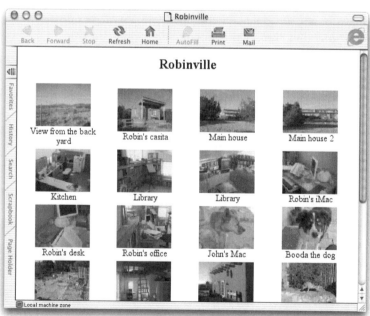

Export your photos as a QuickTime slide show you can give to friends

You can export photos as a QuickTime slide show that plays in the QuickTime player or in a program that supports QuickTime, such as a web browser. The QuickTime slide show can be put on a CD and sent to friends, posted on a web page, inserted into a PDF, or placed in a presentation in AppleWorks (see Chapter 10).

1. Select an Album or a group of photos within an Album or the Photo Library. (The order that photos appear in an Album is the order they will appear in the QuickTime movie.)

2. Click the "Share" view button.

3. Click the "Export" button in the lower pane.

4. In the "Export Images" window, click the "QuickTime" tab to show the QuickTime pane.

5. **Images:** Set the maximum width and height for the slide show images; 640 by 480 pixels is a standard measurement that works well (it's rather large). Set the amount of time that each image will stay on the screen.

6. **Background:** Choose a background color *or* a background image. If some of your photos have unusual dimensions, the empty background area will be filled with the color or image you choose.

7. **Music:** Click "Add currently selected music to movie." The slide show will play whatever piece of music you last chose in the Preferences window (as explained on page 275).

8. Click "Export."

9. In the "Export Images" dialog box, name the file. iPhoto automatically selects the "Movies" folder to save the slide show in.

10. Click "Save."

To open your QuickTime movie, click the "Home" icon in the Toolbar of any Finder window, then double-click the folder named "Movies." Double-click the QuickTime movie file that you just named and saved.

To play your QuickTime movie, click the "Play" button (the big triangle) on the QuickTime Player.

A QuickTime slide show plays in the QuickTime Player. Click the "Play" button (circled above) to play the movie.

Extra tips and information

JPEG and JPG are the same thing.

TIFF and TIF are also the same thing.

Most digital cameras store photos in the **JPEG format,** which combines a high-quality image with effective compression to economize file size. iPhoto works best with JPEG formatted photos, although it recognizes most common formats such as TIFF, PICT, BMP, TARGA, and PNG.

Imported photos are actually located in a folder named **iPhoto Library.** To find this folder, open your Home window, then open the Pictures folder; the iPhoto Library is inside Pictures. The Library folder also contains a folder of the **Albums** you created in iPhoto. But these Albums don't really contain photos, even though you placed photos in them while working in iPhoto. Instead, they contain "references" to photos that have been imported into the Photo Library. This way, you have the same photo in many different Albums without overloading your computer with multiple copies of a photo.

If you plan to have a lot of fun using your digital camera and iPhoto, chances are sooner or later you'll have so many photos in your iPhoto Library that you'll run out of storage space. Plan to back up your iPhoto Library folder regularly by copying it to another disk or burning a CD (as explained in Chapter 12).

Make Beautiful Music with iTunes

With the **iTunes** application, you can create music CDs that will work in just about any regular CD player (and on your iMac), or create digital music files to play while you're working on your iMac. iTunes can convert music files from one format to another (known as "encoding"). iTunes can organize your music files into Playlists (collections). It can create CDs of your customized music playlists. iTunes can connect to the Internet's CD Database and retrieve information about your CDs, including artist, song titles, album name, and music genre. iTunes can connect to dozens of Internet radio stations offering a wide variety of music and talk radio. And it can put on a dazzling, live, visual effects show that's synchronized to the current music selection. What more could you ask? How about this—if you have an **iPod** (Apple's MP3 player available in 5- or 10-gigabyte storage capacities), iTunes will upload and synchronize the iPod with your iTunes Playlist (at least 1,000 songs) using a lightning-fast FireWire connection.

For in-depth information about iTunes, compression, sound quality, custom bit rates, sample rates, and more, get The Little iTunes Book, *by Bob Levitus, available from Peachpit Press.*

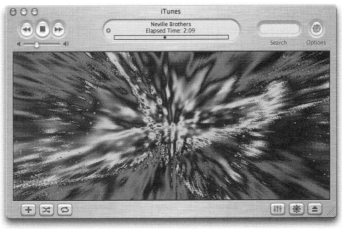

This is the iTunes player with visuals turned on.

Open iTunes for the first time

The first time you open iTunes, the Setup Assistant shows you a welcome window and a series of set-up windows that help you get iTunes ready to use.

1. Click once on the iTunes icon in the Dock. (If the icon isn't in the Dock, you'll find it in the Applications window.)

This is the iTunes icon in the Dock.

2. Click the "Next" button in the "Welcome" window (below).

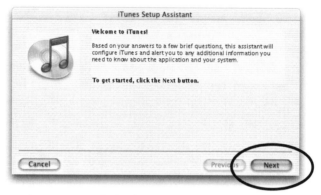

3. In the "Internet Playback" options (shown below), choose

MP3 audio files are music files that are compressed a great deal but still maintain high quality.

"Yes, use iTunes for Internet playback" if you want iTunes to play MP3 audio files when they are available on the Internet (top section of the window below). This is probably the choice for you.

Click "No, do not modify my Internet settings" if you have some other software that you prefer to have play your MP3 audio files.

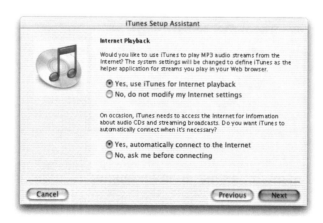

4. Also from the "Internet Playback" options:

> If you have a *full-time Internet connection* such as DSL or a cable modem, choose "Yes, automatically connect to the Internet."
>
> If your Internet connection requires that your *internal modem* dials a phone number, you may prefer the option, "No, ask me before connecting" to prevent your modem from unexpectedly dialing.

Click "Next."

5. In the "Find MP3 files" panel, choose whether you want iTunes to search for any MP3 music files you may already have on your computer.

> If you choose "Yes, find any MP3 files I have on my hard disk(s)," iTunes will search your hard disk, *plus* any other hard disks that are networked to your computer.
>
> If you're on a network of any sort, choose "No, I'll add them myself later" to prevent adding references of files to your music library that don't exist on your own computer.

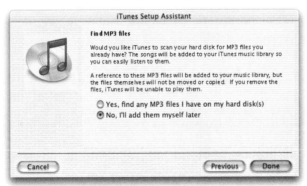

When iTunes searches for MP3 files, it puts a reference to the MP3 file location in the iTunes music library. If you move those MP3 files, iTunes will not be able to play them.

6. Click "Done."

Playing CDs

You can play just about any music CD you stick in your Mac. Make sure your sound is on and turned up (if it isn't, see page 219).

To play a music CD:

Tip: If you want to play songs without putting the CD in your iMac, follow the steps on the next page to put selected songs in the Library.

1. Insert a CD into the drive, label side up.

2. Open iTunes, if it doesn't open automatically:

    If the iTunes icon is in your Dock, click once on it.

    If there is no icon in the Dock, open the Applications folder, find the iTunes icon, then double-click it.

3. The CD icon appears in the "Source pane," as shown below. Click the CD icon to see the song list and other information.

    If you're connected to the Internet, iTunes will automatically go to the CDDB (CD database) web site, retrieve the song titles (if available), and enter the information in the window.

    If you're not connected to the Internet when you insert a CD, song titles will appear as track numbers.

In the Source pane you'll see an icon for the CD that is in your iMac.

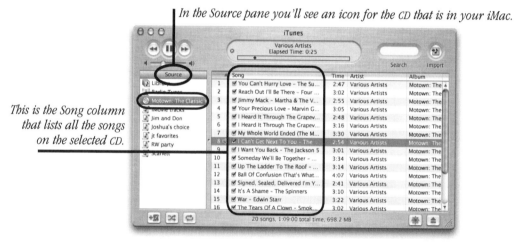

This is the Song column that lists all the songs on the selected CD.

To see the actual song titles, if they have not appeared:

1. Connect to the Internet (if you're not already).

2. From the Advanced menu, choose "Get CD Track Names."

The iTunes Library

Three of the greatest features of iTunes are that you can play music on your iMac without having to insert the original CD, download songs to a portable MP3 player, and burn a customized music collection onto a CD for your personal enjoyment. However, before you can do these things, you must first move the selected songs to the **iTunes Library**—*simply playing songs from a CD does not add them to the Library.* So you must *import* (also called *rip* or *encode*) a music file from a CD into iTunes; this automatically encodes the song as an "MP3" file and places it in the Library. **Then** you can turn to the following page and make Playlists for organizing and exporting your music.

Tip: Each song takes up from 3 to 5 megabytes, at least, of hard disk space, so make sure you have plenty of space before you go crazy with your music files!

To add songs to the Library:

1. Insert a music CD into the drive, label-side up.

2. In the CD list that appears, check each song in the list that you want to add to the Library.

3. Click the "Import" button in the upper-right of the window.

This turns into an "Import" button after you check a song.

An orange icon (a circle with an animated wave symbol) appears next to the track that is being ripped (imported).

When the file is finished, the orange icon is replaced by a green icon (a circle with a check mark), indicating that it has already been imported.

This is how much of my hard disk is filled with music files in the Library.

You may already have music files somewhere on your computer that you want to add to the iTunes Library. There are two ways to do this:

- **Either** go to the File menu and choose "Add to Library...." then find and select your music files.

- **Or** drag a file from any location on your hard disk to the Library icon in the iTunes Source pane.

Creating a Playlist

A **Playlist** is your personal collection of audio files. Your iTunes Library, as described on the previous page, might have hundreds of songs in it; the Playlists organize these songs for you. You can create as many Playlists as you like, the same songs can be in any number of Playlists, and you can arrange the songs in any order by dragging selections up or down in the list. *Before you can burn a CD of songs, you must first put the songs into a Playlist.*

To create a new Playlist:

When you create a new Playlist, the iMac knows you want to change its name, so it highlights the field for you. Just type to replace the existing name.

1. Type Command N, or click the "New Playlist" button at the bottom-left of the iTunes window. A new Playlist icon will appear in the Source pane with a generic name of "untitled playlist," as shown to the left.

2. Change the name of the new Playlist to something appropriate (just type to replace "untitled playlist").

   You can change a Playlist name at any time: Click once on the title, then type a new name in the highlighted field.

To add songs to a Playlist from the Library:

1. In the Source pane, single-click the Library icon to display your Library collection in the Song column.

2. Drag a selection from the Song column to a Playlist icon in the Source pane.

Tip: To select more than one song at a time to drag to the Playlist, hold down the Command key and click on individual songs.

Or to select a range of songs, do this: Click on a song, hold down the Shift key, click on a song lower in the list. Every song between the click and Shift-click will be selected. Let go of the Shift key before you drag a selected song.

*To **de**select a single song, Command-click on it.*

To add songs to a Playlist directly from a CD:

1. Insert the CD whose songs you want to add to a customized Playlist.

2. Single-click the CD icon in the Source pane to open its song list.

3. Drag desired selections from the Song column and drop them on your new Playlist name in the Source pane, as shown at the top of the opposite page.

   NOTE: *When you drag a song directly from a CD to a Playlist, the song is encoded (imported) to the MP3 format and placed in the iTunes Library, just as if you followed the directions on the previous page! So don't do both!*

New Playlist button.

"Songbird" is the name of the CD that is in the iMac and whose songs are showing in the window.

"Robin's Favorites" is the name of the new Playlist. You can see song #10 being dragged over to that Playlist.

To make a new Playlist the easy way (*after* you've added the songs to the Library):

1. In the Source pane, single-click the Library icon to display your music collection.

2. Select the desired songs in the Song column (hold down the Command key and click each song).

   Note: The checkmarks do *not* indicate whether a file is selected. The checkmarks indicate two things: songs that will play when you click the "Play" button, and songs on a CD that will be imported when you click the "Import" button.

3. From the File menu, select "New Playlist From Selection." iTunes will automatically create the Playlist and add the selected items to it. You can change the name of the Playlist.

This is an example of a Playlist called "Joshua's choice."

Now with the Playlist, you can listen to this collection on your iMac, download it to an MP3 player, or burn a CD of this particular collection of songs.

Burn a CD of your customized music collection

The "Burn CD" button is visible when a Playlist is selected in the Source pane.

To burn a CD:

1. Select a Playlist you've created in the Source pane (as explained on pages 310–311).
2. In the Song list, uncheck any songs you do not want recorded on the CD.
3. Single-click the "Burn CD" button (in the upper-right corner), and the button cover opens to reveal the "Burn" icon, as shown below.
4. The Status window will instruct you to insert a blank CD-R.
5. After you insert a disc, iTunes will begin burning the songs onto the disc.
6. When finished, your new CD icon will appear on the Desktop.

  The Multi-Function button in the upper-right corner of the iTunes window will change, depending on what is selected.

Transfer songs to an MP3 player

You can use iTunes to **transfer** one or more Playlists **to an MP3 player,** such as the **Apple iPod.**

1. Connect a supported MP3 player to your iMac using a FireWire or USB cable, and the player's name will appear in the iTunes Source pane.
2. Drag songs from the Library or a Playlist to the MP3 player's name in the Source list. The songs will copy to the player.

If you're using the Apple iPod, you can choose to have iTunes automatically transfer *all* your MP3 songs or just *selected* Playlists to the iPod, or you can manually drag selections to the iPod in the Playlist.

 The iPod is actually a hard disk, so be sure to eject the iPod before you disconnect the FireWire cable! Select the iPod's name in the Source pane, then click the "Eject" button in the bottom-right corner of the iTunes window. Or drag the iPod icon on your hard disk down to the Trash.

For lots of details about the iPod, from the iTunes application menu choose "Help," then choose "iPod Help."

The iTunes Interface

Most of the controls you need are located directly on the **iTunes interface.**
It looks like a lot of details, but most of them are self-explanatory.

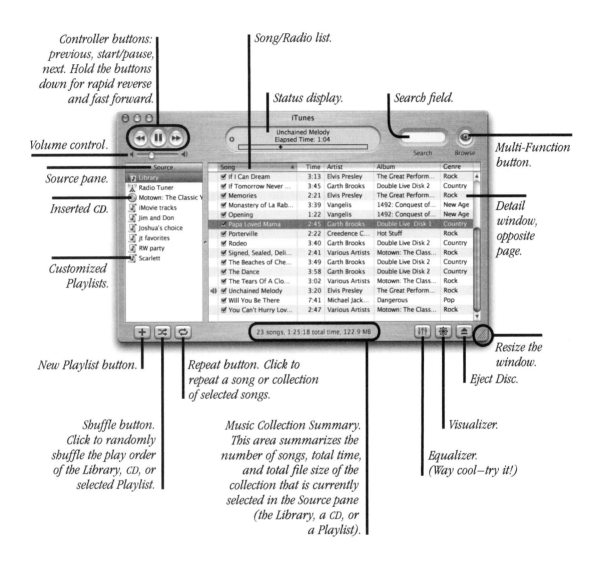

Controller buttons: previous, start/pause, next. Hold the buttons down for rapid reverse and fast forward.

Song/Radio list.

Status display.

Search field.

Volume control.

Multi-Function button.

Source pane.

Inserted CD.

Detail window, opposite page.

Customized Playlists.

New Playlist button.

Repeat button. Click to repeat a song or collection of selected songs.

Resize the window.

Eject Disc.

Shuffle button. Click to randomly shuffle the play order of the Library, CD, or selected Playlist.

Music Collection Summary. This area summarizes the number of songs, total time, and total file size of the collection that is currently selected in the Source pane (the Library, a CD, or a Playlist).

Visualizer.

Equalizer. (Way cool—try it!)

Tip: You can close the iTunes window (click the red button) and your music will continue to play.

Click the green button (the zoom button) to reduce the Player to a little "windoid." Click the green button again to return to the full window.

Play the radio

Radio Tuner gives you an easy way to tune into **Internet radio stations** that are either built into iTunes or whose addresses you have entered. These stations play a wide variety of music, news, and talk show programs, and netcast the "streaming MP3" format.

To play the radio in iTunes:

1. Connect to the Internet, if you're not already.

2. Click the Radio Tuner icon in the Source pane. This will display the radio options in the "Stream" column (the same column that is labeled "Song" when the Source is a CD or your Library).

3. Click the triangle next to a radio category to see the various choices of "streams" (streaming Internet connections).

4. Double-click a stream to begin playing it. iTunes will open the designated web address and "prebuffer" a stream (store a little bit ahead for you). Prebuffering usually takes just a few seconds.

Streaming files download a certain amount of information to your computer before they start playing, then continue to download data as the file plays.

Choose which columns to display in the Radio Tuner window: From the Edit menu, choose "View Options...."

To enter another radio address:

If you happen to know the web address of a streaming MP3 radio station that's not in the iTunes Radio Tuner, you can manually enter it.

1. From the Advanced menu in the upper menu bar, choose "Open Stream...."

2. Enter the web address in the text field in the "Open Stream" window.

3. Click "OK" and be patient for a couple of minutes.

Create and Use an iTools Account

iTools is a collection of online tools provided by Apple that only Macintosh users can access. iTools includes:

- **iCards:** iCards are customized electronic postcards that use Apple's high-quality, professional graphics, or you can use your own great photos. (People other than Mac users can *send* iCards, but you have to use a Mac and have an iTools account to *create* iCards that feature your own digital photos.)

- **Email:** Apple provides a free email service and five megabytes of email server space. (But Apple is not an ISP; you need to have your own Internet Service Provider, as described on page 7 if you want to use Apple's email service.)

- **iDisk:** With an iTools account you have twenty megabytes of free, personal storage space on Apple's Internet servers which can be used to store web pages, photos, and movies; share large files with others; and use as a current source of Mac OS software, software updates, and music files.

- **HomePage:** You can build a free, customizable web site using Apple's web page templates.

Although only Macintosh users can own an iTools account, you can send iCards and email to anyone on *any* computer, and all computer users can access the web site you create and share files from your web site.

Everything in iTools is on the Internet, so you must connect to the Internet before you use any of these features. This is a time when a full-time broadband connection is the best thing to have (actually, it's always best to have a broadband connection, if you're lucky enough).

Create an account

To use **iTools,** you need to register and become a member, but it's free and there are no obligations and you won't get a bunch of junk mail just because you register.

To create your iTools account:

1. Log on to the Internet, open your browser, and go to **www.apple.com.** Single-click the "iTools" tab.

2. On the iTools web page, click one of the iTools icons (iCards, Email, HomePage, or iDisk) to get to the "iTools Login" page, shown below.

3. Click the "Sign Up" button to register and assign yourself a **user name** and a **password.**

   The user name will act as your iTools Email address and for your HomePage web site address. For example, if I designate **"roadrat"** as my user name, my email address will be **roadrat@mac.com** and my iTools HomePage web site address will be **http://homepage.mac.com/roadrat.**

The iTools login screen lets you sign up for iTools membership if you don't have one yet (left side of web page), or you can log in with your existing membership name and password (right side of web page).

Once you've registered, Apple will send an email to your new iTools email address confirming your registration (your Mail application automatically adds your Mac.com account and checks it for email), then you can start using iTools. The iTools web site **(www.apple.com/itools)** will walk you through each step of using each feature.

After you've completed the registration process, you can start using any of iTools features. Click "Start using iTools" to open the iTools web page (shown on the right).

The iTools tab opens this page. Click any of the icons (circled) at the top of the page to open an iTools log-in screen.

Check your Internet preferences

Once you've got your iTools account, check your **Internet preferences** and make sure your member name and password are filled in; if not, enter that information.

1. From the Apple menu, choose "System Preferences...."

2. In the window that appears, click the "Internet" icon. You'll see the pane shown below.

3. After you've checked and entered any missing information, just Quit the System Preferences (Command Q).

If you signed up for an iTools account when you first turned on your Mac, this information is already filled in for you, and your Mail settings are set up as well.

iCards

Anyone can send **iCards** to friends and family, even without an iTools account, but to send an iCard *using your own photo,* you do need an iTools account. An iCard is simply an electronic postcard you can send to anyone on any computer. iCard is better than most e-postcards for two reasons: The quality of the graphics is superior, and iCards are sent straight to the recipient instead of requiring a visit to a web page to "pick up" a card.

To send an iCard:

Note: AOL users will not be able to see iCards! The card and your message turns into crummy ol' text. Dang.

1. Go to **www.apple.com** and click the iTools tab.

2. Click the "iCards" button. You may have to log in with your member name and password if you haven't already.

3. On the iCards web page, as shown below, click on a category. Then click on a specific iCard image to open a full-sized, editable version.

4. On the editable iCard web page that appears, write a message and select a font, then click the "Continue" button.

5. The next page previews your card and lets you address the card to as many recipients as you like.

6. Click the "Send Your Card" button and your customized iCard is sent.

7. A "Thank you" page opens, with the options of sending the same card to someone else or selecting a new card.

Click this button to use photos you've put in your iDisk (as explained on page 323) to make your own customized greeting cards.

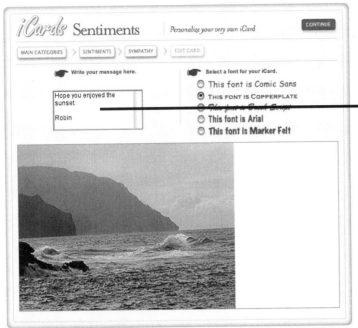

Type a short message here, select a font, then click the "Continue" button in the upper-right corner. Your message will appear next to the photo, as shown in the preview below.

If you want to make changes to your message or change the font, click the "Edit Card" button.

Enter your name and email address in the provided fields. Enter a recipient's email address in the provided field, then click "Add Recipient."

Add as many recipients as you like, one at a time, to the Recipient List, then click "Send Your Card."

Of course, you can always send that one card to just one special person. In that case, enter their email address in the first box, then click the "Send Your Card" button.

Email

When you register for an iTools account, a new Mac.com **email** account is automatically set up for you in your Mail application. If you chose the option of announcing your new email address when you registered for iTools, you will receive a copy of that announcement. You'll also receive a welcome message that confirms your account information.

See the following chapter on Mail for all the details about your Mac.com account and how to use Mail to send and receive your email. It's great.

The first item is a copy of the message that was sent to announce this new email address (see the opposite page).

The second item is an email from Apple with confirmation of your new account.

*This is a **Mac.com** account.*

Extra email features

Although you have the application Mail to do your daily emailing (see Chapter 20), the iTools **Email web page** provides a few extra features. You can use the links on this page to automatically "Forward your mail," set up an "Auto Reply," and "Check your email" (**Webmail,** explained on the following page).

Click the iTools tab, then the "Email" link to get to this page.

To get to the Email page shown below, go to the Apple web site, then click the iTools tab. On the iTools page click the "Email" link in the navigation bar beneath the iTools tab.

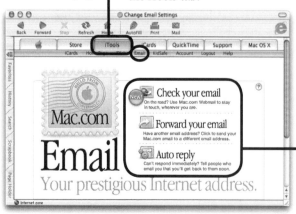

In the iTools Login page that opens, enter your password, then click the "Enter"button. You see the page shown to the left.

Click one of the icons to go to a web page where you can activate that feature.

Check your email on the web

Click the "Check your email" button (previous page) and you can check your Mac.com email from any computer, anywhere in the world. This feature is called *Webmail* because you can use the World Wide Web and a browser on anyone's computer (Mac or PC) to check your mail instead of having to be at your own iMac.

Log in with your iTools member name and password to open a Webmail window that contains your Mac.com email messages. Check mail, send mail, and organize your mail. A shortcut to the login page is **http://webmail.mac.com.**

Forward your email

If you want to forward your messages to another email address, click the "Forward your email" link on the Email page to use the "Change Email Forwarding" form, shown on the right.

Auto reply

If you're going away or under a deadline and won't be checking your mail for a period of time, set up an automatic email response — when people send you a message, they will get an automatic reply telling them that you can't answer their email for a while.

Click the "Auto reply" link on the Email page to use the "Set auto reply" form (shown to the right).

Keep in mind that messages automatically disappear from the Apple server after thirty days, so if you're going to be unavailable for longer than that, you might want to also forward your messages to another account.

iDisk

When you register and become an iTools member, you automatically get twenty megabytes of free storage space on Apple's Internet servers. This server storage space is called **iDisk.** You can mount your iDisk so that it appears on your Desktop just like any other disk to which you have access, then drag and drop files and folders between iDisk and your computer. You can drag movies, photos, and documents to iDisk so they can be shared by other iTools members or used by HomePage in creating web pages.

Open your iDisk

roadrat

If this icon appears on your Desktop but you don't see a window, double-click this to open your iDisk window.

If you haven't already connected to the Internet, do so now. Then from the Go menu at your Desktop, choose "iDisk," or press Command Option I.

If you've never logged on to your iTools account before, you might have to click the button "Open your iDisk" on the Apple web page that appears. After a few moments, an iDisk icon will appear on your Desktop, as shown to the left. (If you've used the Finder Preferences to prevent your disk icons from appearing on the Desktop, press Command Option C to open the Computer window, where you'll find the iDisk icon.)

If you've logged in to your iTools account before, then when you choose "iDisk" from the Go menu, a window opens that displays your iDisk, as shown on the opposite page. Amazing. Don't get confused with these folders that are named exactly the same as the folders in your Home window (why do they do that?!). Keep track of the icon in the title bar—notice it has the magic iDisk crystal ball.

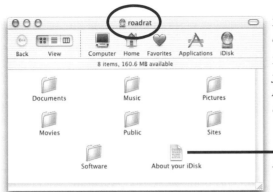

This is an iDisk. The folders you see here are actually on one of Apple's servers!

The icon in the title bar is your only clue that you are not in your own Home folder on your Mac—you have been magically transported to a computer (server) at Apple.

Read this file for more information.

iDisk contents

When you double-click the **iDisk** icon on your Desktop to open its **window,** you're actually looking at files and folders that are on Apple's server, which explains why there may be a delay opening the window (especially if you use a phone modem).

Documents: Drag into this folder any kind of document that you want to store and make available to yourself over the Internet. This folder is private and only you have access to it.

Music: Drag music files and playlists to this private iDisk folder so you can have access to it from anywhere over the Internet.

Pictures: Drag photos, or folders of photos, that you plan to use in a HomePage web site into this iDisk Pictures folder so you'll have access to them when you're building the web page.

Movies: Drag movies that you might use in a HomePage web site into this iDisk Movies folder so you'll have access to them when you're building the web page.

Public: *Other iTools members can access files that you drag to your iDisk Public folder, if they have your iTools member name.* Or, you can open any other Public folder if you have another person's iTools member name.

Sites: The Sites folder stores any web pages that you've created using iTools HomePage. You can also store sites here created with any other web authoring software.

Software: The Software folder contains Apple software, as well as Mac OS X software that you can download by dragging files to your computer, and a folder named "Extras" that contains royalty-free music files you can use in your iMovies. The contents of this folder do not count against your iDisk storage space allotment.

The example above shows an iDisk whose storage space has been upgraded (increased; see page 328), so the status bar shows more space available (160.6 MB) than your iDisk window may show.

If you don't have a high-speed connection, waiting for these files to load can be painful.

HomePage

With **HomePage** you can easily create and publish a single web page, an entire web site, or several sites. Choose from a variety of great looking themes that are designed to display photo albums, QuickTime movies, résumés, newsletters, invitations, and more.

From the iTools web page, click the "HomePage" link to open the page shown below, from which you can build a single web page or a collection of pages.

The "Pages" pane at the top of the window lists web pages you've created using the "Create a page" templates shown at the bottom of the window. To give your site a password, click the arrow button next to "Protect this site."

*In this box, you'll see the list of **pages** you've created with HomePage.*

*If you've created more than one web page, designate one to be the **first page** (the home page): Drag it to the top of this list.*

HomePage Help.

*Select a page in the list, then click the **Minus** button to remove it.*

*To add a new page, click the **Plus** button.*

*Click the **Edit** button to make changes to a selected page.*

*Click each of these links to explore the **categories** of design themes and web page ideas.*

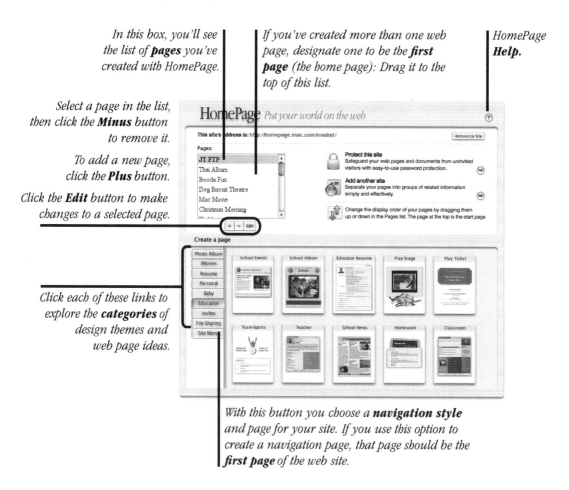

*With this button you choose a **navigation style** and page for your site. If you use this option to create a navigation page, that page should be the **first page** of the web site.*

Overview of the page-building process

Click the Help button at the top-right corner of the web page to open the Help files, there are extensive instructions for working with HomePage. A brief step-by-step **overview of the process** to build and publish a web page is shown below just to show you how easy it is.

1. On the HomePage web page, choose a page category: Click one of the category tabs in the "Create a page" section. Then **choose one of the thumbnail themes** that appears on the right.

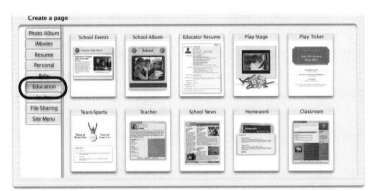

When the "Education" button is selected (far left), this panel shows thumbnails of the "Education" web page themes.

2. When you select a thumbnail, a full-sized version of the page opens in your browser. If you like this theme design, click the "Edit" button in the top-right corner to **open an editable version of this page.**

This preview version of the web page gives you a good idea what the final page will look like, minus photos.

If you want to choose another theme, click the "Themes" button.

If this theme is satisfactory, click the "Edit" button.

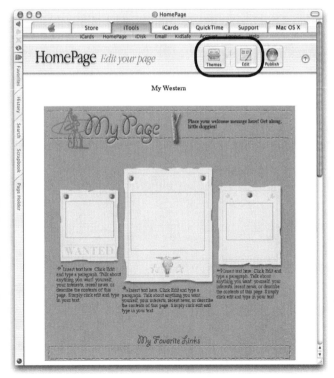

Tip—A file-size reminder: When you drag photos to the Pictures folder on your iDisk, HomePage can access those photos to use on web pages. But make sure the images you place in the Pictures folder are a reasonable size—the smaller an image is, the faster it will download to a web browser. HomePage automatically creates small thumbnail versions of photos for most pages, but those thumbnails usually link to the original full-sized photo that you put in the Pictures folder. If the original photos in the Pictures folder are unnecessarily large, some of your web pages will be painfully slow to download and you'll fill up your allotted server storage space very quickly.

Ideally, photos destined for a web page should be saved in a JPEG format, have a resolution of 72 ppi, and a maximum size of 640 x 480 pixels.

To place a photo or movie, click "Choose" to open the "Choose a file" window.

3. Add images and text.

HomePage accesses all photos and movies from three folders:

To make images available for use in HomePage, log in to your iDisk (see page 322) and drag individual images or an entire folder of images from your hard disk to the **Pictures** folder on the iDisk.

If you plan to use movies on your HomePage, drag QuickTime movies from your hard disk to the **Movies** folder on your iDisk.

If you don't have pictures of your own, you can select from those that Apple has provided in iDisk's **Library folder,** available from the Library tab. You'll see this tab when you click a "Choose" button to place a photo.

To add **images** in designated areas, click the "Choose" button, then from the window provided, select a photo from your Pictures folder, a movie from your Movies folder, or something from Apple's Library folder.

Type your **text** into the various text fields.

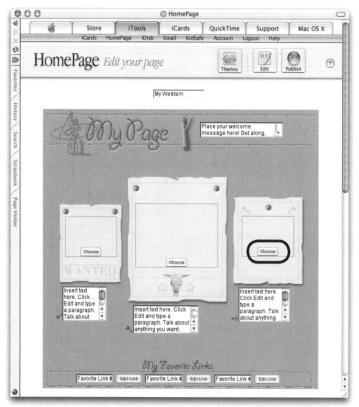

4. **Preview** and **publish** your page: When you've edited the page to your satisfaction, click the "Preview" button at the top-right of the page to proof it, then click "Publish" to publish your page on Apple's servers.

When you've finished building your web page and published it, you'll be presented with a "Congratulations" web page that shows your new HomePage web address and a link for sending an iCard announcement to family and friends.

The address that appears here is the address you give people so they can visit your site. It will always be **homepage.mac.com/ username.**

If you use HomePage to create web pages that show QuickTime movies, you'll drag your movies to the iDisk "Movies" folder. QuickTime movies, even short ones, are large. The 33-second QuickTime movie shown below takes 2.3 megabytes of storage space. If you want to have a large QuickTime movie on your HomePage web site, or lots of small ones, consider upgrading your allotted iDisk space (see the next page).

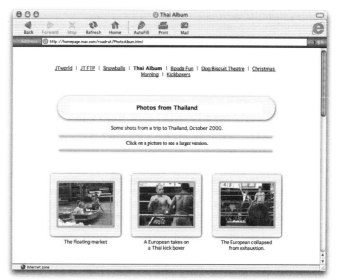

This is an example of a web site full of movies and photos created with Apple's HomePage.

Create a main navigation page

In the main HomePage window you see a "Site Menu" tab in the "Create a page" section, as shown below. With this feature you can create an **optional navigation page** that will provide a *graphic* representation of all the pages in the site.

Click the "Site Menu" button to see thumbnails of design theme choices.

Then click on a theme thumbnail to open an editable, full-size version of the selected navigation page.

Design theme thumbnails.

This navigation page uses the "Modern" theme, as shown above. Enter your customized text into the available text fields and use the small edit buttons on the right to add, delete, and move items on the template page.

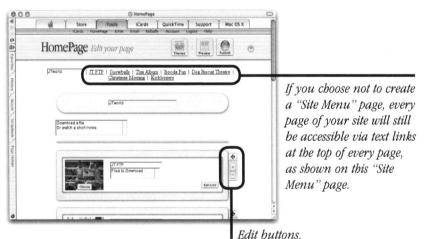

If you choose not to create a "Site Menu" page, every page of your site will still be accessible via text links at the top of every page, as shown on this "Site Menu" page.

Edit buttons.

Buy more iDisk space

You can create multiple sites with HomePage, limited only by the amount of your iDisk storage space on Apple's servers. You can **purchase** up to one gigabyte of **iDisk storage** in addition to the twenty megabytes provided free with your iTools membership. To upgrade your iDisk, go to the iTools web page and click the "Get More Space" link. Or go to the iDisk page and click the "Upgrade now" button.

(e)Mail and Address Book

The Mac OS X application for email is called **Mail.** As you'd expect, Mail lets you write email messages, send messages, and receive messages. Beyond those basic functions, Mail has many useful tools for organizing, formatting, searching, and filtering email.

The **Address Book** is a separate application that works in conjunction with Mail. You can save your favorite email addresses, make a mailing to send a message to a number of people at once, enter an address in a new message with the click of the mouse, and more.

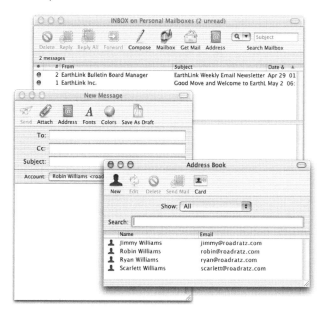

Mail

Mail

The **basic** things you will be doing in **Mail** are checking email messages, replying to messages, and composing new messages. On these next few pages are directions for how to do just that, but there is lots more your Mail program can do for you. You can create folders to organize your mail, create "rules" to filter incoming messages and automatically sort them into special folders, spell-check your compositions, search your mail, and add entries to your Address Book.

But since you probably want to get started right away just using email, jump right in. You must have an Internet connection already set up, as explained in Chapters 1 and/or 15, and you must have **already set up your email account** with Mac.com (or any other provider, as mentioned below). If you haven't set up your Mac.com account yet, and you want one (you don't have to have one), see Chapter 19.

Advanced: If you have an email account with any other provider, you can set it up as an account in Mail so you can use Mail as your email "client"; see pages 348–350. In fact, if you have several email accounts, Mail will check them all for you at the same time (even if they're on different servers), and you can send messages from any account. **Note:** you cannot get your America Online mail through any other client except AOL.

If you have a permanent connection, you can tell Mail to check for your mail every half hour or hour or every five minutes (see page 348 for details). When mail is received, the Mail icon in the Dock will display the number of messages that came in, as shown to the left.

Hey lover man!

The Viewer Window

Mail opens up to the **Viewer Window.** It consists of a customizable "favorites" toolbar, a Status Bar, a Message List pane that lists all your messages in the mailbox, a Message pane that displays a selected message from the Message List, and the Mailboxes drawer which slides in and out of view from either side of the Viewer Window. Each of these is discussed in detail throughout this chapter.

Toolbar,
see page 340.

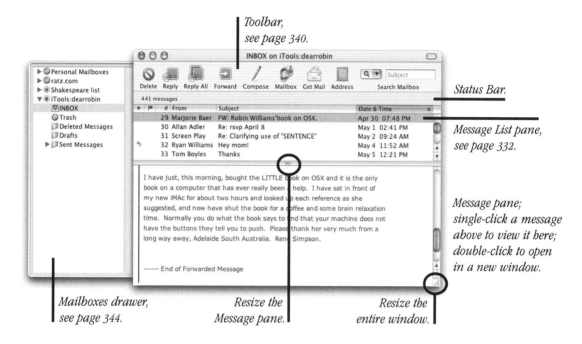

Status Bar.

Message List pane,
see page 332.

Message pane;
single-click a message
above to view it here;
double-click to open
in a new window.

Mailboxes drawer,
see page 344.

Resize the
Message pane.

Resize the
entire window.

Tip: *Depending on your email provider, you may get lots of junk mail or not much. If you get lots and you don't want to have to actually open it to delete it, resize the Message pane so it doesn't show—drag the marker (circled above) all the way to the bottom. Then you will be able to select all the email you don't want and delete it without having to open it at all. To open the mail you **do** want to read, double-click it.*

To check for and read messages:

1. Connect to the Internet (if you're not already connected).

2. Click once on the Mail icon in the Dock to open Mail.

3. Click the "Get Mail" icon in the toolbar.

    Mail checks any "Accounts" you have already set up (to set up other accounts, see pages 348–350). Any account in the Mailboxes drawer that receives new email displays a notice next to the Inbox that indicates how many unread messages are in that Inbox.

4. Your messages will appear in the Message List pane (top). Single-click a message to display its contents in the Message pane (bottom).

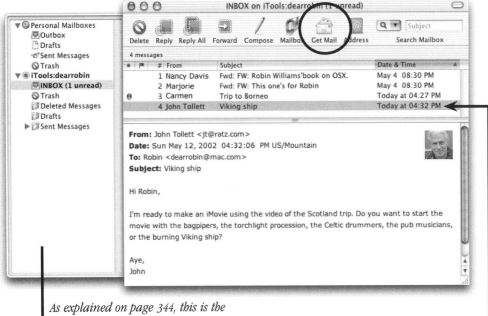

As explained on page 344, this is the Mailboxes drawer. You can see that my account has one unread message.

Single-click a message in this list and it will apear in the lower pane, if the lower pane is open. Double-click a message in the list and it will open in its own, separate window.

To compose and send a message:

1. Click the "Compose" icon in Mail's toolbar to open a "New Message" window (shown below).

2. Type an email address in the "To" field. An email address always has the @ symbol and a "something.com" at the end (or it might be .org, .edu, .gov, etc.). It doesn't matter if you type capital letters or lowercase.

3. Type an email address in the "Cc" field if you want to send a copy to someone. (Cc stands for Carbon copy or Courtesy copy).

   To send the same message to more than one person, type all their email addresses, separated by commas, in either the To or the Cc field. (You can make a "group" address which contains lots of different names, then send to the entire group at once; see pages 354–355.)

4. Type a message description in the "Subject" field.

5. Type a message in the blank message area.

6. Connect to the Internet if you're not already connected.

7. Click the "Send" icon in the "New Message" toolbar.

   Your copy of the sent message will be placed in the Mailboxes drawer, in "Personal Mailboxes," in the "Sent" folder.

To reply to the sender of a message:

1. If the message is not already open, click on the message in the Viewer Window, then click the "Reply" button in the toolbar.

2. A Message window opens which contains the original sender's address in the "To" field, and the original message formatted as a quote as shown below. Type your reply above the quote, then click the "Send" button in the toolbar.

Original sender.

Original sender's subject.

Your new message.

The original message so the recipient knows what you're talking about.

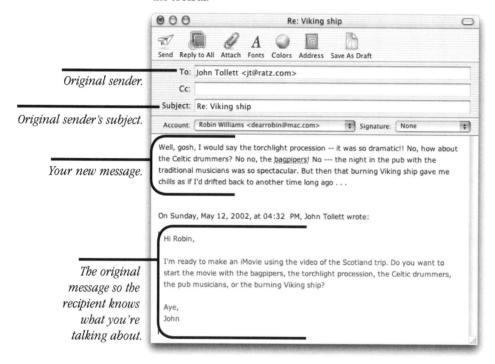

To reply to ALL recipients of a message:

Mail that you receive may have been sent to a number of people, either directly as a Carbon copy (Cc) (now called a Courtesy copy since no one knows what carbon paper is anymore), or secretly as a Blind carbon copy (Bcc). You can choose to reply to all recipients with one email (the reply will not include anyone in the Bcc list).

1. If the message is not already open, select the message in the Viewer Window, then click the "Reply All" button in the toolbar.

2. Type your reply above the original quoted message, then click the "Send" button in the toolbar.

To forward a message you received to someone else:

1. If the message is not already open, select the message in the Viewer Window, then click the "Forward" button in the toolbar.

2. Delete all of the extraneous email addresses—please don't make your recipients scroll through a foot of forwarded junk!

3. Type a personal comment above the original quoted message, then click the "Send" button in the toolbar.

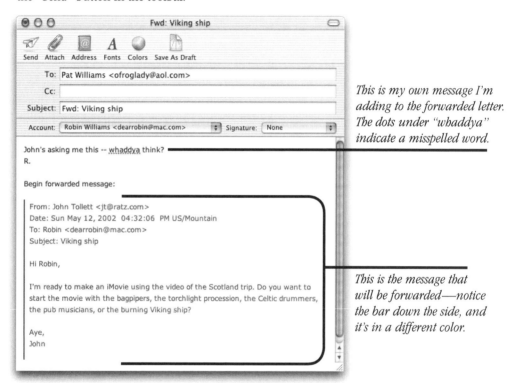

This is my own message I'm adding to the forwarded letter. The dots under "whaddya" indicate a misspelled word.

This is the message that will be forwarded—notice the bar down the side, and it's in a different color.

Tip: *If you won't be able to answer your email for a while, have a message automatically sent to every person who sends you email. This is called an "auto-responder" or "auto-reply." You can set this up on the iTools web page; see page 321.*

Tip: *When you forward a message, **PLEASE** delete all of the extraneous email addresses—please don't make your recipients scroll through a foot of forwarded junk!*

More about composing messages

When you click the **Compose** button to open a "New Message" window, the buttons in the "New Message" toolbar provide easy access to commands that are also in the menu bar at the top of your screen. The following describes what each button is about.

To deliver a message:

Click "Send" to deliver a message. The "Send" button remains gray until you enter an email address in the "To" field of a message. See the example of a message ready to send, below.

To attach a file, like a photograph, to a message:

To attach a file to your message, click the "Attach" button in the toolbar, or choose "Attach" from the Message menu. A dialog box opens so you can find the file you wish to attach. Find the file, select it, then click "Open." (If you don't know how to find files in this open dialog box, please see page 273.)

Another way to attach a file to a message is to drag an icon from the Finder window and drop it in the "New Message" window: Go to the Desktop and either arrange an open Finder window to the side of your screen, or drag that file out of its folder and let it sit on the Desktop. Then when you are in Mail and writing your message, you can reach the file to drag it into the message window to attach it, as shown below. You can attach several files to one email message.

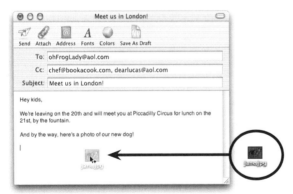

I put the photograph I want to send on the Desktop. Then I opened Mail and wrote my message. Now I can just drag the photo and drop it directly in the message, as shown above.

This is what the attachment looks like in the message area. The recipient can usually just double-click on the icon to open it, or drag it to their Desktop and then open it.

To remove an attachment from a message, *drag* across the icon (don't click on it!) in the message window, then press the Delete key.

To save an unfinished message as a draft:

Some messages may be difficult or time-consuming to write, or you might get interrupted. If you want to finish a message later, click "Save As Draft" in the toolbar, or press Command S. The message will be saved in the Drafts folder that's located in your Mailboxes drawer, as shown below.

To open the Draft ("restore" it) for editing, single-click the "Drafts" icon in the Mailboxes drawer, then double-click the desired draft in the message list (or choose "Restore From Draft" from the File menu). The draft will open in a "New Message" window for you to complete.

It's also a good idea to save a draft whenever you're writing a lengthy letter just in case something happens and your computer goes down—otherwise you'll lose the entire letter. Just press Command S regularly, as you would in any document.

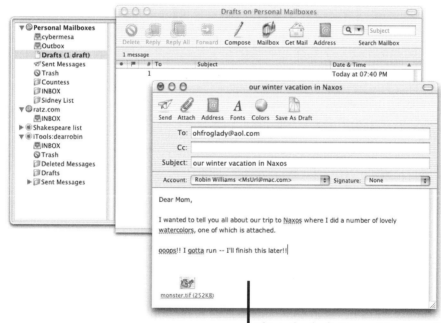

This is the draft. I pressed Command S so it will be saved into my Drafts folder. Later, I'll just open the Drafts folder (single-click it in my Drawer), then double-click the letter to open and finish it.

Change the fonts in your message:

Choose the "Fonts" button in the toolbar to open the Fonts palette. Select text in the "New Message" window (always select the text first!), then select a font family, typeface (regular, bold, italic), and size. The text in the "New Message" window will show style changes as you make them.

If you can't apply formatting to the selected text, perhaps your mail is set up as "Plain Text." Go to the Format menu and change it to "Rich Text Format."

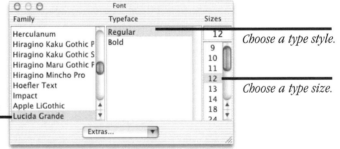

Click a font name to apply it to selected text.

Choose a type style.

Choose a type size.

This is the same Font Panel that TextEdit and other Mac OS X applications use.

Change the color of text in the message:

Choose the "Colors" button in the toolbar to open the Colors palette. The "color wheel" button, as shown circled below, is selected (if not, click once on it).

- **Select text** in a message (just like anywhere else, you must select the text before you can apply any formatting to it), then select a color by clicking or dragging the cursor in the Color palette's color wheel. As you move the cursor around the color wheel, the color swatch in the bottom-left corner changes.

- When you've found a hue of color you like, click the "Apply" button to apply the color to the *selected* text in the message.

- You can also adjust the value (the lightness or darkness) of the selected color by sliding the vertical slider next to the color wheel.

- To save the color for later use, drag the color from the large swatch to one of the wells in the small color swatch collection, located to the right of the magnifying glass.

- Click the magnifying glass to use it as a color picker. Move the magnifying glass anywhere on your screen, then click when the crosshairs of the glass are on top of a color you want to select.

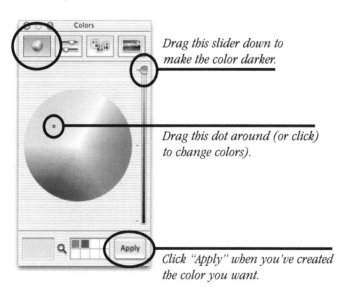

Drag this slider down to make the color darker.

Drag this dot around (or click) to change colors).

Click "Apply" when you've created the color you want.

Customize the Favorites toolbar

The buttons in the **favorites toolbar** are duplicates of some of the commands that are also available in the menu bar across the top of the screen. You can customize this toolbar just like you customize the one in the Finder window.

To add additional tool buttons to the favorites toolbar, go to the View menu and choose "Customize Toolbar...." A pane of buttons appears that represent various functions, as shown below. Drag any of these buttons to the favorites toolbar for easy access.

To remove a button from the toolbar, Command-drag it off the bar.

To rearrange a button, Command-drag it to another position.

Command-click this button at any time to switch the toolbar between icons, icons with text, or just text.

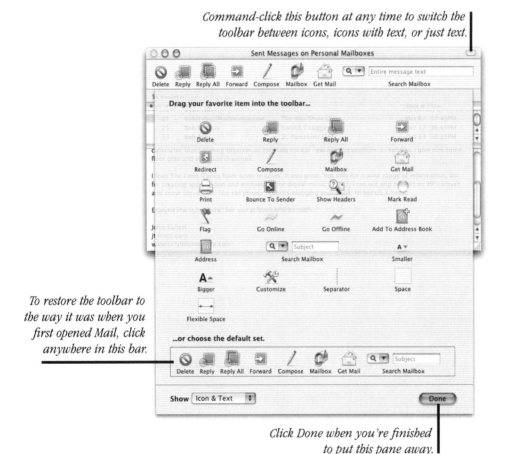

To restore the toolbar to the way it was when you first opened Mail, click anywhere in this bar.

Click Done when you're finished to put this pane away.

Search through your mailboxes

Most of the buttons in the favorites toolbar are self-explanatory, except the **Search Mailbox** button. You can search mailboxes based on the content of email headers (To, From, etc.), or based on the content of the body of a message.

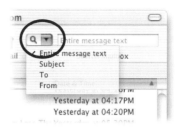

1. In the Mailboxes drawer, select a mailbox to search.

2. Click on the magnifying-glass pop-down menu in the toolbar.

3. Choose the type of content on which to base the search:

   ■ "Entire message text" searches the content of the message body.

   ■ "To," "From," or "Subject" searches the content of a header.

4. Type one or more words in the text field on the right side of the menu.

5. As you type, the Message List pane will display only the files that contain the text you're entering. If multiple messages qualify for the search, the "Rank" column displays a relevance control that indicates the relative ranking of search results. A message with a longer bar in the "Rank" column is more relevant to the search criteria.

Bounce To Sender is meant to discourage **unwanted email:** Select an unwanted message in the List pane, then from the Message menu (across the top of the screen), choose "Bounce To Sender." The sender will receive a reply that says your email address is invalid and that the message was not delivered. The unwanted message is moved to your "Deleted Messages" folder. The recipient cannot tell if the message has been read. Unfortunately, this does not work for most spam (junk email) because spam return addresses are usually invalid (to prevent spammers from being spammed).

Redirect is similar to "Forward," except it doesn't *look* like it was forwarded. Your return address is not in the message body, and the text is not formatted as a quote. Redirected mail shows the original sender's name in the "From" column instead of yours, and shows the time the message was originally composed in the "Date & Time" column of Mail's Viewer Window. When you redirect mail, your name remains in the "To" header at the top of the message so the new recipient will know that you received the message and that you redirected it.

A guide to the Message List pane

The **Message List pane** displays a list of all messages in the currently selected Mailbox. The list is divided into several columns. The Message List pane provides different views of a list, depending on which column is selected.

The columns of information

The **column headings** are all explained on these pages. Besides the default headings that appear, you can choose to show two additional columns.

From the View menu, choose:

- "Show Contents Column" to show email attachments.

An attachment is a file, separate from an email message, that you can "attach" and send along with an email.

- "Show Message Sizes" to show email file sizes, including *attachments,* in a column. If you don't know who a message is from, it's a good idea not to open the attachment.

Also from the the View menu, you can choose to **hide** the Number, Contents, Flags, and Sizes columns.

To change the column widths, position the pointer over the gray dividing line in the column headings, then press-and-drag the column left or right.

To rearrange the list according to the column heading, just click the heading at the top of a column. The blue column heading is the one that items are currently arranged by.

These are the column headings. Click a heading to sort the messages by that column.

The first column is the Message Status column, as explained on the following page.

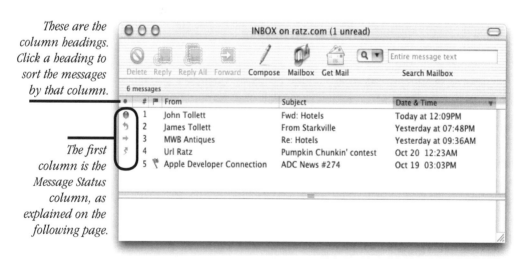

A guide to the icons in the Message Status column

The **Message Status** column (•) uses different icons to indicate if you've read the message, replied to it, forwarded it, or redirected it. These icons are applied automatically when one of those actions takes place. In addition, you can manually mark an email that you've already read as "unread." You can use this as a reminder to go back and read a message more carefully, or to make a message stand out in the list: Select a message or multiple messages, then from the Message menu, select "Mark As Unread."

Click the column heading to group similar Categories, such as unread or returned messages, together in the list. Click again in the column heading to reverse the order of the list.

Message Status **icons** give visual clues to the status of messages.

Blue orb: Message has not been read.

Curved arrow: Message was replied to.

→ Right arrow: Message was forwarded.

Segmented arrow: Message was redirected.

Number column: In a series of email exchanges, it may be useful to know in what order messages were received. The Number column keeps track of the order for you. Click the **#** symbol in the column heading to arrange messages by order. Click again in the column heading to reverse the order of the list.

Flags column: Mark a message as "flagged" when you want it to stand out in the list, or if you want to temporarily tag a group of related messages. **To search for flagged files** in a list, click the "Flag" column heading; all flagged messages will move to the top of the list. Click the heading again to reverse the order and put flagged messages at the bottom of the list.

Subject column: This column shows the text that the sender typed into the Subject header of their email message. Click the heading of the column to show the subjects in alphabetical order; click again to reverse the order of the list.

Date & Time column: This column displays the date and time you received a message. Click the heading of the column to show messages in the time sequence they were received; click again to reverse the order of the list.

Using the Mailboxes drawer

The **Mailboxes drawer** slides out from either side of the Viewer Window, depending on how much screen space is available to the left or right.

Besides the Mailboxes that appear automatically when you create new accounts, you can manually create new Mailboxes at any time to customize the storage and management of your email accounts (page 347).

To open (or close) the Mailboxes drawer, single-click the Mailbox button in the toolbar. **Or** drag the edge of the drawer. **Or** go to the View menu and choose "Show Mailboxes."

*The **Personal Mailboxes** section holds the Outbox, Trash, Drafts, and Sent Messages folders for all of your non-Mac.com accounts, as well as folders you've created for storing files.*

You can see here that Mail is checking two different Mac.com accounts (the apple icons), as well as an account forwarded from my web site at ratz.com (the @ icon), plus my ISP account (cybermesa, under "Personal Mailboxes").

I created a number of folders (mailboxes) and told Mail to send certain messages into those mailboxes (use the Account Options pane in the Accounts preferences). For instance, I am on the Sidney Family/Edmund Spencer email list, and that email goes directly into the "Sidney List" mailbox.

Send mail from a different Mailbox account

If you only have one account, skip the next couple of paragraphs.

Some people, like me and my partner John, get email at several different addresses, each coming from a different server. You might have an account from your ISP, one from your own web site, one at work, and an iTools account as well. **Mail can check all of your email accounts at once,** once you set them up. When you answer mail, you can choose to have it answered from any one of your accounts, no matter to which account the original message was mailed.

To set up your other accounts so Mail can check them all, see pages 348–350.

If you have more than one account in the Mailboxes drawer, the "New Message" window provides a pop-up "Account" menu that contains the names of all accounts you've created. From the pop-up menu, choose the account that you want the message sent *from*.

To change the default account in Mail, drag another account to the top of the list in the Mailboxes drawer (below Personal Mailboxes).

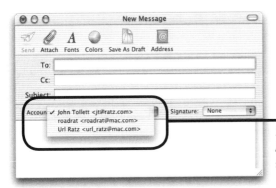

This is John's Mail. If he received an email to his ratz.com account, he could answer it with a return address from any of his other accounts.

What do the little circular icons mean?

Accounts in the Mailboxes drawer are marked with either a blue **@ icon** or a red **Apple icon.**

Email in accounts marked with the blue @ symbol is actually being stored on your computer's hard disk.

Email in accounts marked with the Apple icon are *not* on your computer. They are on an Apple IMAP *server* far away, but you can view them and manipulate them. There's important information about storing your mail on Apple's IMAP server on the following two pages.

*server: A big computer that is **not** the one you're sitting at.*

IMAP vs. POP

Apple's Mail program can handle two types of incoming mail "protocol": **IMAP** and **POP** (or POP3, to be specific). A protocol is a particular set of standards or rules having to do with communications between computers.

*Email from a POP account is stored on **your** hard disk.*

POP3 (Post Office Protocol 3) is a protocol in which the server automatically downloads the mail to your computer when you check mail, then *deletes* the mail from the server. With POP you cannot read mail *until* it has been downloaded to your computer. POP works best for users who always use one computer on which email files are stored and managed.

You can choose to leave your mail on the POP server after it has been downloaded to your iMac (see page 350; use the Account Options pane), but it's not a good idea—it will make your service provider mad to have all of your email clogging up space on their server, plus your mailbox will eventually get full and won't accept new mail.

*Email from an IMAP account is stored on a **remote** server (not your hard disk).*

IMAP (Internet Message Access Protocol) is a protocol that receives and *holds* email on a server for a certain amount of time, typically thirty days. IMAP allows you to view email before deciding whether or not to download it to your computer.

One advantage of IMAP is that you can manage your email from multiple computers because the email files are kept on the IMAP server for storage and manipulation. This means if you check your mail on one computer while you're away from home, say in Glasgow, you can come home and check your mail and get the same messages at home that you read in Glasgow.

America Online uses an IMAP server. That's why you can choose whether or not to download a file, and your email disappears automatically after thirty days whether you like it or not.

Another advantage is that you can choose *not* to download email that has large attachments, or email from people you don't want to hear from. You can wait until it's convenient, until you know who an attachment is from, or you can just delete unwanted or unsolicited email and attachments before they ever get to your computer.

When you sign up for a free Mac.com email service through iTools, you're assigned a five-megabyte mailbox on Apple's IMAP mail server. All messages within an account, *even deleted messages,* are stored on Apple's server for one month by default, unless you designate a different length of time. If you get more than five megabytes of mail and attachments, people will not be able to send you any more email at that account until you clear it out.

To choose how long your deleted Mac.com email remains stored on Apple's IMAP server before it's totally erased:

1. From the Mail menu, choose "Preferences…."

2. Click the "Viewing" button in the favorites toolbar.

3. In the pop-up menu "Erase deleted mail when," you have the options of "Never," "One day old," "One week old," "One month old," and "Quitting Mail."

If you choose to "Never" erase deleted mail, you'll eventually fill up your five-megabyte allocation on the server and you won't be able to receive new mail. To avoid this, copy important mail to your computer as explained below.

Tip: You can also drag an entire mailbox from an IMAP account in the Mailboxes drawer to "Personal Mailboxes." This will make a copy of the mailbox and its contents on your computer.

If you choose any of the other options for erasing deleted mail, plenty of IMAP server space will remain available, but you still won't have a permanent copy of your email unless you **create a new Mailbox** on your computer and copy the email that you want to keep into that Mailbox.

Create a new mailbox for permanently storing selected email messages:

1. Open the Mailboxes drawer (click the Mailbox button).

2. Click the "Personal Mailboxes" folder to select it so your new Mailbox will be created within the Personal Mailboxes folder. You want to create the new "local" Mailbox (which is really a folder) inside the Personal Mailboxes folder because messages and folders stored here will be on your Mac's hard drive, not on the Apple server.

"Local" means it is on your hard disk, as opposed to "remote," which means it is on someone else's hard disk, usually far away.

3. From the "Mailbox" menu, choose "New Mailbox…."

4. Type a name in the "New Mailbox name" field, then click OK.

5. In the Viewer Window, select the emails you want to keep and drag them to your new, local Mailbox.

Notice that the messages you just moved to your new, local Mailbox have *disappeared* from the Inbox they were in.

Select any remaining, unwanted messages that remain in the IMAP Inbox and click the "Delete" button in the toolbar. The deleted messages will remain on Apple's server for the length of time you specified in Mail Preferences (above), unless you remove them manually.

Tip: To permanently delete messages, from the Mailbox menu, choose "Empty Deleted Messages." The Mailbox menu may show "Compact Trash," "Empty Deleted Items," or "Empty Trash," depending on how you set up Mail.

Accounts

Set up a new account

Use **Mail Preferences** to create new mail accounts, edit existing accounts, and to customize Mail's behavior.

To open Preferences and get the Accounts pane:

1. From the Mail menu, choose "Preferences...."

2. The "Mail Preferences" toolbar shows six buttons representing different Categories of preferences. Click **Accounts.**

   The **Description** list shows all the email accounts you've created.

   To **create** a new account, see the opposite page.

   To **edit** the preferences of an existing account, select the account in the list, then click "Edit" to show the "Account Preferences" sheet (or double-click the account name). See the following pages for a description of the "Account Preferences" pane.

   To **remove** an account from the list, select it, then click "Remove."

Check accounts for new mail: Set how often you want to check for new mail. This only works if Mail is open (if the triangle is under its icon in the Dock). If you don't have a full-time, always-on connection to the Internet (such as DSL or cable modem), you'll probably want to select the "Manually" option to avoid having your modem dialing and trying to connect when you least expect it.

Play sound when new mail arrives: Choose various sound alerts when email appears, or "None."

Create Account: You may have more than one email account in your life. For instance, you might have one that is strictly for business, one for friends and family, one for your lover, and one for your research. Mail can manage them all for you—just add new email accounts to the Mailboxes drawer.

1. From the Mail menu, choose "Preferences...."

2. Click "Accounts" in the toolbar, then click "Create Account."

3. You should see the "Account Information" pane; if not, click the tab.

Mail cannot get your AOL email. Nothing can get AOL email except AOL (although you can use any browser anywhere in the world and go to www.aol.com to get your mail).

Tip: If you're setting up another account type, the mail service provider can tell you what name to use. Tell them you need to know the "incoming" mail server name, also known as the "POP address." (It's probably something like "mail.domainname.com," where "domainname" is the name in your email address, such as mail.ratz.com)

4. Choose an **Account Type** from the pop-up menu.

   Choose "Mac.com Account" if you're setting up an email account that you created using the Apple iTools web site.

   If you're setting up an account that comes from some other service provider, they can tell you if they use POP, IMAP, or UNIX (it's most likely POP).

5. In the **Description** field, type a name that will identify the account in the Mailboxes drawer. You can name it anything, such as "Lover Boy" or "Research Mailing List."

6. If you're setting up a Mac.com address, the **Email Address** field will be automatically filled in with your Mac.com email address.

7. **Host name** is the "incoming" email server name. If your account type is "Mac.com Account," the host name will automatically be filled in with "mail.Mac.com."

—continued

8. If you're setting up a Mac.com account, **User name** and **Password** are the same ones you chose when you signed up for a Mac.com account through Apple's iTools web site. You should have seen a web page verifying this information.

If you're setting up a POP or UNIX account, your user ID and password may have been assigned by your provider, or they may have been chosen by you. *These are not necessarily the same user ID and password that you use to access your email.* If necessary, ask your provider for the user ID and password information.

9. **SMTP Host** refers to the "outgoing" email server address; this is always your ISP.

Mac.com is **not** an ISP (see page 18). For instance, I have several email accounts, but I *pay* Cybermesa in Santa Fe for my Internet connection; Cybermesa is my ISP. My SMTP host is **mail.cybermesa.com.** If your ISP is ATTBI, your SMTP host is probably **mail.attbi.com.** EarthLink is **pop.earthlink.net.**

10. The **SMTP User** and **SMTP Password** fields are disabled unless you've checked the option "Use authentication when sending mail." As a deterrent to spam (unsolicited email, usually junk mail), this option instructs the mail server to verify your identity and password as someone who has permission to send outgoing mail through the server. The SMTP User ID and the SMTP Password for a Mac.com account would be the same as the Host User name and Password above. Apple's IMAP email server recognizes SMTP authentication, but not all servers do.

If you're setting up an account other than Mac.com, ask your service provider if they support this feature. Or just leave it unchecked.

The **Account Options** tab lets you customize more settings, depending on whether you're creating an IMAP account (such as a Mac.com account) or a POP account (most others). The useful options are self-explanatory; just ignore anything that doesn't make sense.

Address Book

Address Book

The **Address Book** works both independently and in conjunction with Mail to create Address Cards that store contact information for individuals or groups. When *Mail* is open, you can automatically create an Address Book entry for anyone who sent mail to you. When *Address Book* is open you can automatically address email to an individual or group. You can search the Address Book by name, email address, or by a user-defined Category.

If an address can be found in Address Book, the complete address is automatically filled in for you when you start to type it in the "To" field of a message header.

The **Address Book window** consists of the Toolbar, Search bar and Show menu, Address Card pane, and the vCard at the bottom of the window.

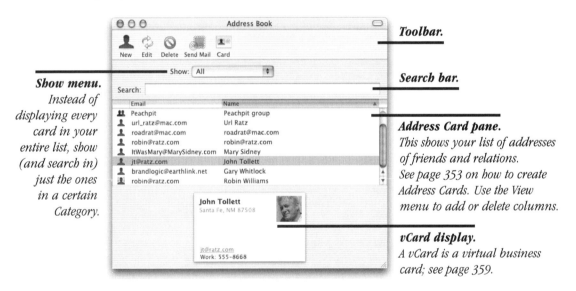

Toolbar.

Show menu.
Instead of displaying every card in your entire list, show (and search in) just the ones in a certain Category.

Search bar.

Address Card pane.
This shows your list of addresses of friends and relations.
See page 353 on how to create Address Cards. Use the View menu to add or delete columns.

vCard display.
A vCard is a virtual business card; see page 359.

Address Book

To open Address Book, do one of the following:

- If Mail is open, go to the Window menu and choose "Address Book," *or* press Command Option A.

- If Mail is open and you see a "vCard" in a message, single-click on the blue underlined name of the vCard.

- If Mail is not open, go to the Applications window (click on the Applications icon in any Finder window), then double-click on the Address Book icon.

- If you use Address Book regularly or want it accessible even when Mail is not open, add its icon to the Dock.

The **Address Card pane** lists the Address Cards according to the group you've chosen in the "Show" pop-up menu, as well as the "Available Fields" (or columns of information) you've chosen from the View menu in the main menu bar.

The **Show** menu lists different Categories that you can sort your addresses into, such as Home, Work, Buddy, Group. An address can be in more than one Category. A group list is automatically placed in the Group Category.

To sort the Address Cards by the column heading, click on a column heading. To reverse the order, click the small triangle in the heading.

To rearrange the position of columns, drag a column heading left or right to a new position.

Add an Address Card to Address Book

An **Address Card** contains the email address of your contact person, plus you can add lots of other information to the card, such as phone and fax numbers, birthdates, names of their children, and more. **To add a card,** first open Address Book in any of the ways mentioned on the opposite page, then:

- To automatically create an Address Card for someone who sent email to you, select their email message in the Message List window (in Mail). Then press Command Y or choose "Add Sender To Address Book" from the Message menu.

- In the Address Book, go to the File menu and choose "New," or click the "New" button in the toolbar to open an "untitled Address Card." Enter the appropriate information and click "Save."

- **Or** If someone sent you a vCard (virtual business card, explained on page 359), drag it from their email message to the Address Book window, as shown below.

Tip: If you plan to use FAXstf to send faxes from your iMac, be sure to fill the fax number in the Address Card here because FAXstf uses it.

*This is a **vCard** in an email message. Drag it into the list of the Address Book and drop it anywhere in that pane.*

Create a Group (a private mailing list)

A **Group,** or private mailing list, in Address Book is a sub-collection of your email addresses so you can send a message to everyone in that Group at once. You might have a Group for your family, a different Group for your fellow office workers, and a Group for your rugby team or chess team. The same address can be in more than one Group.

To create a new Group, do one of the following:

- From the File menu in the Address Book, choose "New Group."

- **Or,** if you've customized the toolbar (as explained on page 360) to include the "New Group" button, click it.

- **Or** Command-click to select multiple cards in the Address Card List, then from the File menu, choose "New Group From Selection."

Each method opens an "untitled Address Card" window designed to include a Group of email addresses and assign a Group name, as shown below.

Enter a Group name and description, then click the **Categories...** button and select one or more Categories (if you like—it's not critical). A Group list is auto-matically placed in the Group Category as well as any other you select. See page 358 for details about Categories.

This is the group list of addresses.

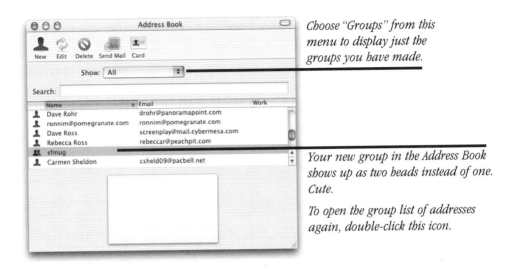

Choose "Groups" from this menu to display just the groups you have made.

Your new group in the Address Book shows up as two heads instead of one. Cute.

To open the group list of addresses again, double-click this icon.

To add an email address to the Group: In the Group list window shown on the opposite page, type a new address in the "Address" field, then click the "Plus" button. **Or** drag an Address Book entry from the Address Book window and drop it in the list pane of the Group window.

To remove an address from the Group: In the Group list window shown on the opposite page, select the address and click the "Minus" button.

To send email to the entire Group:

Select a Group in the Address Book window (click once on it), then click the "Send Mail" button in the toolbar. Mail opens and a "New Message" window opens, addressed to the Group. **Or** in the New Message window, type the name of the Group in the "To" field, as shown below.

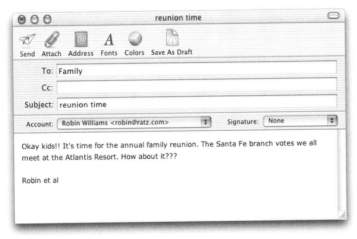

Tip: You can choose whether the email will be addressed to the group name, as shown to the left, or will display each individual email address in the group:

Open Mail, then from the Mail menu (not the Address Book menu), choose "Preferences...."

Click the "Composing" button.

Check or uncheck "List private group members individually."

Details of an Address Card

You can add lots of information to **Address Cards** so they become quite useful. Besides contact information, you can keep track of birthdays, meetings, shoe size, notes, and more.

To expand the Address Card and store more contact information, click the triangle above the "Save" button.

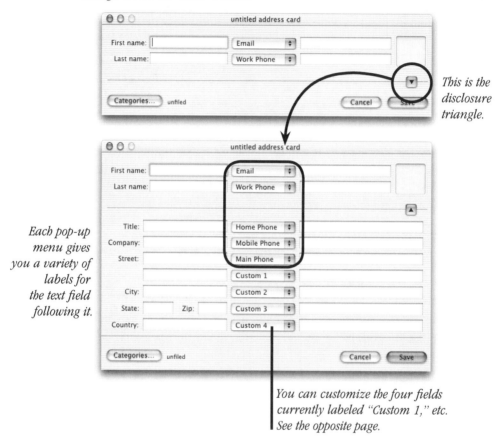

This is the disclosure triangle.

Each pop-up menu gives you a variety of labels for the text field following it.

You can customize the four fields currently labeled "Custom 1," etc. See the opposite page.

From the first five pop-up menus (circled, above), **choose the label** you want to apply to the field.

Customize any of the other four fields as explained on the opposite page.

Define the Custom labels of an Address Card

You can **define your own labels** for the four "Custom" pop-up menus. These four options will apply to every one of your Address Cards. You can change the *labels* at any time, although the *data* in the fields won't change to match the new label.

To define the Custom labels:

1. From any one of the four "Custom" pop-up menus, choose "Edit...."
   A sheet will drop down from the title bar, as shown below.

2. Name the "Custom Fields," then click "Save."
   You don't have to name all four of them at this point.

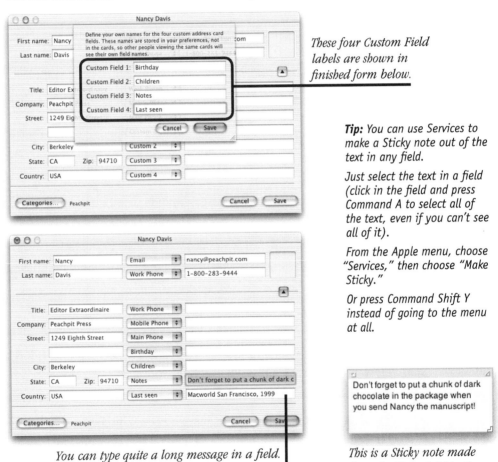

These four Custom Field labels are shown in finished form below.

Tip: You can use Services to make a Sticky note out of the text in any field.

Just select the text in a field (click in the field and press Command A to select all of the text, even if you can't see all of it).

From the Apple menu, choose "Services," then choose "Make Sticky."

Or press Command Shift Y instead of going to the menu at all.

Don't forget to put a chunk of dark chocolate in the package when you send Nancy the manuscript!

You can type quite a long message in a field. To show the information in custom fields in the Address Book window, use the View menu and choose from the "Available Fields."

This is a Sticky note made from the Notes field in the Address Card.

Make a new Category for addresses

You will eventually have quite a few email addresses in your list. To keep them organized and make it easier to find what you need, you can create separate **Categories** and file each Address Card into a Category. Then from the "Show" pop-up menu in the Address Book window, you can choose to show just one Category at a time.

One Address Card can be in as many Categories as you like. Categories are also helpful when conducting a search for email addresses because you can limit the search to just certain Categories.

Several Categories have been made for you already. You can add to the existing list, and you can delete any that you make.

The Categories listed in bold are the ones Apple made for you; you cannot delete these.

The Categories you create will not appear in bold type.

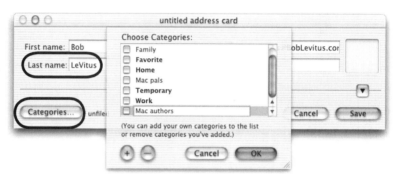

To file a card into a Category, double-click any Address Card to open the detail window, as shown above. Click the "Categories..." button in the bottom-left corner to show the "Choose Categories" sheet. Select a category from the existing list.

To make a new Category, double-click any Address Card. Click the "Categories..." button in the bottom-left corner to show the "Choose Categories" sheet, as shown above. Click the "Plus" button to create and name a new Category.

To make a new Category appear in the "Show" pop-up menu, you have to quit Address Book, then open it again. Hopefully Apple will fix that.

To remove a Category that you created, select it, then click the "Minus" button.

To display the Categories in the Address Book main window, choose a Category from the "Show" pop-up menu (other than "All"). Only cards that have been filed in the chosen Category will appear in the Address Book window.

Create vCards

A **vCard** is a virtual business card. When you receive a vCard from someone, it has a .vcf extension (virtual card file) and appears in your email message as an attachment. Address Book automatically creates a vCard for every contact in your list.

To create a new Address Card from a vCard that someone sent you, drag the vCard icon from the Mail window to the Address Book window.

To see the vCard for anyone in your Address Book, select that person's entry, then click the "Card" button in the toolbar. The vCard that appears at the bottom of the Address Book window provides a quick view of the essential contact information. **To hide the vCard,** click the "Card" button again.

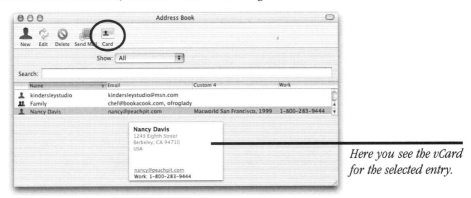

Here you see the vCard for the selected entry.

Attach your vCard to outgoing messages

You can **attach your vCard** to email messages. (But keep in mind that some people don't appreciate getting a vCard because it's another file that has to be downloaded, and if it's attached to every email you send someone, they have to download it everytime they hear from you.)

To add your vCard to an email message, open a "New Message" window (open Mail, then click the "Compose" button in the toolbar). From the Address Book, grab the small icon (the head-and-shoulders silhouette) next to your email address and drag it to Mail's "New Message" window.

vCards can **include images** to help identify Address Book entries, as shown on the following page. But support for vCards in Mail is limited at this time. Currently, when you attach a photo to your Address Card, the photo is not automatically sent with the vCard. If you want to include your photo, you have to send it as an attachment. After sending a photo, the recipient can drag your vCard into their Address Card list, as explained on the following page, and *your* photo will appear on *your* vCard in *their* list.

Customize the Address Book toolbar

To customize the toolbar, hold down the Control key and click on the toolbar. From the contextual menu that appears, choose "Customize toolbar...." Drag any button from the customize toolbar sheet (shown below) up to the toolbar and drop it.

Display the toolbar:

From the "Show" pop-up menu, choose "Icon & Text," "Text Only," or "Icon Only."

Or cycle through these "Show" choices when the customize toolbar sheet is not visible: Command-click on the clear button at the top-right corner of the Address Book window.

Or Control-click on the toolbar, then from the contextual menu, choose one of these three toolbar views.

The **Separator** is a visual device to help organize items in the toolbar. The only buttons that are not on the toolbar by default are the "New Group" button and the "Directory" button.

New Group: Opens an "untitled Address Card" window so you can create a group of email addresses. See page 354 for details.

Directory: Refers to LDAP (pronounced *el dap*) directories. LDAP (Lightweight Directory Access Protocol), is a scaled-back version of DAP (Directory Access Protocol), a protocol for accessing large, searchable, online directories of information, similar to phone books, over a network, or on the Internet. LDAP is referred to as "lightweight" because it's less complicated and easier to implement than DAP.

Mail and Address Book can look up email addresses and contact information in LDAP directories, if you have access to such a directory. Chances are you do not have access to an LDAP directory unless you're on a large network, in which case you should have the network administrator help you set up access, which may require special software. There are public LDAP directories on the Internet, and Mac OS X will enable you to access those in the near future.

iMovie: Be a Movie Mogul!

Making movies is incredibly fun and easy with **iMovie.** Connect a digital video camera to your computer with a FireWire cable, launch iMovie, and you're ready to create home movies with sound tracks, transitions between scenes, special effects, and customized titles.

If you didn't get a **FireWire cable** with your camera, check the small box that came with your iMac—often there is a FireWire cable in it. If you don't have a cable and need to order one, go to **www.cameraworld.com**.

Digital video (DV) requires a lot of disk space: One minute of raw DV footage uses about 220 MB of hard disk space. A four-minute iMovie that contains sound tracks, transitions, and titles may use 4 to 6 *gigabytes* of disk space.

If you're serious about making iMovies, or if you just can't control yourself after making your first iMovie, buy an extra, very large FireWire drive to use when working with video. You'll be surprised how fast you can fill a dedicated 80 GB hard drive when you start making movies.

This is the icon that designates a FireWire port. **FireWire** *is a type of connection that is fast enough to handle the transfer of video to your computer.*

With iMovie you can create memorable moments so easily. Here are my friends Tim Thomas and Lew Nelson toasting at Macworld. Where are Phil and Leigh??

An overview of the basic steps

Making an iMovie consists of **five basic steps.** This chapter will walk you through each step.

1. Import video clips to the shelf (below).

2. Edit the clips (pages 364–365).

3. Place edited clips into the movie Timeline (page 366).

4. Add transitions, titles, effects, and audio (pages 369–371).

5. Export the iMovie (page 374).

As you shoot video, keep in mind that every time you start and stop the camera, iMovie will interpret that as a "scene." Each scene will appear in its own little slot on the "shelf." You can then rearrange the order, edit each scene individually, and much more. Of course, you can always split a scene, cut from one scene and make a separate one, etc., but it's good to keep the scene divisions in mind as you shoot.

Import clips to the Shelf

Before you can **import,** of course, you must connect the camera to the Mac.

Connect your camera:

1. With the camera off, plug one end of the FireWire cable into the camera and the other end into the Mac's FireWire port.

2. Put the camera into VTR mode (VTR stands for Video Tape Recorder).

3. Open iMovie.

4. Turn on the camera. In a couple of seconds, the monitor area will display the words "Camera Connected," as shown below.

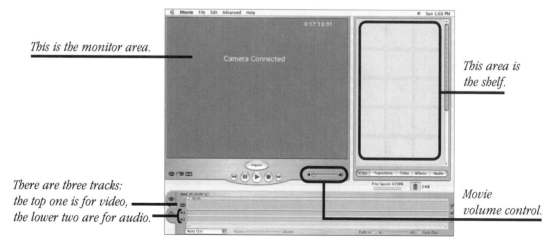

This is the monitor area.

This area is the shelf.

There are three tracks: the top one is for video, the lower two are for audio.

Movie volume control.

Preview the raw footage:

1. In the iMovie interface, click the "Camera mode" button, circled below.

2. Then click the "Play" button to play the video in the iMovie monitor.

At this point you are just *previewing* the video. iMovie will not digitize and import any video until you click the "Import" button. To economize disk space, preview your footage, then rewind and import just the best of it.

Import video footage into iMovie:

1. Click the "Play" button to view the raw footage.

2. When you see footage you want to import, click the "Import" button (circled, below). The Import button is blue when it is selected and importing files. You can back up while in Play mode (click the Reverse arrows), but not while Importing.

3. To stop importing, click the "Import" button again. Each time you start and stop importing, iMovie will place that segment (called a "clip") into a separate slot on the "shelf" at the upper-right corner of the iMovie window.

If you have plenty of disk space, you can let the camera run. iMovie will import all "scenes" (individual segments that were created when you started and stopped the camera, as described on the opposite page) as separate clips and place them on the shelf.

*Note: The Camera mode button will automatically switch to **Edit mode** (the button to the right) whenever you click on a clip or the shelf. You need to be in Edit mode to create your movie.*

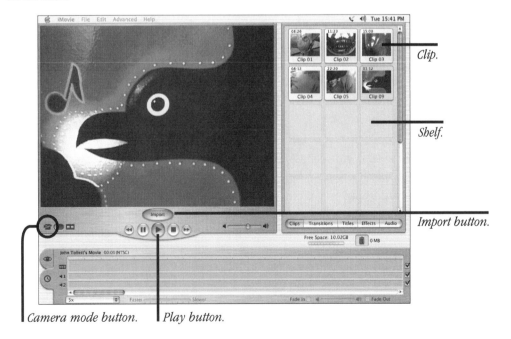

Clip.

Shelf.

Import button.

Camera mode button. *Play button.*

Edit clips

Many **clips** are longer than necessary and should be **trimmed** or **cropped.**

- Trimming, in iMovie, means to select and delete *unwanted* video frames either at the beginning or the end of a clip.

- Cropping means to delete all frames in a clip *other than* the selected frames.

To display and preview a clip:

1. Click a clip on the shelf to select it. The clip is displayed in the monitor. A blue "scrubber bar" appears, as shown below. The scrubber bar represents the time length of the clip.

2. Preview the entire clip by dragging the Playhead (the large white triangle) across the scrubber bar, or click the "Play" button.

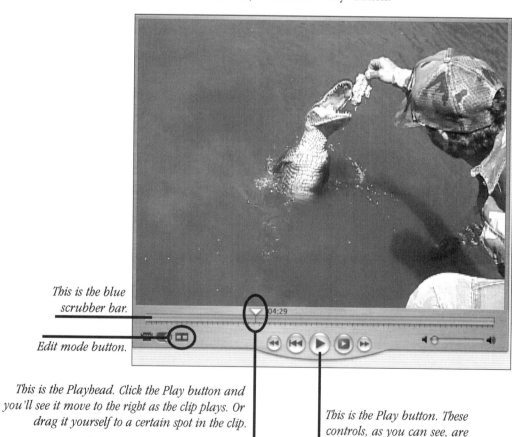

This is the blue scrubber bar.

Edit mode button.

This is the Playhead. Click the Play button and you'll see it move to the right as the clip plays. Or drag it yourself to a certain spot in the clip.

The number indicates how many seconds have elapsed in the clip.

This is the Play button. These controls, as you can see, are just like the controls on any other media player.

To trim a clip:

1. Click directly beneath the scrubber bar to show the crop markers, two small triangles. Drag the crop markers to select the frames at the beginning or the end of a clip that you *want to delete.*

2. From the Edit menu, choose "Clear" to delete all of the selected frames.

To crop a clip:

1. Click directly beneath the scrubber bar to show the crop markers, two small triangles. Use the crop markers to select a range of frames in the clip that you *want to keep.*

2. Drag the crop markers individually to select a range of frames. The selected frames are highlighted in yellow.

3. From the Edit menu, choose "Crop" to delete all of the frames that were *not* selected.

Tip: When you crop or trim a clip on the shelf, the deleted data goes in the Trash, located just below the shelf. Once a clip is in the Trash, you can't take it out.

Because even a moderate amount of editing results in a huge amount of Trash, you can preserve disk space if you keep an eye on the Trash and empty it occasionally: From the File menu choose "Empty Trash...."

The circles point out the crop markers.

This shows a selection of the clip that is going to be cropped. After choosing "Crop" from the Edit menu, this section is all that will remain of the clip.

After you've edited a clip, you're going to drag it to the **Timeline** at the bottom of the iMovie window, as explained on the following page, so you can put your movie together.

But when you crop and trim clips as described above, you eliminate the possibility of ever going back later to use segments of clips that you deleted. You might want to keep the original, unedited footage available and accessible. In that case, **copy and paste** a clip segment.

To copy and paste a clip:

1. Use the crop markers to select a range of frames that you want to add to your movie.

2. Press Command C to copy the selection.

3. Click in the Timeline at the bottom of the iMovie window.

—continued

4. Press Command V to paste the selection into the Timeline.

If there are already other clips in the movie track, you can place the copied selection wherever you want: click on an existing clip in the movie track. Type Command V and your selection will be pasted *to the right* of the clip you clicked on.

If later you decide that you need a longer segment from that original clip (to sync with a music track, for instance), the clip in its entirety is still on the shelf instead of forever lost in the Trash.

Place clips in a movie

There are two overlapped editing areas at the bottom of the iMovie window: the **Timeline** (indicated by the clock icon) and the **Clip Viewer** (indicated by the eyeball icon). If you put a clip in either the Timeline or the Clip Viewer, it automatically appears in the other area.

Click this to display the Clip Viewer (bottom of next page).

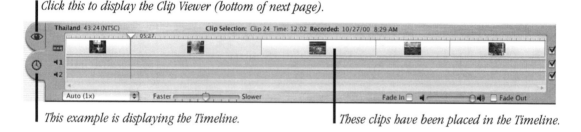

This example is displaying the Timeline.   *These clips have been placed in the Timeline.*

The Timeline

Use the **Timeline** to arrange the order of clips, add transitions between clips, add effects, create titles, and add audio to your movie.

To add clips to the Timeline:

- **Either** drag the clips you created from the shelf to the Timeline.

- **Or,** as explained above, copy segments of clips and paste them into the Timeline.

To rearrange clips in the Timeline:

1. Click on a clip in the Timeline to select it.

2. Press Command X to delete it from its current position in the Timeline.

3. Next, select a clip (click on it) in the Timeline immediately to the left of where you want the new clip.

4. Press Command V to paste the clip to the right of the selected clip.

The **Zoom** pop-up menu lets you view the Timeline at different zoom levels. Higher zoom levels show the Timeline in greater detail for precise editing. Lower zoom levels show more clips in the Timeline, to reduce the amount of scrolling necessary.

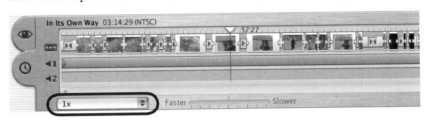

A low zoom level makes more clips visible in the Timeline.

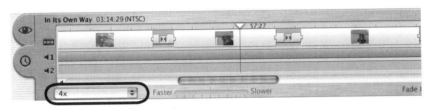

A higher zoom level makes it easier to precisely place the Playhead or to drag a sound track to a certain position. When you use very short clips, you need a higher zoom level to see them clearly.

The Clip Viewer

You can also use the **Clip Viewer,** shown below, to place and rearrange clips, add transitions and effects, and create titles. You cannot work with sound tracks while using the Clip Viewer, but, unlike in the Timeline, you *can* drag clips out of the movie and back to the shelf.

To place clips in a movie using the Clip Viewer:

Either drag clips from the shelf to the Clip Viewer, or use the copy-and-paste technique explained on pages 365–366.

To rearrange clips in the Clip Viewer:

Simply drag a clip to a new location.

This is the Clip Viewer.

You can rename these clips. Just click on the clip number to highlight the text, then type the name.

Preview the assembled clips

To **preview** your movie, move the Playhead (the white triangle) in the Timeline to the beginning of the movie, or wherever you choose, then click the Play button.

Notice that if you click on a specific *clip* in the Timeline, only that clip shows and plays in the monitor. To load the entire movie into the monitor, click anywhere in the Timeline *except* on a clip (click in the Timeline above the clips or in one of the audio tracks).

Each of these segments represents a clip in the movie.

Click this button to play your movie in full-screen mode on your iMac.

The small shapes between clips are "transitions" that affect how one scene blends into the next.

When the monitor displays the entire movie, the scrubber bar is divided into segments. Each segment is a separate clip in the movie. The small objects that appear between clips in the Timeline are the transitions that were dragged from the Transitions window to the Timeline, as described on the opposite page.

Add transitions, titles, effects, and audio

If your movie requires precise synchronization between music tracks and video footage, it's best to assemble all your clips in the Timeline before adding transitions and effects because transitions and effects can alter clip lengths. For some movies, this may not be an issue.

Transitions

A **transition** is a visual effect that creates a bridge from one scene to the next scene. It might be a cross dissolve, a fade out, a spinning image, or any of a wide variety of other effects.

To add a transition effect between two clips:

1. Click the "Transitions" button beneath the shelf to reveal the Transitions window, as shown below.

2. Click on a transition to see its effect previewed in the small preview window. The "Preview" button plays the effect full-size in the monitor, but the preview may be too slow to be very useful.

3. Use the "Speed" slider to determine the time length of the transition.

4. Drag the selected transition to the Timeline (or Clip Viewer) and drop it between two clips of your choosing.

To delete a transition at any time: select it in the Timeline and hit the Delete key.

To change a placed transition: select it in the Timeline, make changes in the Transitions window, then click "Update."

A limited number of transitions come with iMovie, but you can download others from the Apple web site at www.apple.com/imovie, or buy collections of transitions and effects from third-party vendors.

Cross Dissolve vs. Overlap:

The Cross Dissolve transition smoothly dissolves from one scene to another, retaining full motion of the first scene until it dissolves away.

The Overlap effect freezes on the last frame in a scene as it dissolves into the next scene.

Titles

A **title** is text that you place in its own frame or on top of a scene. A title can show credits, act as a caption, or add comments. There are many styles of titles to choose from and you can use different typefaces, sizes, and colors.

To add titles to your movie:

1. Select a clip in the Timeline (click once on it).

2. Click the "Titles" button beneath the shelf, then select a title style.

3. Type your title text into the text fields at the bottom of the window.

4. Use the font pop-up menu to select a font.

5. Use the font slider to enlarge or reduce the type.

6. Click the "Color" box to choose a color from a palette.

7. By default, a title is superimposed over a video clip. If you want to super-impose a title over a black background instead of a clip, check the "Over Black" box. This option creates new frames for the title sequence and does not affect other clips. It does, however, add to the length of your movie.

8. If you plan to export the movie as a QuickTime file, check the "QT Margins" box to allow the title to expand within the limitations of the QuickTime margin.

   If you plan to show it on the television, make sure this button is *not* selected or your type may be cut off on the edges, or leave it unchecked all the time to play it safe for any media.

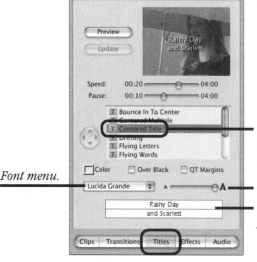

9. Drag your selected title style from the list of styles to the desired position in the Timeline.

Font menu.

Choose your style here.

When finished with your title, drag this same line down to the Timeline.

Font size slider.

Type your title here. Different effects give you different amounts of space for text.

Effects

An **effect** is a visual distortion or alteration that is applied to a clip. The effect may be used for aesthetic reasons, or for visual impact. A limited number of effects come with iMovie, but many more are available from third-party vendors.

To add effects to a clip in your movie:

1. Select a clip in the Timeline (click once on it).
2. Click the "Effects" button beneath the shelf.
3. Select an effect from the effects list.
4. Use the "Effect In" and "Effect Out" sliders to set the amount of time it takes for the effect to fade in and to fade out.
5. If there are other settings sliders below the effects list, set those as well.
6. When you're satisfied with the effect, click the "Apply" button.

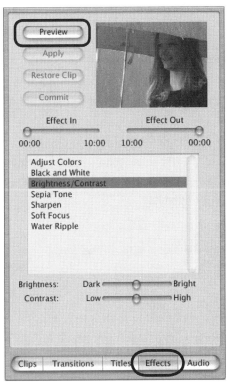

The Preview button plays the effect full-sized in the monitor window of iMovie.

Click the "Restore Clip" button to restore a clip to its original state after applying and previewing an effect.

Once you click the "Commit" button, you cannot restore a clip to its original state (which is a good reason to use the copy and paste technique for clips as explained on page 365–366).

Add audio clips to your movie

Place as many **audio clips** in a sound track as you like. Drag audio clips to other positions or to another track, if necessary. Audio clips can overlap in the same track or in separate tracks. When two audio clips overlap, both are audible, although you can adjust the volume of individual sound tracks with the clip volume control slider beneath the Timeline.

*Use these checkboxes to **mute** the sound of a clip in a video track or in either of the audio tracks.*

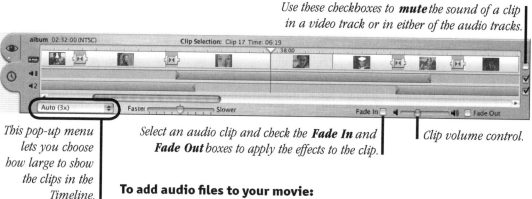

This pop-up menu lets you choose how large to show the clips in the Timeline.

*Select an audio clip and check the **Fade In** and **Fade Out** boxes to apply the effects to the clip.*

Clip volume control.

To add audio files to your movie:

1. Click the "Audio" button beneath the shelf.

2. Position the Playhead (the white triangle) in the Timeline where you want the recording to start.

3. The top of the audio window contains a Library of sound files that you can drag to either of the audio tracks at the bottom of the Timeline. Select a sound from the library and drag it to a point in one of the sound tracks where you want it to start playing.

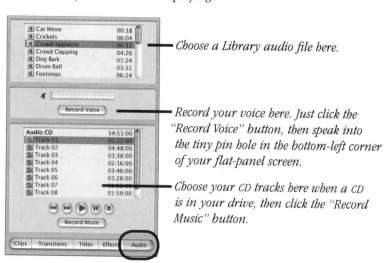

Choose a Library audio file here.

Record your voice here. Just click the "Record Voice" button, then speak into the tiny pin hole in the bottom-left corner of your flat-panel screen.

Choose your CD tracks here when a CD is in your drive, then click the "Record Music" button.

To import an MP3 or AIFF sound file:

1. From the File menu, choose "Import File...."

2. In the "Import File" window, navigate to an MP3 or AIFF file that is stored on your computer, select it, then click "Import." The entire audio file is placed in one of the audio tracks.

   Some of your MP3 file names may be gray, which means you can't use them in the movie because iMovie can only import MP3s that support the QuickTime format.

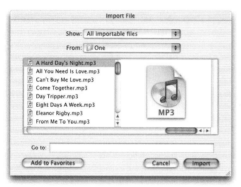

Files that can be imported are shown in the Import File window.

To import a CD sound track:

1. Insert a CD into your CD drive.

2. To review CD tracks without importing them, click the Play button.

3. To record the song, select a CD track from the "Audio CD" list.

4. In the Timeline, move the Playhead (the white triangle) to a point where you want to start recording.

5. Click the "Record Music" button. Click "Stop" when you've recorded as much of the CD track as you want.

To adjust and edit the audio clips:

Adjust the placement of an imported audio file in the Timeline by dragging the file's purple bar left or right. **Edit the start and stop point** of audio clips by moving the audio crop markers at either end of the audio clip's purple bar in the audio track. To fine-tune the placement of an audio crop marker, click it, then use the left and right arrows to move it.

Export your iMovie

Once you've finished creating your movie, you can store it on your hard drive, but that uses a lot of disk space, and the only place you can show it is on your computer. Since iMovies are usually large, from several gigabytes on up, you can't pass them around on a Zip disk or even on a CD. So you need to **export the movie.** Fortunately, iMovie is able to export movies in several formats, depending on the final intended use of the movie.

To export your movie:

1. From the File menu, choose "Export Movie...."

2. The "Export Movie" dialog box appears. From the "Export" menu, choose to export "To Camera," "To QuickTime," or "For IDVD." Each option is explained below.

- **Export To Camera:** Put a writable tape in your camera and put the camera in VTR mode. Make sure it is connected to your computer with a FireWire cable, then click the "Export" button.

  Exporting your edited movie back out to your digital camera puts the movie on the digital video tape in your camera. The tape in your camera can store from 30 to 180 minutes of movies, depending on the model of your camera. You can attach your camera to a TV to show your edited movies, or you can transfer movies from your camera to a VHS tape. If your movie contains scenes that are in slow motion or reversed, iMovie will tell you that it needs to render those scenes before it can export the movie.

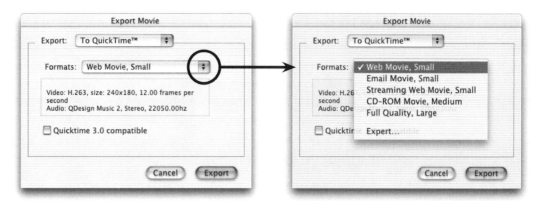

- **Export To QuickTime:** QuickTime format is a popular standard for multimedia files. It compresses movies so that their sizes are manageable for transport and delivery, either on the web or other media.

  From the "Formats" pop-up menu, select one of the compression options, then click "Export." The "Expert…" option in the pop-up menu lets you customize "Image Settings," "Audio Settings," and "Internet Settings."

If you want to ensure that your QuickTime movie can be viewed by someone with an older version of QuickTime Player, click the checkbox next to "Quicktime 3.0 compatible."

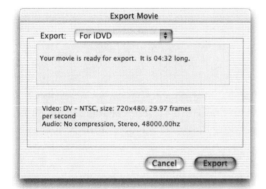

- **Export For iDVD:** This option creates a QuickTime file that can be used with Apple's iDVD software. iDVD is amazing software for putting a collection of movies onto a DVD disc that will play on your computer (if you have a supported DVD drive) and will also play on most popular commercial DVD players. Exporting for DVD actually saves your movie in a QuickTime format, but with different compression settings from those used for other types of QuickTime files. If some scenes in your movie need to be rendered because they use a motion effect such as slow motion, iMovie alerts you that it needs to render those scenes before you can export the movie.

Extra tips

If your selected music track plays just a few seconds too long past the end of the video or ends too soon, select a clip or a transition somewhere in the movie and slow it down using the **motion effects slider.** This slider is located beneath the Timeline, next to the Zoom pop-up menu. This is an easy way to help synchronize the length of a movie with an audio track. *However,* notice that I've turned off the audio on the video track (the checkbox on the far right side of the Timeline is *not* checked). Slow motion or fast motion will distort the audio of a clip.

- **Either** select a clip in the Timeline, then drag the slider left (Faster) or right (Slower).

- **Or** select a transition between two clips, then drag this slider left or right.

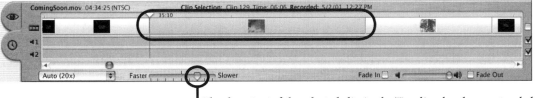

The duration of the selected clip in the Timeline has been extended by moving the motion effects slider to the right.

In the Timeline, the selected clip will actually appear longer or shorter as you move the slider towards "Slower" or "Faster."

Located above the Timeline, next to the Trash, the **Free Space status bar** alerts you to how much free space is left on the disk or partition being used for your movie. The bar indicator is color coded to indicate the amount of free disk space.

Green: More than 400 megabytes available.

Yellow: Less than 400 megabytes available.

Red: Less than 200 megabytes available.

If you have less than 100 megabytes of free disk space, you cannot import more video until you remove clips from the shelf or empty the iMovie Trash.

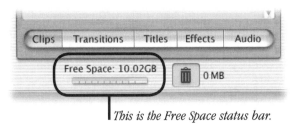

This is the Free Space status bar.

The QuickTime Player

The **QuickTime Player** plays audio, video, and QTVR (QuickTime Virtual Reality) movies. In addition, it can display still image files in almost every mainstream format (JPEG, TIFF, PICT, GIF, PSD, PNG, BMP, and others). If you create an iMovie or an iPhoto Slide Show, you can save them as QuickTime movies. Some multimedia content available on the Internet is automatically opened by QuickTime. You can use QuickTime to listen to Internet radio stations, watch headline news, or watch the latest movie trailers. You may hear someone refer to a QuickTime audio file as a "movie." Any type of QuickTime file (audio or video) is referred to as a "QuickTime movie."

QuickTime Player

You can play QuickTime movies in QuickTime Player or in any application that supports QuickTime, such as most popular browsers, some word processors, and in PDF files. Use QuickTime Player to play movies that you downloaded to your computer, that you created on your computer, or that exist on the Internet.

To open QuickTime Player:

There are several ways to **open** QuickTime Player. These first three methods open the QuickTime Player with the movie loaded and ready to play.

- Double-click a QuickTime file on your computer.
- Single-click on a QuickTime link on a web page.
- Drag a QuickTime file's icon on top of the QuickTime application icon, either in the Dock or in the Applications folder.

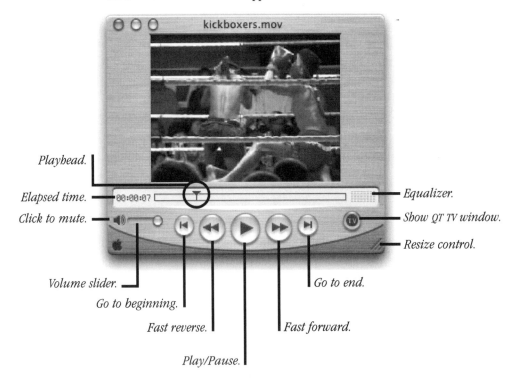

QuickTime TV

If you use either of the next two methods, a version of the Player **opens** that contains QuickTime content links and your personal QuickTime Favorites.

- Click on the QuickTime Player's icon in the Dock.
- Open the Applications folder, then double-click the QuickTime application icon.

Click this button to collapse the player to a small size that shows only the audio track and controller buttons.

Two tabs are visible in this window: a **QuickTime TV** tab and a **Favorites** tab (the heart icon). The QT TV pane contains a collection of preset QuickTime TV channels that offer a variety of content including news, sports, weather, music, and music videos. You can get links to additional entertaining content at **www.apple.com/ quicktime.**

Click any icon in the QT TV pane to connect to that site's streaming QuickTime content. For details about the Favorites pane, see the next page.

The Favorites pane in QuickTime TV

The **Favorites** pane (the heart tab) is a convenient place to store your favorite QuickTime content links. In Favorites, you can add links to streaming QuickTime movies on the Internet, QuickTime movies that are on your local computer, and almost any image file on your computer.

To add an image file to Favorites, drag its icon to the Favorites pane.

To add streaming QuickTime content from the Internet to Favorites:

1. Click on a streaming QuickTime movie link on a web page to start playing the movie.

2. From the QTV menu, choose Favorites, then choose "Add Movie As Favorite." The movie is not *copied* to your computer. Instead, a *link* to the online movie is created in Favorites.

To add a QuickTime movie that's on your computer to Favorites:

1. Drag the movie's QuickTime file icon to the Favorites pane.

2. **Or** double-click the QuickTime movie to open it. From the QTV menu, choose Favorites, then "Add Movie As Favorite."

The Favorites pane gives you instant access to your favorite QuickTime content located on the Internet and on your computer, plus almost any kind of image file that you want to access easily and quickly.

To remove a Favorite:

- **Either** Control-click on a Favorite, then from the pop-up menu, choose "Delete Favorite."

- **Or** select a Favorite using the arrow keys, then press Delete.

The views in Favorites

You will see different channels in different **views.** Some of the channel content providers, such as ESPN (shown below, left) play streaming audio in the QuickTime player. Others open and play content in the full multimedia version of the player that includes streaming audio and streaming video (below, right).

QuickTime Player adjusts its appearance to the type of content it needs to play:

The Player above is connected to a streaming radio station.

The Player on the right is connected to a site that streams audio and video.

Change the Poster Frame

The thumbnail image that appears in Favorites is called the **Poster Frame.** A Poster Frame is one frame of a movie that is used as a preview, or thumbnail image. By default, the Poster Frame is usually the first frame in a movie. If the first frame of your selected movie is not visually descriptive enough, you can choose any frame to use as the Poster Frame. (You can only do this to movies that are actually stored on your hard disk, not those that are streaming in from the Internet.)

To change the Poster Frame:

1. Open the movie in QuickTime Player.

2. Drag the Playhead (the black triangle in the video track) to select the frame you want to use as the Poster Frame.

3. From the Movie menu, choose "Set Poster Frame."

4. Press Command S to save your changes, then close the movie.

5. Drag the QuickTime movie's icon to the Favorites window.

Streaming content *is multimedia content that downloads partially to your computer, then starts playing while your computer continues to download the "stream." Streaming content does not remain on your computer. Streaming makes it possible to deliver live content or content that would take up too much disk space on a computer.*

Play QuickTime movies

There are several ways to play QuickTime movies.

To play a QuickTime movie that's stored on your computer:

robin.mov

This is what a QuickTime movie icon looks like.

- ▪ **Either** double-click on the QuickTime movie's icon.

- ▪ **Or** from the File menu, choose "Open Movie in New Player...."
  Navigate to a QuickTime movie, select it, then click "Open."

- ▪ **Or** locate a movie file, then drag the file icon on top of the QuickTime
  Player icon.

To play a QuickTime movie located on the Internet:

Most QuickTime movies you encounter on the Internet are links on a web page that you simply click to play. The Louvre Museum web page, shown to the left, offers a virtual tour with links to many QTVR movies (QuickTime Virtual Reality), which are 360-degree panoramic photos that you can pan and zoom in on. The large and small QuickTime logos on the web page are links that offer a choice of both large and small QuickTime movies for viewers who have fast or slow Internet connections.

The larger of these little icons indicates that a file is large; the smaller icon indicates the file is small.

If you know the specific web address:

If you know the specific web address of a QuickTime movie, from the File menu, choose "Open URL...." Type the address in the text field, then click "OK." The trick is that the address must be a complete path name to the QuickTime file, and not just to a web page.

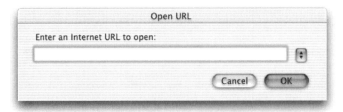

QuickTime Player audio options

When you play a QuickTime movie, you can adjust the left/right speaker balance and the bass/treble levels of QuickTime movies with **Sound Controls.**

To show or hide Sound Controls:

- **Either** go to the Movie menu and choose "Show Sound Controls" to show the controls in the status window.

  Choose "Hide Sound Controls" when you don't want them visible.

- **Or** click on the small equalizer on the right side of the status window, if an equalizer is visible, to show the Sound Controls.

  Click the equalizer again to hide the Sound Controls.

Click the small equalizer to show or hide the Sound Controls.

The small equalizer on the right side of the movie track gives a visual representation of the audio.

The preferences for QuickTime Player

The **QuickTime Player Preferences** give you a few more options for customizing the behavior of the Player.

From the QuickTime Player menu, choose "Preferences," then choose "Player Preferences…" to open the General Preferences window, as shown below.

Select your choices for the **options** listed for Movies, Sound, Favorites, and Hot Picks. They're self-explanatory.

If you're using QuickTime to listen to **Internet Radio** while you work, select "Play sound when application is in background" to let QuickTime audio continue to play when another window is active and when the Player has been minimized in the Dock.

The **Hot Picks** option connects to the Internet and takes you to QuickTime's currently featured content whenever you open QuickTime Player.

Uncheck the Hot Picks item unless you have a full-time broadband connection or your modem will automatically try to dial and connect to the Internet whenever you double-click on QuickTime Player.

More about Your iMac

You can live a long time without reading this section, but the more you read, the more you will feel in control of your computer. This section covers some odds and ends that can be quite useful to you, such as creating aliases to make it easy to open files, how to use Sherlock to find documents you thought you misplaced, what those "extensions" at the ends of file names are, and more. Skim through the section, and when you're ready to absorb it, just read what you need.

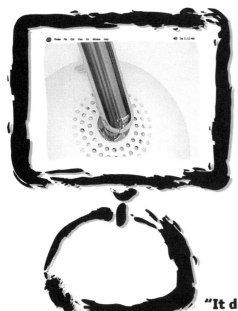

"It doesn't even look like a computer."

PC curmudgeon

Other Things You Might Need to Know

There are several other things you should know that can help you be more productive and add to your understanding of how your iMac works.

In this chapter, I'm assuming that you know how to use the mouse, make new folders, drag items from one place to another, open windows, and how to do the basic things that entail working on your iMac. If you don't understand a term used in this chapter, check for it in the index.

Extensions and file names

In Mac OS X, every file name has an **extension** (whether you see it or not), which is a short abbreviation at the end of a file name, preceded by a period, such as *.jpg*. This extension tells the Mac what to do with the file.

robin's story.rtf   robin's story

The extension is so important to some files that if you take it off, the Mac doesn't know what to do with the file when you try to open it. In the example above, the Mac cannot open the file on the right, even though it is exactly the same as the file on the left, minus the .rtf extension.

You can add your own extension to the end of a file name if you know the exact characters for your document, or you can just let the Mac add the correct one for you—what you *don't* want to do is add an extension without knowing that the *Mac* has added an extension to your extension.

To make sure that doesn't happen, or to make sure you get the extension you want, you can choose to see the extensions on a file-by-file basis. If you prefer, choose a global setting so you *always* see the file extension or you *never* see it.

To make the extensions visible or invisible on an individual basis:

1. Select a file, then go to the File menu and choose "Show Info, *or* press Command I.

2. From the pop-up menu, choose "Name & Extension."

3. Check or uncheck the box to "Hide extension."

Notice when you hide the extension, it is hidden from the file name you see on the Desktop (shown at the top of the Info window), but the "File system name" that the Mac uses retains the extension.

To hide or show extensions globally:

1. From the Finder menu, choose "Preferences...."

2. Check or uncheck the box to "Always show file extensions."

   If you choose to always show them, you won't inadvertently add your own extension as well.

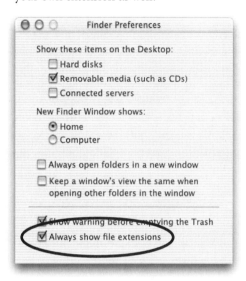

Illegal characters in file names: Do not start file names with a hyphen or period. Do not use a colon (:) or a slash (/) anywhere in the file name.

chapter8   chapter8.dock

Adding an extension of .dock to this folder turned the folder into a "dockling." Unfortunately, Apple does not provide a list of extensions that you should avoid. (When I removed the ".dock" extension, it turned back into a folder with all of its files intact.)

Below is a list of some (not all) common file extensions you might see.

Document extensions

.doc   Word document
.txt   Plain Text
.rtf   Rich Text Format
.rtfd Rich Text Format
       Directory
.pdf   Portable Document
       Format
.psd   Photoshop file
.qxp   QuarkXPress
       document
.pps   PowerPoint
       Show
.xls   Excel spreadsheet
.mov   QuickTime movie

Backup your work!

Backup your work! To back it up, just copy any file you don't want to lose and burn it to a CD or DVD, as explained in Chapter 12.

You should do this to every file you want to keep, especially your own documents. In the event the file on your hard disk gets lost or trashed or your hard disk dies, you will have this extra copy. In fact, you should make **two copies** of anything important, and store the second copy away from the premises; it won't do much good to have a second backup if your office burns down or is broken into and all of your disks stolen.

As your backup disks, you can use CD-R (recordable) discs or CD-RW (rewritable) discs. A CD can hold 650 megabytes of data. The iMac's CD-burning application can burn a CD-R only one time, while you can burn several "sessions" onto CD-RWs. However, CD-Rs are so inexpensive that I prefer using them over the more expensive CD-RWs.

If your iMac has a "Super Drive," you can backup files onto DVDs. A DVD can hold 4.5 gigabytes of data.

You already have an extra copy of your system software and applications on the CDs that came with your iMac—store them in a safe place.

If you download software or important files from the Internet directly to your iMac, be sure to make backup copies onto discs.

Backup your iPhoto Library

The **iPhoto Library** contains all the photos that have been imported by iPhoto, plus any Albums you created. Make backup copies of the iPhoto Library regularly. Then you can delete photos in iPhoto so you don't fill up your hard disk with unnecessary photo storage. If you decide you need a photo you've removed from your iMac, you can copy it back to your computer from the backup disc (as explained in Chapter 12).

To find the iPhoto Library: Click the Home button in the Toolbar of any Finder window, then double-click the "Pictures" folder. The "iPhoto Library" folder is inside; back it up.

Backup your iTunes Library

Also backup the **iTunes Library.** Music files are large and take up a lot of disk space. If you've imported songs to copy to a CD, but don't need them on the hard disk any more, copy them to a backup disc and delete them from the iTunes Library to conserve disk space.

To find the music files in the iTunes Library, click the Home folder in the Toolbar, then open the "Documents" folder. The "iTunes" folder contains all the music files stored in your iTunes Library. Backup that folder.

Backup your iMovie files

iMovie project folders are very large and can take a lot of disk space—about a gigabyte per minute of movie. Make backups of them for safe storage and to prevent your iMovie obsession from gobbling up all your hard disk storage space.

Very short iMovies that you save in the editable iMovie format can be backed up onto DVDs because there is 4.5 gigabytes of storage space on a DVD, but longer iMovies will not fit even on a DVD. If you make a lot of iMovies, buy an external hard disk to store them on; that will be your backup. John uses an eighty-gigabyte external hard disk just for storing iMovies.

The Show Info window

Show Info is a small window that gives you pertinent information about any selected file.

To open a Show Info window, select a file's icon (single-click on it) then press Command I, *or* from the File menu choose "Show Info."

The kind of information you get depends on what type of file is selected, as shown below and on the opposite page.

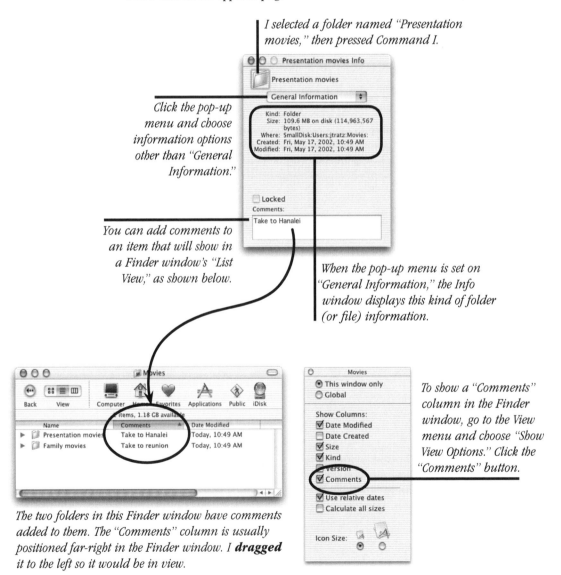

I selected a folder named "Presentation movies," then pressed Command I.

Click the pop-up menu and choose information options other than "General Information."

You can add comments to an item that will show in a Finder window's "List View," as shown below.

When the pop-up menu is set on "General Information," the Info window displays this kind of folder (or file) information.

*The two folders in this Finder window have comments added to them. The "Comments" column is usually positioned far-right in the Finder window. I **dragged** it to the left so it would be in view.*

To show a "Comments" column in the Finder window, go to the View menu and choose "Show View Options." Click the "Comments" button.

Click the pop-up menu to show other file information. You can even use Show Info to create custom icons for your files and folders (see page 407).

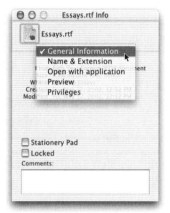

The Info pop-up menu.

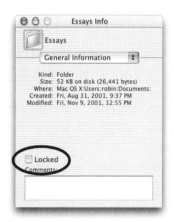

Lock *a file (if you have the privileges to do so). Locking a file prevents accidental changes. No one can print a locked file.*

Click the "Play" button to play a QuickTime movie in the Info window.

Preview some text documents, PDFs, most images, and most movies right here in the Info window.

Take advantage of aliases!

Macworld alias.mov

An alias has a tiny arrow in the bottom-right corner of the icon. Often it's very difficult to see!

An **alias** is an "empty" icon that *represents* the real thing. When you double-click an alias, the alias goes and finds the real file and opens the real one.

Aliases are especially useful for applications. You see, most applications must stay in the folder they were installed into because when the application opens, it calls upon resources within its folder. If you store the application icon itself (without all of its resource files) in a different folder or on your Desktop, you run the risk that the application won't be able to function properly. That's where the alias comes in: You make an alias, which *represents* the application, and you can put that alias anywhere. In fact, you can make a dozen aliases of the same application and store them in all sorts of handy places. When you double-click an application alias, it goes into the original folder and tells the real application to open.

Let's say you have an application you use frequently—your word processing program, for instance. You can make an alias of AppleWorks or Quicken or whatever you use and put it just about anywhere. You might want to put it right on your Desktop, in a folder full of application aliases, or in your Home folder. Since you can have many aliases of the same file, you can put aliases to the same item in several places.

Aliases only take up about 2 or 3K of disk space (which is a really tiny bit), so you can make lots and store them all over the place, wherever they come in handy.

You can make aliases of applications, documents, partitions, folders, utilities, games, etc. Aliases are wonderful tools for organizing your work—anything you want to use is only one double-click away from wherever you are. Remember, an alias is just a picture that goes and gets the real file.

Using aliases

Before I tell you *how* to make them, here are ideas for **using aliases** so you will *want* to make them (how to make an alias is on the following page).

- Store aliases of documents in two or three places at once, including right on your Desktop. For instance, you may want to keep budget reports in folders organized by months, as well as in folders organized by projects. When you update the real document, every alias will open the updated document.

- Leave aliases of applications neatly organized directly on your Desktop. This makes your applications available to you for the **drag-and-drop trick of opening files,** including files from other applications.You can drag any document onto the icon of an application to open the document. Many applications can open files created in other programs, so if you come across a file from a program you don't have or perhaps you don't know where it came from, you can drag the unknown file over the top of aliases that are sitting on your Desktop. Any icon that changes color when you drag the document on top of it will try to open that document.

- You might find you use a particular utility regularly. If so, put an alias of that utility right on your Desktop.

- Put aliases of all your applications in a folder, then put that folder in the Dock. When you want to open an application, just *press* on that folder icon in the Dock to get the pop-up menu and choose your application from there (shown to the right).

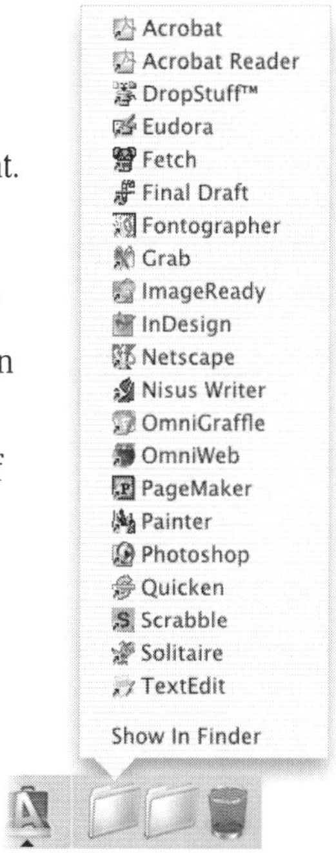

> 🄰 Acrobat
> 🄰 Acrobat Reader
> 🄳 DropStuff™
> 🄴 Eudora
> 🄵 Fetch
> 🄵 Final Draft
> 🄵 Fontographer
> 🄶 Grab
> 🄸 ImageReady
> 🄸 InDesign
> 🄽 Netscape
> 🄽 Nisus Writer
> 🄾 OmniGraffle
> 🄾 OmniWeb
> 🄿 PageMaker
> 🄿 Painter
> 🄿 Photoshop
> 🄀 Quicken
> 🅂 Scrabble
> 🅂 Solitaire
> 🅃 TextEdit
>
> Show In Finder

This is my folder of the applications I use most often. Putting all of these in the Dock would make the Dock too small and crowded.

Automatic aliases

There are a several places on your computer where the Mac **automatically creates an alias** for you:

When you drag an item into the *Dock,* the original item doesn't actually *move* to the Dock—the Mac puts an alias in the Dock. That's why you can delete the icon from the Dock in a puff of dust and you still have the original file in your folder.

When you drag an item into any Finder window *Toolbar,* the Mac automatically puts an alias in the Toolbar.

The *Recent Places* menu that appears in "Save As" and "Open" dialog boxes, as well as the Apple menu, uses aliases that are automatically created (you can customize the number of items in the Recent menu: use the General preferences).

When you drop a file on the Favorites icon in the Toolbar, *or* when you select a file and use the Favorites command in the File menu ("Add to Favorites," or press Command T), the Mac automatically puts an *alias* of the file in the *Favorites folder.* (See page 53 about Favorites.)

Making an alias

Making an alias is so easy:

1. **Select** the item you want to make an alias of (click once on it).

2. Then choose one of these four easy ways to make an alias:

   a. From the File menu, choose "Make Alias."

   b. Or press Command L instead of going to the File menu.

   c. Or hold down the Control key and click on the item you want to make an alias of. A contextual menu will pop up, as shown below; choose "Make Alias."

After you choose "Make Alias," the new alias will be sitting right on top of the original file. Just drag it to where you want to keep it.

   d. Or hold down Command Option and drag the file—if you drag it to a *different* folder or to the Desktop, when you let go you'll have an alias with the word "alias" removed from its name; if you drag to somewhere else in the *same* folder, you'll have an alias with the word "alias" at the end of it.

You can also **make an alias of any open document:**

1. Save the open document.

2. Drag the tiny picture in the title bar and drop it on the Desktop or in any folder. You'll notice the pointer has a tiny arrow attached to it, which is a *visual clue* that you are in the process of making an alias.

The **new alias icon** will look the same as the original file and will be named the same, with the word *alias* added (unless you used the Command-Option–drag trick). If you want to remove the word "alias," first move the alias out of the folder the original file is in because you cannot have two files with the same name in one folder.

Drag the icon to wherever you want to keep it. Rename it if you like. The new file does not have to have the word "alias" in its name. *And it doesn't matter if you move the original file* —the alias can always find it.

Details of aliases

Making aliases is easy, but here are some **details** you should understand.

- An alias isn't a *duplicate* of anything; it's just a **pointer** to the real thing. If you double-click an *alias* of Quicken, you'll open your *original* Quicken application, even if the original Quicken is stored in a completely different folder.

- If you **delete** an alias, you don't delete the original — the original is still stored on your hard disk. So you can keep revising your filing system as your needs change. Don't want that *alias* of Budget Charts cluttering up your Project Plans folder any more? Fine; throw it away. The *original* Budget Charts is still where you stored it.

- If you put an item into an *alias* of a **folder,** the item actually gets put into the *original* folder.

- You can **move** an alias and even **rename** an alias. The Mac will still be able to find the original and open it whenever you double-click on the alias.

- Even if you move or rename the **original** file, the alias can still find it.

- If you **delete** the *original* file, the Mac does *not* automatically delete any of the aliases you created for that file. When you double-click on an alias whose original has been trashed, you will get a message telling you the original could not be located.

Important note: An alias is not a copy of a file—it is just a pointer. Although you can throw away any alias, do not throw away the original file!

Finding the original file that is linked to an alias

Sometimes you want to find the original file that the alias is linked to. For instance, maybe you need to get something from an application's folder, but you don't want to dig down through all the other folders to get there.

To find the original file belonging to an alias, follow these simple steps:

1. Click once on the alias to select it.

2. From the File menu, choose "Show Original," **or** press Command R. The original file will appear in front of you, selected.

Customize the Finder window Toolbar

You can **customize the Toolbar** to suit your working habits. You can *rearrange* items, *remove* any of the existing icons, and *add* icons of folders, applications, files, servers, and more. Once you rearrange or add new items to a Toolbar, they appear in the Toolbar of every Finder window.

To rearrange items in the Toolbar:

> Just drag them (for some items you have to hold down the Command key and drag). As you drag sideways, other icons move over to make room. When you have an item positioned where you want it, let go.

To customize the Toolbar using the "Customize Toolbar" pane:

1. Open any Finder window.

2. Hold the Shift key down and click the Hide/Show Toolbar button.
   Or from the View menu, choose "Customize Toolbar...."

3. From the pane that appears, press-and-drag any icon you like into the Toolbar and drop it there (if you change your mind, just drag the icon off the Toolbar and drop it on the Desktop; it will disappear).

This little menu changes how the icons are displayed in the Toolbar. Choose each one to see how it looks. The last one you choose is the one that will apply to the Toolbar when you close this pane.

This "Separator" icon is in the process of being dragged into the Toolbar.

Click "Done" when you are finished.

If you add more icons than will fit, a tiny double-arrow icon appears at the end of the Toolbar, indicating there are more items in the Toolbar. Click on that double-arrow and a tiny menu will appear with the other items listed; you can select from that menu.

Icons in the Customize Toolbar pane

Some of the **icons in the Customize pane** represent items you already have in your Toolbar. They exist because it's possible to remove every single item from the Toolbar, even the Back button, and you might one day want something back that you previously removed. Below is a list of some items and what they do:

Path: An open window represents the contents of a disk or a folder. Click the Path button to see where the current disk or folder is located. A menu appears, showing the folders inside of folders, etc., where the item is stored. Choose any folder from the menu to open it. (Clicking this button is exactly the same as Command-clicking on the title bar.)

Eject: If you click the "Computer" icon in the Toolbar and *select* a removable disk in that window (click once on its icon), you can then click this Eject button to eject the *selected* disk. This button doesn't work if you select the disk icon on the Desktop—you have to select it in the Computer window.

Burn: If you have a writable CD or DVD drive, you can click this button to begin the burn process, as explained in Chapter 12.

Customize: Click this button to open the Customize pane (the one shown on the opposite page).

Separator: Drag this into position on the Toolbar to create a dividing line between groups of icons.

New Folder: Click this to put a new folder in the *active* window.

Delete: Click this to delete any *selected* item(s) in the window. The item you delete will go into the Trash basket.

Connect: Click this to connect to any other computers in your office that are already networked.

Find: Click this to open Sherlock, which you can use to find files on your computer or information on the Internet (see Chapter 24).

Documents, Movies, Music, Pictures, Public: Each of these represents one of the folders in your "Home." Put its icon in your Toolbar, then you can just click to access that folder. Or you can drop files onto the *icon* in the Toolbar and the files will actually go into the real *folder.*

Default set: Drag this entire block up to the Toolbar and it will replace everything you have customized and make the Toolbar exactly how it was when you first turned on your iMac.

View Options

You can customize the appearance of Finder windows. From the View menu, choose "Show View Options," or press Command J.

Once this dialog box is open (as shown below), you'll notice that its title bar changes its name depending on which window is *active*. That is, once you open it, you can open a whole bunch of other windows and whichever window is in *front*, the one that has the three buttons in color, is the one that this View Options box will apply to. Even if you have only one window open, if you switch to another folder in that same window, this View Options box will switch to displaying the options for the new contents.

What you see in the View Options box also depends on which *view* the active window is displaying. For instance, if you have a window in *Icon View* and you click its button to change the window to *List View*, the View Options box will change, as shown below. (There are no options for Column View.)

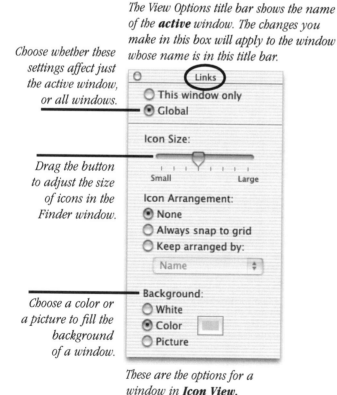

*The View Options title bar shows the name of the **active** window. The changes you make in this box will apply to the window whose name is in this title bar.*

Choose whether these settings affect just the active window, or all windows.

Drag the button to adjust the size of icons in the Finder window.

Choose a color or a picture to fill the background of a window.

Choose which columns to show in a List View window.

*These are the options for a window in **Icon View**.*

*These are the options for a window in **List View**.*

Finder Preferences

There are a couple of items in the **Finder Preferences** that refer to using Finder windows. These options are global, meaning they will apply to all windows on the Desktop until you go back and change them.

To open the Finder Preferences:

1. Make sure you are at the Finder/Desktop. Look at the menu bar: If the menu item next to the apple is not "Finder," then click once on an empty spot on the Desktop, or click on a Finder window.

2. When you see "Finder" in the menu bar, click on it and choose "Preferences..." from the menu. You'll get the box shown below.

   ▪ Whenever you open a new Finder window, it automatically opens to the "Computer" level. You probably don't need to use much on the Computer level; everything you need is in your "Home." In the Finder Preferences you can choose to have **new Finder windows open to your Home level** instead.

   ▪ If you are an experienced Mac user, you're probably accustomed to a new window opening every time you double-click a folder icon, instead of the contents of the new folder *replacing* what was already in the window. In the Finder Preferences you can choose to **have a new window open every time you double-click a folder.**

   ▪ If you prefer one window view over another, it might make you crazy that you never know what view the next folder will appear in. You can choose that all views *in the window you're working in* will stay the same as the view you have currently selected. That is, if you set a window to Icon View, all the folders that open *within that window* will be in Icon View.

These are the options that apply to Finder windows, as explained above.

Force Quit

Sometimes an application gets a little squirrelly and you have to force it to quit. You might not be able to get to the application's File menu to choose "Quit," but there are several other things you can do. You can also use these techniques to **force quit** applications that you're not using at the moment, but that might be causing trouble.

In Mac OS X when one application goes down, it doesn't take the rest of the computer down with it, as happened in previous operating systems. And if you're a Mac user from way back, you'll be happy to learn that force quit in OS X actually works.

To force quit an application:

1. From the **Apple menu,** choose "Force Quit...."

2. In the dialog box that appears, click once on the name of the application you want to quit.

3. Hit the Return or Enter key, or click the "Force Quit" button.

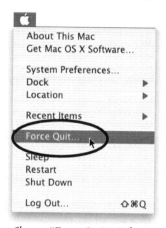
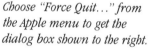

Choose "Force Quit..." from the Apple menu to get the dialog box shown to the right.

Choose the application you want to force quit, then click the button.

Instead of going to the Apple menu, you can press **Command Option Escape** to get the "Force Quit Applications" dialog box shown above. (Remember, *hold down* Command and Option, then *tap* the Escape key. The Escape key is in the upper-left corner of your keyboard, and it has "esc" on it.)

Or:

- Hold down the **Option key and press** on the application's icon in the Dock (don't click—*hold* the button down). The menu that pops up typically says "Quit," but with the Option key down it changes to "Force Quit." Choose that item and it will force quit the selected application.

The Dock menu for TextEdit (the selected application) shows "Quit."

With the Option key down (either before or after you choose this menu), "Quit" changes to "Force Quit."

Relaunch the Finder

If you have trouble in the **Finder** (at the Desktop), you can't *quit* the Finder. But you can **relaunch** it which might clear up weird little problems you may be having. Relaunching the Finder does not affect your other applications or open windows.

To relaunch the Finder:

1. From the **Apple menu,** choose "Force Quit...," *or* press Command Option Escape.

2. In the dialog box, click once on "Finder."

3. Click the Relaunch button.

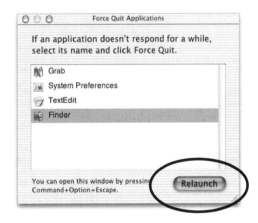

Log in as the root user

There is another user on the Mac, called the **root user,** or superuser. By logging into this account, you can change any file on the entire Mac, even system files that you as the Administrator are not allowed to touch. By default, the root account is disabled in Mac OS X because it is phenomenally easy to destroy your entire system with the click of a mouse. But sometimes you try to throw away items you created or you might try to install software into the Applications folder and the Mac yells at you that it's not possible, usually because you don't have sufficient privileges. And you wonder, "Well, I'm the only person who has ever used this machine—if I don't have privileges, *who on earth does!?*" This is when you might have to log in as the **root user.** It's not something you want or need to do often, and you don't want to leave your computer sitting around with the root user available because as the root user, you (or anyone using your machine) has access to read, write, and destroy any file on the Mac, including all other user files.

But if you need to do it, log in as the root user, do what you need to do, then log out and **disable the root user** when you're done. You must know the Administrator's short name and password to do this.

NetInfo Manager

This is the NetInfo Manager icon in the Utilities folder.

To enable the root user and log in:

1. Click on the Applications icon in any Finder window, or go to the Go menu and choose "Applications."

2. In the Applications window, open the Utilities folder.

3. In the Utilities window, find and double-click "NetInfo Manager."

4. In the NetInfo Manager window, click the padlock icon in the bottom-left corner.

5. In the dialog box that appears, type in the *short* name of the main Admin of the Mac, plus that Admin's password. It must be the name of the main, original Administrator—not a user who has been granted administrative status. Click OK.

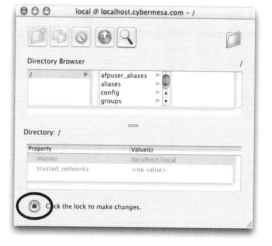

6. From the Domain menu, slide down to "Security," and then choose "Enable Root User," as shown to the right.

(If the root user has already been enabled, this item says "Disable Root User"; skip to Step 9.)

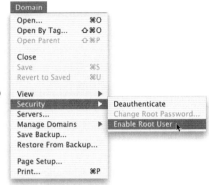

7. If there is not a root password already, you will be asked to create one. Use the standard password guidelines: difficult to figure out, a combination of letters and numbers, no non-alphanumeric characters, no spaces, etc. Capital letters and lowercase letters are different characters in a password. *Write this password down somewhere!!*

After you type the password the first time, you'll be asked to type it again to verify it. Click the Verify button.

8. You have now enabled the root user. The padlock in the NetInfo window will automatically shut—you'll get a message that you must "re-authenticate" to make any more changes. Quit NetInfo.

9. Next you need to **log out** so you can **log in** as the root user. But before you log out, go to the Login preferences pane (in the System Preferences). Click the "Login Window" tab.

10. Check the "Display Login Window as" radio button to display "Name and password entry fields." *Or,* if you want to keep the list of user accounts that displays the photos the users have chosen, then check the box to "Show 'Other User' in list for network users." Either choice will give you an edit box where you can log in as the root user.

This option is active when you choose the "List of users" radio button.

11. From the Apple menu, choose "Log Out…." In the Login window that appears, type "root" as the user name, and type the root password you assigned earlier. Voilà. You can now delete files that you weren't allowed to delete earlier. Be careful.

12. When you're finished doing your root business, log out, log back in as yourself, and **disable root access** in the NetInfo Manager (Steps 1–6).

Locking a file

You can see information about every file icon in a **Show Info** window (details about Show Info are on page 392). One of the things you can do in a Show Info window is **lock** a file so no one can make changes to it.

> **To get a Show Info window:** In the Finder, click once on an icon, then press Command I, *or* go the the File menu and choose "Show Info."

There is a "Locked" checkbox in the lower-left corner of the Show Info window. If you check this box (click once on it), this file cannot be renamed or inadvertently thrown away—as soon as it hits the Trash, a dialog box comes up telling you a locked file cannot be thrown away. It also becomes a **read-only** file: anyone can open and read the file, but no one can save any changes to it. You can't even change the Show Info comments. This is handy for sending around copies of a document and ensuring no one accidentally changes anything.

> **To lock the file,** click in the checkbox.

> **To unlock the file,** click in the checkbox again. If there is no ✔, the file is unlocked.

*Tip: If Mac OS X yells at you because a file is locked, but the "Locked" button is not checked in **Show Info**, it may have been checked in OS 9 in **Get Info**. Restart your Mac in OS 9, unlock the file, then go back to OS X.*

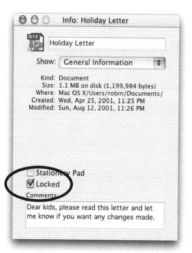

If you look very closely at a locked file, you'll see a tiny padlock in the lower-left corner.

This message can mean a file is locked.

As you can see, this isn't a very secure way to safeguard a file—all anyone has to do is Show Info and unlock it. It's just a way to prevent things from happening to the file accidentally.

You'll find there are a number of files you cannot lock, including all of your Home folders. Apple is trying to protect you from yourself.

Moving icons

To move icons, simply press-and-drag them. You can put any icon into or drag any icon out of any *folder* icon.

- When you drag an icon (or any file, no matter what it looks like) from one place to another **on the same disk,** the computer **moves** it to the other place.

- When you drag a file **from one disk to another disk,** the computer **copies** it to the other disk. For details about copying, see Chapter 12.

Creating your own icons

You can **create your own icons** and apply them to any existing icons, and you can copy icons from one file and apply them to another.

Ryan's Writings

I changed the standard folder icon, above, to a photo of Ryan, below.

- Open an OS X graphic program like AppleWorks (paint or draw). *Or* use any clipart or photo image instead.

- In the graphic program, create the little picture that you want as your icon. No matter what size you make the art, the Mac will reduce it to an appropriate size as it becomes the new icon. But if you make it too large, it will be unrecognizable when reduced.

Ryan's Writings

This is actually a folder.

- Select the image you created or found; copy it (from the Edit menu).

- Go back to a Finder window.

- Click once on the icon whose picture you want to replace. From the File menu, choose "Show Info" (*or* press Command I).

- Click once on the icon that appears in the upper-left of the Show Info window (to the right, circled).

- From the Edit menu, choose "Paste" (*or* press Command V).

- Close the Show Info window (press Command W).

Click here to select the icon's image, either to paste in a new one or to clear out an existing one.

To change an icon back to the original, select its tiny icon in the Show Info window; from the Edit menu, choose "Cut." The original icon will reappear.

The "Classic" environment

Mac OS X is a fabulous operating system. But at the moment, there are many applications that can't run in OS X because every application has to be rewritten for the new system. So, when necessary, applications that can't run in Mac OS X will automatically open in Mac OS 9. These applications are considered "Classic applications."

Opening Classic

If you double-click on a Classic application, it will open OS 9 for you, but I've found there are fewer problems if I open Classic first, and *then* open the application.

System Preferences icon.

To open the Classic environment:

1. Open System Preferences: either click on the icon in the Dock, *or* go to the Apple menu and choose "Preferences...."

Classic icon.

2. In System Preferences, click on the Classic icon, *or* choose "Classic" from the View menu.

3. In the Classic preferences pane, click the "Start" button. It takes a minute or two for Classic to get up and running.

If you want Classic to start up everytime you turn on your iMac, check this box.

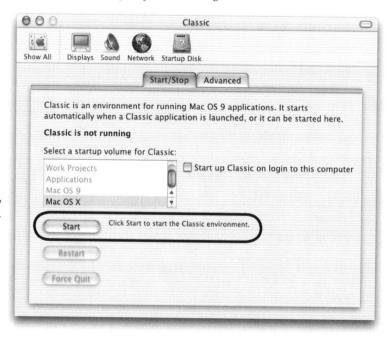

4. While Classic is starting, you'll see the small window shown below, with the status bar telling you how much more time it will take, relatively.

If you want to see the whole "Desktop" and the extra files that are loading into Mac OS 9, click the triangle in the bottom-left corner of this small window.

Click here.

5. You'll see the OS 9 Desktop as it loads, as shown on page 24.

Some applications are what's called "Carbon," which means they can open in both Mac OS 9 and OS X. Sometimes an application is *capable* of opening in OS X, but some of its features depend on "extensions" installed in Mac OS 9. In this case, you need to open the application in Classic (Mac OS 9) to get full functionality. **To force an application to open in Classic,** use the Info window: single-click on the application icon to select it, then press Command I to open the Info window, shown below.

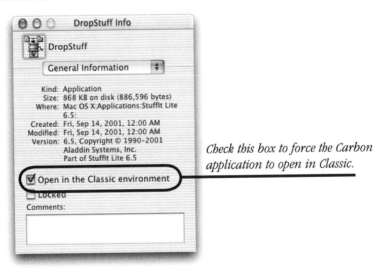

Check this box to force the Carbon application to open in Classic.

If you have Mac OS X on your machine but you start up your Mac with OS 9 most of the time, you'll need to know lots more about OS 9 than we can tell you in this book. If so, please read *The Little Mac Book, seventh edition,* from Peachpit Press.

Apple System Profiler

Apple System Profiler

The **Apple System Profiler** (in your Utilities folder) is the place to go to find out your Mac's serial number, all the details about your hardware and software, memory chips, every application on your hard disk, and more. You won't need to use it very often, but it's good to check it out so you know what information is available here. If you ever have to call tech support, they will probably ask you to open this.

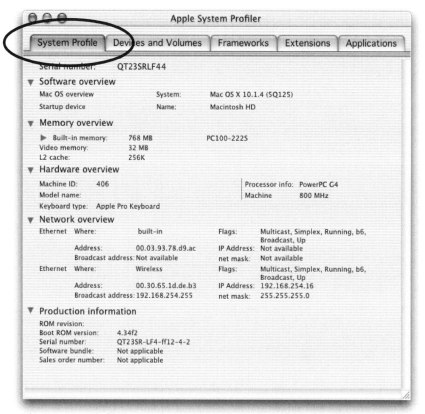

This "System Profile" pane shows me which version of the software this computer is running, how much memory it has, what kind of keyboard I have, my serial number, and more stuff that I don't even know what it is.

Sherlock:
Find it on Your iMac or on the Web

If you click the Sherlock Holmes hat you see in the Dock, you'll get the application shown below, called **Sherlock.** Sherlock is the tool you use to find any file on your hard disk, or to find things on the Internet like old friends, shopping bargains, definitions of strange words, research articles, entertainment, and more.

First *click on this "channel."*

Second, *type in the name of a file to find its location on your hard disk.*

Third, *click this button to have Sherlock search your hard disk for the desired file.*

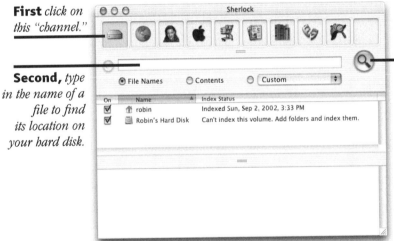

Click any of the other "channels" to log on to the Internet (providing your connection is set up first) and find various sorts of information.

Note: *If **America Online** is your only email/Internet service, you must first open and log on to AOL before you can use Sherlock to search the Internet!*

Channels

The buttons across the top of Sherlock represent what Apple calls **channels,** or customizable sources of information. Position your mouse over any of the buttons and pause a few seconds—a hint, called a "help tag," appears that tells you what that channel can help you find, as shown to the left. Try it.

When you position the pointer over a channel, a Help tag appears that tells you what that channel is for.

Across the row in the example below, the channels are Files, Internet, People, Apple, Shopping, News, References, Entertainment, and a channel called My Channel that you can customize. Plus there are empty slots where you can add other customized channels and your own icons.

Click on a channel to select it; the contents in the middle panel will change with each channel. Try it.

This is the Search button. After you have typed in a request, click this button to have Sherlock find it.

*This **channel** is selected (notice the slightly darker shade).*

*In this **edit box,** type in what you want to find (details on opposite page).*

*Depending on the channel you choose, you'll have different options in this **middle panel.** Click different channels, above, to see how the list in this panel changes. Sherlock will search only the items that are checked.*

After a search, the results will appear in this middle panel.

*The information in this **lower panel** is different for different channels. The details of selected results will appear here.*

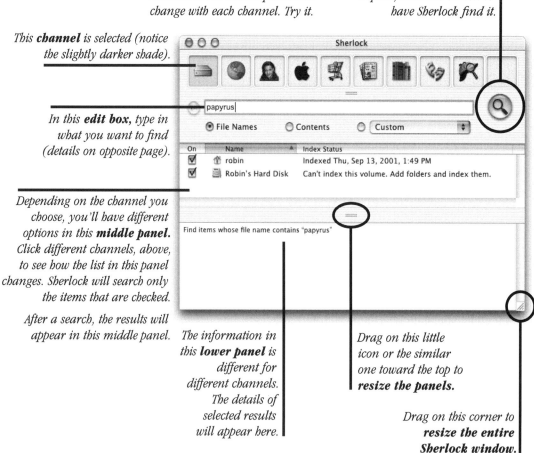

*Drag on this little icon or the similar one toward the top to **resize the panels.***

*Drag on this corner to **resize the entire Sherlock window.***

Find a file on your hard disk

A *file* is anything on your hard disk. Documents, folders, applications, fonts—everything is considered a file. Every file on your Mac is represented by an icon and has a **name.** Sherlock can find files by their names.

This is the Sherlock icon in the Dock.

To search for a file on your hard disk:

1. From the Dock, click the Sherlock icon (shown to the right).
   Or go to the Desktop and press Command F.

2. Click the first channel button, the one with the picture of a computer (circled, below; it's probably already selected).

3. In the middle panel of the window you'll see the name of your hard disk and Home, as shown below. Depending on how your computer is set up, you might see other items in that panel, such as any "partitions" you might have, or any disks that are mounted (CDs, Zips, etc.). Make sure there is a checkbox in any disk you want to search.

4. In the edit box (see below), type a word that is in some of the file names on your computer. For instance, type "letter" or "setup."

5. Make sure the round radio button for "File Names" is checked (shown below).

6. You'll notice in the lower panel that Sherlock reiterates what you are looking for.

7. Click the Search button (the round, green one with the magnifying glass). Then turn this page and continue.

Tips: It doesn't matter whether you type capital or lowercase letters—Sherlock will find "Love Letter" even if you search for "love letter."

*Spaces, however, **do** matter. That is, "love letter" will not find "loveletter."*

If you don't know the exact name of the file, just type any part of it that you think is in the file name, such as "love."

*Choose the **Files channel** to search for files on your hard disk.*

*Type your request in this **edit box.***

Make sure this button is selected so Sherlock will search for your request in a file's name (as opposed to its contents).

Click this button to search.

Right now this panel reminds you of what you are looking for.

Opening a found file

Sherlock will take several seconds to search your entire hard disk. The results will look something like those shown below. In the **middle panel** of the window is a list of all the files that have your request in the file name; **click once** on any one of those files, and in the **lower panel,** Sherlock will tell you where that file is stored.

When necessary, click this Back button to return to the list of volumes you just left. There is no "Forward" button to return to this window—you'll just have to click the Search button again.

Click once on the file you were looking for, and in the lower panel you'll see exactly where that file is stored.

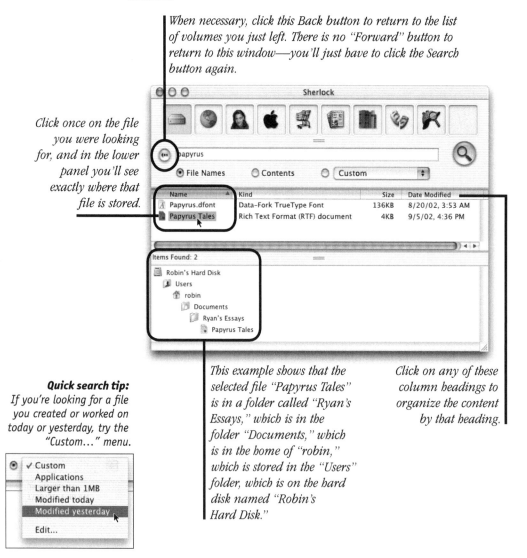

Quick search tip:
If you're looking for a file you created or worked on today or yesterday, try the "Custom..." menu.

This example shows that the selected file "Papyrus Tales" is in a folder called "Ryan's Essays," which is in the folder "Documents," which is in the home of "robin," which is stored in the "Users" folder, which is on the hard disk named "Robin's Hard Disk."

Click on any of these column headings to organize the content by that heading.

Once you have located the file you want, there are several things you can do. First, click once on the file name in either the middle or the lower panel of Sherlock to select that file. Then do one of the following:

- **To open the file,** double-click the file name, or single-click the file name to select it and press Command O. This will, of course, also open the application that the file was created in.

- **To open the folder** in which the file is stored, press Command E.

- **To print the item** (if it's a document), press Command P.

- **To move the item,** drag it to wherever you want, outside of Sherlock.

- **To copy the item,** hold down the Option key and drag the file somewhere outside of Sherlock.

- **To delete the item,** drag the file from the window to the trash basket, or select the file and press Command Delete.

- **To find the original of an alias,** select its icon and press Command R.

Tip: Click on a file name to select it, then go to the File menu to see what your options are for that particular type of file.

For the following technique, you must select the file in the *middle* panel—it won't work if you select the file in the lower panel.

- ▼ **To make an alias of the file,** hold down the Command and Option keys and drag the file to the Desktop or into a folder; let go and an alias will appear (see Chapter 23 for information about aliases).

Do a new search without losing the previous search

After you've done one search, you can **start another** without eliminating the search criteria or the results from the first search. Just go to the File menu in Sherlock and choose "New Window," or press Command N. You can have any number of search windows open at the same time.

How to quit Sherlock

When you want to put the Sherlock *window* away, click in the little red button in the upper-left corner of the window.

When you want to put the Sherlock *application* away (that is, you want to quit), press Command Q or choose "Quit Sherlock" from the Sherlock menu.

Search a specific folder

Sometimes you want to **search one particular folder** or several folders instead of every mounted disk. That's easy to do. (Sherlock calls all folders or disks "volumes.")

To search a particular folder:

1. First:

    - **Either** find the icon for that folder on your Desktop or in a Finder window. Drag the folder icon and drop it in the middle panel of the Sherlock window.

    - **Or** from the Find menu in the menu bar across the top of the screen, choose "Add Folder...." Then use the dialog box to navigate to the folder of your choice. Select the folder and click "Add."

2. Back at the Sherlock window, make sure there is a check in the box next to each folder you want to search.

3. Continue with the search as you did on the previous pages.

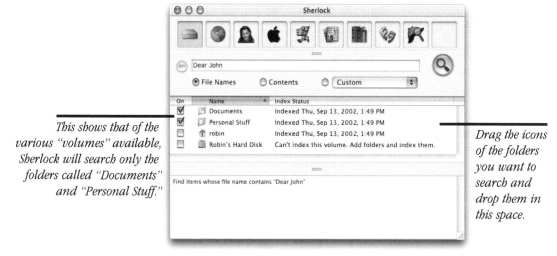

This shows that of the various "volumes" available, Sherlock will search only the folders called "Documents" and "Personal Stuff."

Drag the icons of the folders you want to search and drop them in this space.

To remove a folder from Sherlock:

1. Select the folder you want to remove. You must select the *name* of the folder. That is, clicking in the checkbox does not select the folder to remove it.

2. From the Find menu, choose "Remove Folder."

The Contents button and indexing

Sherlock will **search through the contents** of most text files. For instance, maybe you're working on a research project and you've created dozens of files on the topic of chess. You want to find all the papers in your collection that mention "en passant." That's when you click the "Contents" button; instead of searching for just the *name* of a file, Sherlock will actually read the *contents* of files. For instance, you might have written an article that you named "Special Moves in Chess," and in the article itself you wrote about the en passant move, but you also mention en passant in three other articles with different names—Sherlock will find every file that includes the phrase "en passant" in the text.

BUT Sherlock cannot search the contents of your files *until* it has first **indexed** every file. That is, Sherlock has to read every file on your computer and then organize every word into a database that it can search when you request it. Logically, if you write more articles after Sherlock has indexed the files on your hard disk, Sherlock has to index things again to update and add those new files to its database.

*Sherlock cannot search the text in **every** file. It can search files saved in Rich Text Format, Plain Text, most PDF documents, and some word processing documents. If you have lots of files you want to search and Sherlock can't do it, buy Adobe Acrobat and learn to use it. It's amazing.*

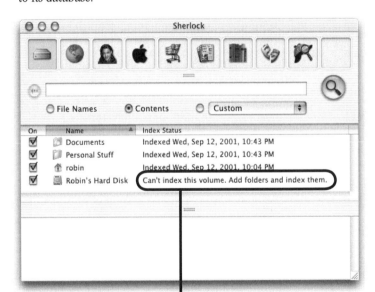

*Users (like you and me) are not allowed to change the "first level" of the computer; the first level is the hard disk or partition that holds the operating system. Because a user can't change it, that level **cannot be indexed.** As the note says, you can add individual folders from that disk into Sherlock (as explained on page 368) and index the individual folders. (This message does not mean to add folders to that disk.)*

To search the Internet, Sherlock has to go to the Internet, which means you must have your Internet connection already set up and working before you use this feature of Sherlock.

Internet

People

Apple

Shopping

News

Reference

Entertainment

When you choose any of the Internet channels and go to the web, you'll get advertisements in the very bottom portion of Sherlock.

Find something on the Internet

Besides searching your disk, Sherlock will also search the Internet and the web. Each of the buttons across the top of Sherlock is called a "channel." Each channel is set up to search specific areas of the web (except the very first channel, which finds files on your computer). When you click on a channel to select it, you'll see the middle panel of Sherlock change to fit the channel's specifications. Try it.

To search the Internet:

1. Open Sherlock (click the Sherlock Holmes hat in the Dock or press Command F when you are at the Desktop).

2. Click once on the "Internet" channel (the globe).

   If you are looking for a person, click the "People" channel button instead of the "Internet" channel. If you're looking for news, reference material, or Apple support information, click the appropriate channel. If you want to go shopping, take a look at pages 420–421.

3. Type in the item you wish to look for. If it is a phrase, put quotation marks around the phrase; for instance, if you are looking for a recipe for chocolate pecan pie, type "chocolate pecan pie" in quotes.

   If you don't use the quotes, Sherlock will find every web page with the word "chocolate" on it, plus every page with the word "pecan" on it, plus every page with the word "pie" on it. But with the phrase enclosed with quotes, you should only get pages that contain the entire phrase "chocolate pecan pie."

4. Click the Search button (the big one with the magnifying glass).

   If you have a full-time connection, Sherlock will jump on it and do the search.

   If you have a dial-up account, Sherlock will log on to the Internet through your ISP (Internet Service Provider).

   If you use AOL you must first open and log on to AOL before you click the Search button.

5. You will get a list of "results," as shown on the opposite page. Click once on a result, and details of that web page will be displayed in the lower panel (also shown).

6. To go to that web page, either double-click the title in the middle panel of Sherlock, or single-click the underlined link in the lower details panel. Read the captions on the opposite page.

2. *Click the channel that you want to search.*

3. *Type in what you're looking for.*

4. *Click the Search button.*

5. *Click once on a result to see details below, or double-click to go directly to that web page.*

Using the scroller or arrows, scroll through this list of results.

6. *To go to this web page, single-click this link.*

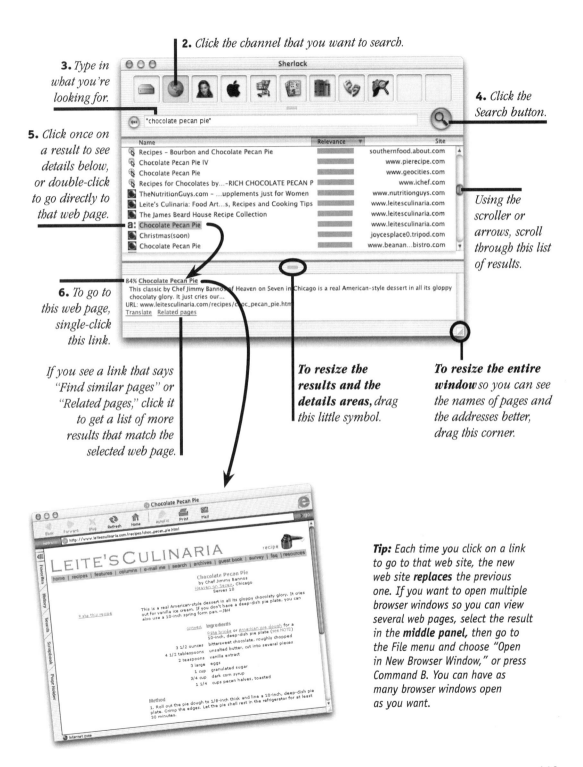

If you see a link that says "Find similar pages" or "Related pages," click it to get a list of more results that match the selected web page.

To resize the results and the details areas, *drag this little symbol.*

To resize the entire window *so you can see the names of pages and the addresses better, drag this corner.*

Tip: *Each time you click on a link to go to that web site, the new web site **replaces** the previous one. If you want to open multiple browser windows so you can view several web pages, select the result in the **middle panel,** then go to the File menu and choose "Open in New Browser Window," or press Command B. You can have as many browser windows open as you want.*

Shop on the Internet

Sherlock doesn't just *find* items for sale on the Internet—it actually provides you with their prices and availability. Amazing.

Keep in mind that what Sherlock finds is dependent on what is offered for sale *through the selected search sites;* in the case of the Shopping channel, you can see below that Sherlock is only looking through selected sources. That is, if you want to compare prices of a down jacket from Lands End, L.L. Bean, and Orvis, Sherlock is not the right tool to use. But considering there are literally millions of items for sale in the search sites listed in Sherlock, it's not a bad place to look for many things.

Search using the Shopping channel just as explained on the previous pages:

1. Click the Shopping channel button.

2. Type in your request (use quotation marks for phrases).

3. Click the Search button; wait for the results.

4. Double-click the result of your choice to go to that web site, **OR:**

5. Single-click your choice to see more details in the lower panel, then if you still want to go to that site, click the link in the lower panel.

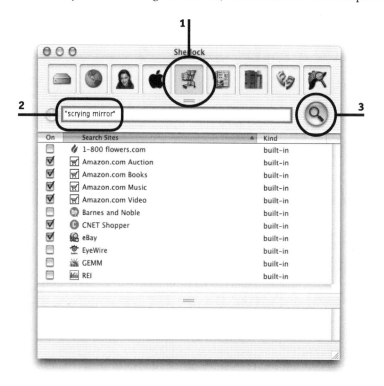

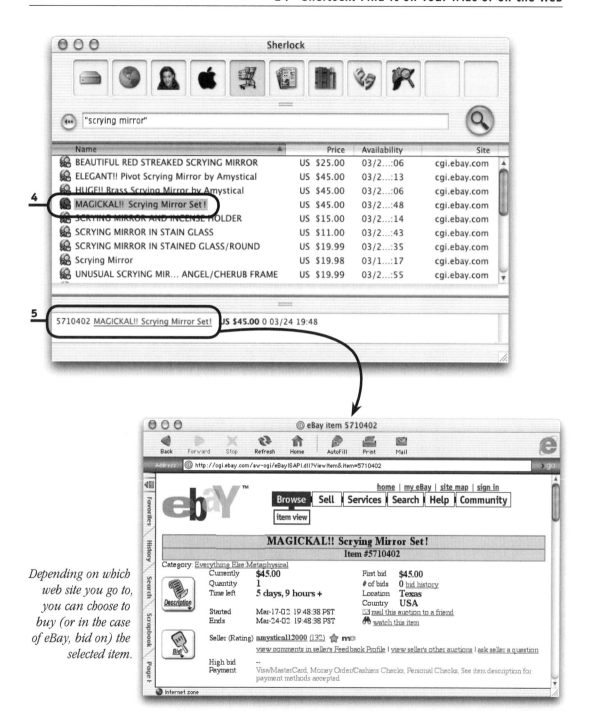

Depending on which web site you go to, you can choose to buy (or in the case of eBay, bid on) the selected item.

Boolean operators

The intimidating term "Boolean operators" (good name for a rock band) simply refers to using words like AND, NOT, and OR in your search. For instance, in the example below, I was able to find only research information that had the words "Mary Sidney" *plus* the word "Countess" on the page. If I did a search for just "Mary Sidney," I would have gotten a huge number of genealogy sites in the results.

Most of the search engines on the web use Boolean operators. For more information, go to just about any search engine site and click the "Help" button or the "Advanced Search" button, and look for information about Boolean operators.

I clicked the "Reference" channel to search for encyclopedia and reference articles.

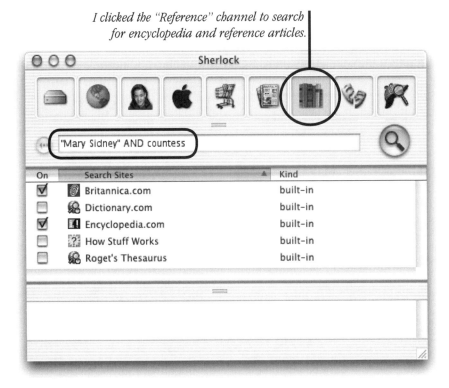

What's a Peripheral, a Hub, and a Port?

This chapter describes those places on the back or side of your computer where you plug things in **(ports)** and the things you plug into them **(peripherals).** You can spend years on your iMac without knowing the information in this chapter because one of the greatest things about the iMac is that if a cable fits into a port, it's the right match. It's not possible to plug something into the wrong place. So you don't really have to know anything about the back of your computer—if it fits, plug it in and move on. But when you get to the point where you want to know the difference between a FireWire port and a USB port and an Ethernet port, then dive into this short chapter.

What is a peripheral?

Tip: To find out the latest information about iMac peripherals and adapters and everything related, go to *www.macintouch.com/ imacusb.html.* Also check the Apple site at *www.apple.com.*

A **peripheral** is any item (or "device") that is outside of the main computer enclosure, but attached to it. Your mouse, keyboard, and printer are actually peripheral devices. Scanners and external hard disks are peripherals. If you have the Apple Pro Speakers, they are peripheral devices.

What is a port?

A **port** is a socket, a kind of receptacle, on the back of a computer (or on the backs of peripheral devices). The port is where you connect the peripheral device. A port is very different from a regular socket like electrical sockets in the wall, in that information goes both ways through a port. A wall socket sends power in only one direction—to a device. A port sends information back and forth between the computer and the device.

There are lots of different kinds of ports, and peripherals are made to match a certain port type. For instance, you might have *USB* ports, to which you can only connect USB devices, such as *USB* printers.

The cables that connect peripherals to your iMac (or to another peripheral) have **connectors** on the ends. The connectors match the ports. On an iMac, if the connector matches the port, it works. You can't plug a connector into the wrong port.

Below are pictures of all these ports so you'll know exactly what you have.

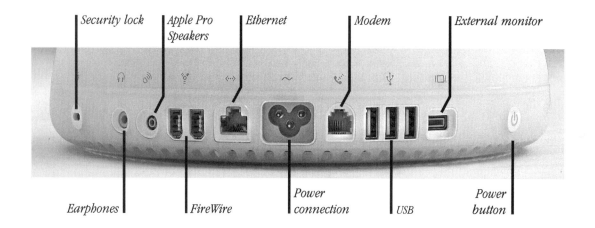

Security lock | Apple Pro Speakers | Ethernet | Modem | External monitor

Earphones | FireWire | Power connection | USB | Power button

What is USB?

You'll probably hear the term "USB" often, as well as "peripheral." The acronym USB stands for Universal Serial Bus (which you don't have to remember). A "bus" is the system of wires, ports, and programming that a computer uses to connect peripherals and communicate with them. Until the iMac, Apple used a different sort of bus on Macintoshes, and so this switch to the USB is a big deal; it's the new technology that many (especially older) peripherals can't connect to.

On the iMacs with the flat screen, all the ports are on the back side, as illustrated on the opposite page. You'll plug all of your peripherals into this place. The USB ports are the rectangular ones in the middle. Notice you have three of them, and your keyboard is already plugged into one. Your printer, one that either has a USB connector or uses an adapter, will plug into the other port.

What is a connector?

Connectors are the parts on the ends of the cables that actually make the connection to the other device. The connector is the part that tells you what kind of cable it is—an Ethernet cable has a very different connector from a FireWire cable, which is very different from a USB cable (as illustrated on the following pages).

Every connector is either **male or female;** take one look and you can guess why. The male or female shape is a very important identifying feature. When you start connecting lots of things together (like to project a presentation from the computer to a large wall screen), you will find yourself looking for either a male or female connector.

Another identifying feature of connectors are the **pins,** or slender metal prongs on the male versions (not all connectors have pins). The number of pins is particularly useful in describing what you need. For instance, I once needed a cable for a video card that I installed in my computer. I didn't know exactly what kind of cable I needed, so I counted the little pin holes and told the guy I needed a 15-pin connector and he thought I knew what I was talking about.

The **shape** is important. Some connectors are long and skinny, short and fat, rectangular or round, etc. Many connectors have identifying symbols that match the symbol on the port. On the next few pages are illustrations of the most common symbols that identify both the connectors and the ports.

This is what an RJ45 Ethernet port looks like, and the symbol that identifies it.

Ethernet ports

Ethernet (pronounced *eether-net*) is the most common *networking* system for local area networks (LANs), which means the computers that are connected together are close enough to be connected with cables (as opposed to a wide area network, a WAN). iMacs have Ethernet ports which look like large phone jacks. You can use Ethernet in your home or small office to connect several computers so you can send files back and forth.

Your printer might have an Ethernet port, in which case you can send data to the printer much faster than through the USB port. Even if it doesn't have an actual Ethernet port, you can get adapters for some printers so you can add the printer to your Ethernet network. In my office we use EtherMac iPrint Adapters from Farallon to network our good ol' workhorses—eight-year-old Apple LaserWriters.

This is the port for an internal modem, and the symbol that identifies it. Don't get the modem port confused with the larger Ethernet port.

You also have a **modem port** for your *internal* modem, which looks exactly like an RJ11 phone jack (because it is), so don't get it confused with the Ethernet port. The Ethernet port is larger than the internal modem port.

This is what an AAUI port looks like, and the symbol that identifies it.

AAUI ports

Your iMac doesn't have an **AAUI port,** but you may want to connect to another computer that does have one. The AAUI port (which stands for Apple Adapter Unit Interface) takes a variety of adapters for different networking systems, but the symbol for its port is the same as the symbol for an Ethernet port because Ethernet has become the most commonly used local area network. You can buy an Ethernet adapter for this port, called a *transceiver,* so you can connect your old computer to your new iMac that has an actual Ethernet port.

USB ports

There are three **USB ports** on the back of your iMac, plus two others on the keyboard (the upper-left and upper-right corners of the keyboard). USB stands for Universal Serial Bus, which replaces both the Apple Desktop Bus and the serial ports (older types of ports). With USB, input devices (like mice and keyboards) as well as scanners, printers, Zip drives, and other devices can all connect into the same ports.

This drawing shows two USB ports and the symbol that identifies USB.

You can't "daisy chain" USB devices, like you can FireWire devices (below), but you can buy a **hub**. The hub connects into one of the USB ports on the iMac, and several devices can plug into the hub. You can connect another hub to the first one, and so on, so you can supposedly connect up to 127 USB devices to one Macintosh. I don't know why you would, but you could.

One of the greatest things about USB devices is that you can **hot swap** them; that is, you can connect and disconnect devices such as keyboards, mice, Zip drives, printers, or scanners without having to shut down the computer like you do with SCSI, serial, and ADB devices. Just don't swap devices while they're doing something, like copying to a Zip or scanning a photo or printing.

This is a USB hub. The back connector goes into the computer's port, and the front connector leads to a USB device.

FireWire ports

FireWire is Apple's trademarked version of the standard called IEEE 1394. It's a high-performance "serial bus" for connecting up to 63 devices through one port on your iMac.

This symbol identifies a FireWire port.

The big deal about FireWire is this: It's extremely fast; you can connect 63 devices in any which way you like, such as in a star or tree pattern, and up to 16 in a single chain; you can hot swap them in and out without having to turn off the computer; they connect with a simple snap-in cable.

You can connect a vast array of consumer electronics to FireWire, such as digital cameras, video tapes, and camcorders, as well as DVD (digital video disk), plus hard disks, optical disks, and printers.

You might hear the FireWire ports called IEEE, but IEEE actually stands for the professional society, Institute of Electrical and Electronics Engineers, and IEEE 1394 is a standard they developed. For instance, the Ethernet standard is IEEE 802.3.

These are the two ends of a FireWire cable.

Serial ports and parallel ports

You iMac doesn't have a **serial port** or a **parallel port,** but your printer might, in addition to a **USB port.**

The **serial port** is the little round one with lots of holes. There are two data wires in a serial cable, so the port can send and receive information at the same time.

A **parallel port** is a big, horsey-looking port that looks like it came from a PC, which it did. Parallel ports transfer data through eight wires, so all eight bits in a byte can go through the line at once (in parallel). Sounds like it should be fast, but most parallel ports are not capable of sending and receiving data at the same time, which slows them down. Some PCs use the parallel port to connect to printers.

Until recently, almost all printers for the Mac were "serial printers," which means they connected to a serial port on your computer. But, newer Macs (such as your iMac) don't have serial ports; they've been replaced with USB.

This is the back side of an Epson printer.

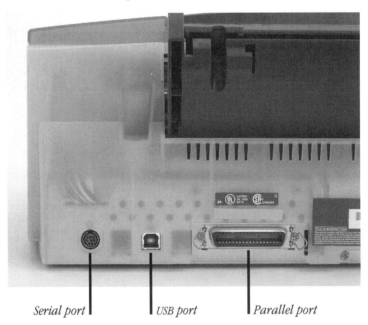

Serial port   *USB port*   *Parallel port*

"Your computer gives you an attitude."

Ms. Robin Williams

The Index

John Tollett and Robin Williams

We live on several acres just south of Santa Fe, New Mexico, where we can see every sunrise and sunset, every moonrise and moonset. And we can see the ski trails on the mountain. Between us we have four kids and several dogs. John has lots of electronic equipment and Robin has lots of books.

Other books by Robin

The Little Mac OS X Book

The Little Mac Book, seventh edition (for Mac OS 9)

The Little iBook Book
    (and John Tollett)

The Mac is not a typewriter

The Non-Designer's Design Book

The Non-Designer's Type Book

The Non-Designer's Web Book
    (and John Tollett)

The Non-Designer's Scan and Print Book
    (and Sandee Cohen)

Robin Williams Design Workshop
    (and John Tollett)

Robin Williams Web Design Workshop
    (and John Tollett and Dave Rohr)

Windows for Mac Users
    (and Cynthia Baron)

A Blip in the continuum
    (and John Tollett)

How to Boss Your Fonts Around (for Mac OS 9)
    and several other books

Colophon

We created this book on several Macintoshes running Mac OS X, sharing files across the office. We used Adobe InDesign 2.0, which is fabulous, especially the book features. Wow. The fonts used are the Tree family from [T-26], Garamond Condensed from Adobe Systems, and ITC Officina Sans from ITC.